NORTH AMERICA in FOCUS

VOLUME 6

A Region-by-Region Guide to Nations, Legacies & Landscapes

M. MILLER-YIANNI

Copyright and Credits

Publisher: Martin Miller-Yianni, Bulgaria

First Printing Edition 2026

ISBN - 978-619-7742-74-9 (paperback)
ISBN - 978-619-7742-75-6 (ePub)

A CIP catalogue record for this book is available from:

The National Register of Published Books in Bulgaria
bulevard 'Vasil Levski' 88,
1504 Sofia,
Bulgaria

Cover Image/Title Page: ChatGPT Creation

CONTENTS

INTRODUCTION

North America in Focus sets out to offer a clear-eyed, readable account of a continent that has shaped—and been shaped by—centuries of encounter, conflict and exchange. Bringing together history, culture and national identity, the book explores North America's countries from their Indigenous foundations and early civilisations through colonisation, independence and into the pressures and possibilities of the present day. It is written in plain, careful British English and rests on solid scholarship, without losing sight of the human stories that give the continent its character.

Each country profile combines narrative history with essential context on population, economy and political life. Key individuals, landmark events, UNESCO World Heritage Sites and familiar cultural reference points—from the birth of jazz in New Orleans to the global pull of Hollywood cinema or the enduring symbolism of the Maple Leaf—help ground broader themes in everyday experience. The aim is not simply to list facts, but to show how people have lived, argued, created and governed across this vast and varied land.

Chapters open with short vignettes intended to draw the reader in: a council fire among the Haudenosaunee, the restless optimism of a nineteenth-century settler heading west, or the careful negotiations that reshaped Canada's constitution in the late twentieth century. Throughout, the tone avoids academic heaviness. Whether discussing the legacy of Mesoamerican civilisations, the consequences of Atlantic slavery, or the long shadow of the Cold War, the writing seeks clarity and balance rather than jargon or grand theory.

As part of the *World Continents in Focus* series, the book follows a consistent and practical structure. Each country is covered in a self-contained profile of around 1,000 words, allowing the reader to move straight through the continent, dip into comparisons—between Caribbean Island states and continental powers, for example—or quickly consult a specific topic such as Arctic sovereignty, trade agreements, or migration routes. Teachers may find sections useful for lessons on independence movements or civil rights; travellers can orient themselves within cultural regions and landscapes; students can follow the role of rivers, borders and resources in shaping settlement and trade.

The book does not shy away from complexity. It places technological innovation alongside economic inequality, Indigenous survival alongside colonial displacement and global influence alongside internal division. Silicon Valley and the Rust Belt, booming metropolitan centres and sparsely populated hinterlands, long-standing traditions and rapid social change all sit side by side, reflecting a continent that resists simple description.

At a time when information is often reduced to headlines or soundbites, *North America in Focus* offers a considered, coherent guide. It is intended to be useful without being superficial and compact without being reductive. Whether the reader is settling an argument about geography, planning a journey across borders, or trying to make sense of contemporary political and social tensions, this volume aims to provide reliable orientation. More than a reference work, it is an invitation to understand North America as it has been lived: a place of deep histories, contested ideas and constant reinvention.

A BRIEF HISTORY OF NORTH AMERICA

North America, shaped by ancient Indigenous civilisations, successive waves of migration and transformative political experiments, stretches from the Arctic tundra to tropical rainforests and coral-fringed seas across immense distances. Comprising sovereign states, overseas territories and diverse nations within nations, the continent's history is one of encounter—between peoples, empires and ideas across time. From pre-Columbian societies to settler colonialism, industrial power and contemporary global influence, North America has continually redefined itself in response to internal and external pressures. This account traces the continent's historical development, regional character and modern challenges, presented in British English and a broad comparative perspective.

Ancient Foundations (Prehistory–15th Century)

Human presence in North America dates back at least 15,000 years, with early peoples migrating across Beringia from Asia during periods of lowered sea level. Over millennia, complex societies emerged, adapting to diverse climates and landscapes. The Ancestral Puebloans of the American Southwest built cliff dwellings and irrigation systems, while the Mississippian culture (c. 800–1600) raised vast earthen mounds at Cahokia, rivalling medieval European cities in scale, organisation and influence.

In Mesoamerica, the Olmec civilisation (c. 1500–400 BCE) laid cultural foundations later developed by the Maya, whose city-states excelled in astronomy, mathematics and hieroglyphic writing. The Aztec Empire (c. 1300–1521) dominated central Mexico from Tenochtitlan, sustaining millions through chinampa agriculture and complex tribute systems. Across the north, Inuit, Haudenosaunee (Iroquois) and Plains nations forged sophisticated political systems and ecological knowledge adapted to harsh environments, seasonal change and long-distance interaction.

Conquest, Colonisation and Resistance (16th–18th Centuries)

European arrival reshaped the continent irrevocably. Spain's conquest of the Aztec Empire (1519–1521) and subsequent colonisation of Mexico and the Caribbean introduced Christianity, new governance structures and devastating epidemics. France established fur-trading networks along the St Lawrence and Mississippi rivers, while Britain's Atlantic colonies grew through agriculture, trade and enslaved labour.

Indigenous resistance persisted—from the Pueblo Revolt (1680) to sustained warfare across the Great Plains. In the Caribbean, plantation economies transformed islands such as Cuba and Jamaica, built on the transatlantic slave trade. By the late 18th century, North America was a mosaic of empires, Indigenous nations and creole societies.

Revolutions and Nation-Building (18th–19th Centuries)

The American Revolution (1775–1783) marked a turning point, creating the United States and inspiring republican movements elsewhere. Canada followed a different path, remaining within the British Empire while developing self-governing institutions after 1867. Mexico's war of independence (1810–1821) dismantled Spanish rule, yet ushered in decades of political instability.

The 19th century was defined by territorial expansion and conflict. The United States pushed westward through treaties and wars, culminating in the displacement of Indigenous peoples via policies such as the Trail of Tears. The Mexican–American War (1846–1848) redrew borders, while the US Civil War (1861–1865) resolved the question of slavery at immense human cost. Industrialisation accelerated urban growth across the continent.

Modern Era: Power, Integration and Tension (20th–21st Centuries)

The 20th century saw North America emerge as a centre of global influence. The United States became a superpower after two world wars, shaping international institutions and Cold War alliances. Canada expanded its welfare state and multicultural identity, while Mexico underwent revolution (1910–1920) and later industrial modernisation.

Economic integration deepened through agreements such as NAFTA (1994), binding Canada, the United States and Mexico into shared supply chains. Yet disparities remain stark. Contemporary challenges include migration pressures, racial inequality, Indigenous reconciliation, climate change and political polarisation. Technological innovation flourishes in hubs from Silicon Valley to Toronto, while environmental risks—from Arctic thaw to Caribbean hurricanes—intensify.

Cultural and Regional Identity

North America's identity is plural and contested. Hundreds of Indigenous languages endure alongside English, Spanish and French. Cultural expression ranges from Navajo weaving and Inuit carving to jazz, hip-hop and Caribbean calypso. Sporting traditions—baseball, basketball, ice hockey—command continental loyalty, while cuisine reflects layered histories: Mexican maize, Cajun spice, Canadian maple and Caribbean rum.

Migration continues to redefine society, sustaining North America's reputation as a continent shaped as much by movement as by place.

NORTHERN AMERICA

Countries and Territories: Canada, Greenland, Saint Pierre and Miquelon

Legacy: Indigenous resilience, Arctic exploration, settler governance.

Today: Climate change in the Arctic; reconciliation with First Nations; Greenland's strategic importance.

UNITED STATES OF AMERICA

Regions: Northeast, Midwest, South, West

Foundations: Constitutional republicanism, frontier expansion, industrial might.

Now: Global cultural reach; political division; technological and military dominance.

MEXICO

Core: Mesoamerican civilisations, Spanish colonial rule, revolutionary nationalism.

Present: Manufacturing integration with North America; cultural influence; security and inequality challenges.

CENTRAL AMERICA

Countries: Belize, Guatemala, Honduras, El Salvador, Nicaragua, Costa Rica, Panama

Traits: Ancient Maya heritage, plantation economies, Cold War interventions.

Pulse: Migration pressures; democratic strain; Panama's canal economy.

THE CARIBBEAN

Countries: Cuba, Haiti, Dominican Republic, Jamaica, Bahamas, Trinidad and Tobago, Barbados and others

Past: Plantation slavery, colonial rivalry, revolutionary movements.

Challenges: Climate vulnerability; tourism dependence; post-colonial identity.

ISLAND TERRITORIES & STRATEGIC OUTPOSTS

Areas: Greenland, Caribbean territories, Pacific-facing coastlines

Niche: Trade routes, military positioning, environmental frontlines.

Ties: Balancing local autonomy with global power interests.

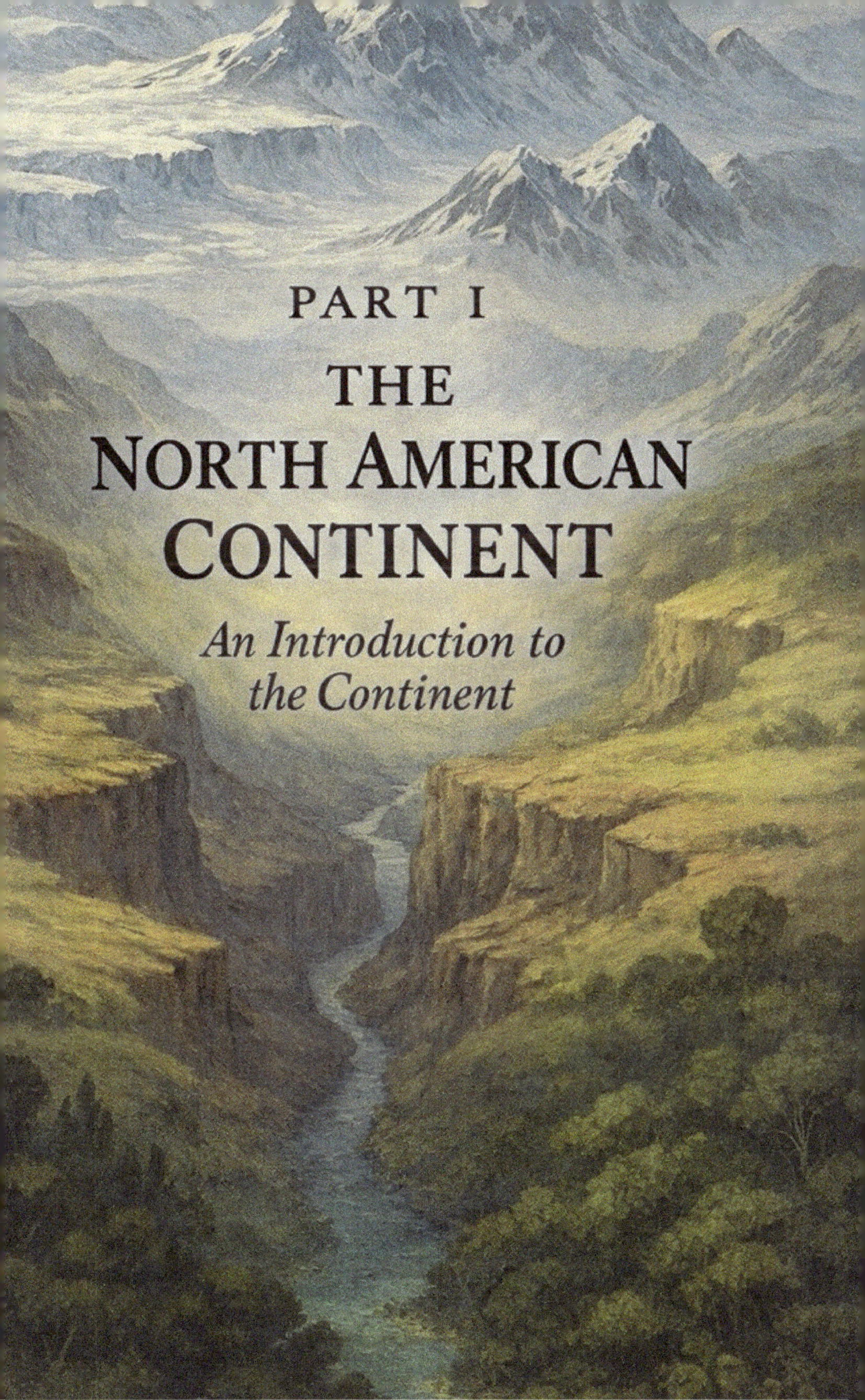

PART I
THE NORTH AMERICAN CONTINENT
An Introduction to the Continent

Overview

North America is a continent of striking contrasts and monumental scale, extending from the permanent ice of the High Arctic to the humid rainforests and coral-fringed shores of the Caribbean. As the world's third-largest landmass, its geography reflects immense geological age and powerful natural forces. Spanning more than five thousand miles from the Aleutian Islands of Alaska to the narrow Isthmus of Panama, the continent encompasses an exceptional range of landscapes, climates and ecosystems. Its name, drawn from the Florentine navigator Amerigo Vespucci, was gradually adopted by European mapmakers as the breadth and diversity of these lands became better understood.

Geological Foundations and Physical Framework

The physical structure of North America rests upon ancient geological foundations. At its centre lies the Canadian Shield, a vast expanse of Precambrian rock forming the continent's oldest core. Scoured by successive ice ages, this region is characterised by thin soils, innumerable lakes and extensive boreal forest, dominating much of Canada and extending into the northern United States.

To the east rise the Appalachian Mountains, among the oldest mountain ranges on Earth, their rounded ridges stretching from eastern Canada through the United States into northern Mexico. In contrast, the western edge of the continent is defined by the younger and more rugged Cordilleran system, including the Rocky Mountains, Sierra Nevada and coastal ranges that run from Alaska through Canada and the United States into Mexico and Central America.

Between these mountain systems lie the broad interior lowlands. The Great Plains sweep southward from Canada through the United States into northern Mexico, while the Central Lowlands are shaped by vast river systems. Farther south, the land narrows through Central America, where volcanic highlands, fertile valleys and coastal plains dominate the landscape.

Along the Atlantic, Pacific and Caribbean margins, coastal plains and islands form environments ranging from mangrove swamps to sandy beaches and coral reefs.

An Array of Climates and Environments

North America's climates are governed by latitude, topography and ocean currents. In the far north of Canada and Alaska, Arctic tundra prevails, with permafrost, brief summers and specialised plant and animal life. South of this lies the great boreal forest, a continuous belt of coniferous woodland stretching across Canada and into the northern United States.

The continental interior, particularly across the United States and southern Canada, experiences some of the world's most pronounced seasonal contrasts. Cold Arctic air and warm tropical air frequently collide, producing severe thunderstorms and tornadoes, especially across the Great Plains.

Along the Pacific coast, moist ocean air brings heavy rainfall to coastal forests from Alaska to northern California, while rain shadows behind the mountains create the deserts of the American Southwest and northern Mexico. Central America, lying closer to the equator, is largely tropical, with wet and dry seasons supporting rainforests, cloud forests and rich agricultural lands.

The eastern side of the continent, including much of the United States, eastern Canada and the Caribbean, enjoys climates moderated by warm ocean currents, though it is vulnerable to hurricanes originating in the Atlantic. The Caribbean Island nations—such as Cuba, Jamaica, Haiti, the Dominican Republic, Barbados, the Bahamas, Trinidad and Tobago and the smaller island states including Antigua and Barbuda, Saint Lucia, Grenada, Dominica, Saint Kitts and Nevis and Saint Vincent and the Grenadines—are predominantly tropical, supporting lush vegetation and diverse marine ecosystems.

Major Waterways

North America's rivers and lakes are central to its geography and history. The Mississippi–Missouri river system drains much of the central United States, carrying water from the Rocky Mountains and Appalachians to the Gulf of Mexico. This vast watershed has long supported agriculture, trade and settlement.

In Canada, the Mackenzie River drains the north-western interior into the Arctic Ocean, while the St Lawrence River links the Great Lakes to the Atlantic, forming one of the world's most important inland shipping routes. The Great Lakes themselves—Superior, Michigan, Huron, Erie and Ontario—represent the largest group of freshwater lakes on Earth by surface area.

On the Pacific side, rivers such as the Columbia and Colorado have carved dramatic landscapes, the latter famously forming the Grand Canyon. In Central America, shorter but powerful rivers descend rapidly from highlands to the sea, while in the Caribbean, freshwater resources are more limited and closely tied to rainfall patterns.

Natural Riches and Human Reliance

The continent's varied environments support an extraordinary diversity of life. From polar bears and caribou in the Arctic, to bison on the plains, jaguars in the forests of Mexico and Central America and coral species in Caribbean waters, North America's biodiversity is both extensive and emblematic. These ecosystems provide essential services, including climate regulation, soil fertility, freshwater supply and coastal protection.

Agriculturally, North America is one of the most productive regions on the planet. The prairies of Canada, the Midwest of the United States, the valleys of Mexico and the fertile volcanic soils of Central America sustain major crops such as wheat, maize, rice, coffee and sugar cane. Beneath the surface lie abundant mineral and energy resources—oil, natural gas, coal and metals—that have shaped the economic development of Canada, the United States, Mexico and several Caribbean nations.

Scope and Continental Definition

This guide considers North America in its full continental sense, encompassing Canada, the United States and Mexico; the nations of Central America from Belize to Panama; and the island states of the Caribbean. Together, these countries form a region of immense physical diversity and cultural richness. While Greenland is geographically part of the North American landmass, its historical and political associations lie largely with Europe and it occupies a distinct position.

Upon this vast physical stage—of ancient rock, shifting climates and abundant life—the human history of North America has unfolded. From Indigenous civilisations to colonial encounters and modern nation-states, the continent's natural foundations continue to shape the societies that inhabit it, a story explored in the chapters that follow.

Chapter 1

The Continental Framework

Defining the Physical Stage

North America presents itself first and foremost as a continent of immense physical proportions and startling natural variety. This foundational chapter sets out the key geographical realities that underpin every aspect of its ecological and human story across time and space. It is a landmass defined not by uniformity but by extremes: from the frozen, treeless plains of the High Arctic to the humid rainforests of Central America and the reef-fringed shores of the Caribbean. To understand the nations, histories and cultures that have developed here—Canada, the United States, Mexico, the countries of Central America and the island states of the Caribbean—one must first grasp the vast and sometimes unforgiving physical stage upon which they emerged and continue to evolve.

That stage was set hundreds of millions of years ago by the slow, inexorable forces of plate tectonics, volcanism and glaciation acting over immense geological timescales. Their signatures are written into the continent's mountain chains, river valleys and coastlines. Beyond the visible scenery, these ancient processes established enduring constraints and opportunities, shaping soil depth, mineral wealth, water availability and the natural corridors that guided early migration, trade and settlement across the continent.

Major Landforms

The continent's physical architecture can be imagined as a broad, shallow bowl flanked by mountainous rims to east and west, with the land narrowing into a complex tropical bridge in the south and dissolving into an archipelago of islands to the south-east, creating striking regional contrasts.

At the ancient, stable centre lies the Canadian Shield: a vast, saucer-like expanse of Precambrian rock forming the geological heart of North America. Glaciers scraped it bare and moulded it into a rugged landscape of exposed bedrock, thin soils and innumerable lakes, extending across much of Canada and into parts of the northern United States, shaping ecosystems and settlement.

To the east of this core rise the Appalachian Mountains—old, worn highlands whose once jagged peaks have been softened into long ridges and fertile valleys by deep time and erosion. They stretch from Atlantic Canada southwards through the eastern United States, forming a forested barrier that shaped early movement, defence and patterns of settlement.

The western edge of the continent presents a more youthful, restless landscape. Here the Cordilleran systems rise in a sequence of parallel ranges from Alaska through Canada and the United States and into Mexico, including the Rockies, Sierra Nevada, Cascades and Sierra Madre. Taller and sharper than the Appalachians, these ranges remain tectonically active, with earthquakes and volcanoes testifying to the forces still at work along the Pacific margin today.

Between these mountain bookends lie the vast interior lowlands: the Great Plains and the Central Lowlands. The Great Plains extend from the Canadian prairies deep into the United States and into northern Mexico, a broad sweep of grassland and deep soils supporting agriculture. To the east, the Central Lowlands are drained by immense river systems and open towards the Gulf of Mexico and the Caribbean, facilitating trade and communication.

Southwards, the continent narrows into Central America—where folded ranges and volcanic chains run close to both coasts. Here, steep slopes, fertile volcanic soils and narrow coastal plains create a densely varied topography in a compressed space, with passes and valleys carrying outsized strategic, economic and cultural importance.

Beyond the mainland, the Caribbean is a world of its own: a scatter of island arcs and low limestone platforms shaped by tectonics, reef growth and sea-level change over long periods. The larger islands—Cuba, Hispaniola (Haiti and the Dominican Republic) and Jamaica—include mountain interiors and broad valleys, whilst smaller states such as Antigua and Barbuda, Dominica, Grenada, Saint Lucia, Saint Kitts and Nevis and Saint Vincent and the Grenadines are often steep, volcanic and tightly bounded by the sea. The Bahamas and Barbados present different forms again: low-lying carbonate islands and uplifted limestone, where freshwater and soil are scarce and settlement has long been conditioned by delicate natural limits. Trinidad and Tobago lie close to South America yet remain part of the Caribbean system, with forested hills and coastal wetlands that connect Atlantic and Caribbean environments.

Together, these landforms shape drainage, soils and natural barriers, creating regional identities that influenced isolation or exchange and determined where farming flourished, where cities rose and where movement was channelled through plains, valleys and navigable waters over centuries.

The Climate

The climate of North America is among its most defining and dynamic features, driving biological diversity and setting hard boundaries for human life and economic activity. It is shaped by latitude, atmospheric circulation, ocean currents and topography. The continent's great north–south reach places it within nearly every climatic zone, from polar ice and tundra to tropical rainforest. Prevailing westerly winds, combined with the immense wall of western mountains, create stark contrasts between wet coastal slopes and arid interiors through the rain-shadow effect.

In the far north of Canada and Alaska, Arctic and subarctic climates dominate: long, dark winters, short cool summers and widespread permafrost that limits both vegetation and construction. South of this lies the boreal forest, where strongly continental conditions produce extreme seasonal swings affecting ecosystems and livelihoods.

Across the interior—from the Canadian prairies through the American Midwest—the temperate continental climate brings four distinct seasons.

Here, the open plains allow air masses to collide with little restraint: frigid Arctic air surges south, warm humid air pushes north from the Gulf and dry air spills east from the high interior. The result is volatility on a grand scale, including the powerful thunderstorms and tornado outbreaks associated with the central plains.

The western mountains produce a mosaic of climates compressed by elevation and exposure. Windward slopes intercept Pacific moisture, supporting temperate rainforests along parts of the Pacific Northwest and coastal British Columbia, whilst leeward basins descend into steppe, scrub and desert in the American Southwest and northern Mexico. Farther south, the Mexican highlands temper tropical latitude with altitude, creating climates that can shift sharply within short distances.

Central America is largely tropical but varies with elevation and coastal orientation. Caribbean-facing slopes are often wetter, whilst Pacific coasts tend towards marked wet and dry seasons. Volcanoes and cloud forests sit above lowland jungles and even small shifts in wind or sea-surface temperature can transform rainfall patterns with significant consequences for agriculture, water supply and stability.

The Caribbean is defined by warm temperatures, trade winds and the rhythms of the Atlantic hurricane season. While the sea moderates temperature, it also fuels storms. Hurricanes and tropical storms shape coastlines, ecosystems and settlement patterns from the Bahamas and Cuba through Jamaica, Hispaniola and the Lesser Antilles, bringing periodic destruction alongside the life-giving rain on which island freshwater supplies depend.

Across all regions, climatic extremes—floods, droughts, blizzards, heatwaves and storms—have repeatedly tested human resilience, encouraging innovation in settlement, architecture and land use, whilst periodically imposing sharp limits on security, growth and long-term sustainability.

The Waterways

North America's hydrological systems form a connective network that sustains ecosystems, supports economies and binds distant regions together across political boundaries. The continent's defining watershed is the Mississippi–Missouri–Ohio system, draining much of the interior United States and carrying water and sediment to the Gulf of Mexico. For centuries it has served as a corridor of movement, commerce and agriculture, shaping the development of cities and the fortunes of regions.

To the north, the Mackenzie River drains a vast portion of north-western Canada into the Arctic Ocean. To the east, the St Lawrence River links the Great Lakes to the Atlantic, forming one of the great inland navigation routes of the world. The Great Lakes themselves—Superior, Michigan, Huron, Erie and Ontario—are vast freshwater seas and a foundational resource for both Canada and the United States.

On the Pacific slope, rivers such as the Fraser and Columbia run from mountain headwaters to the sea, supporting salmon runs, hydroelectric power and coastal ecosystems. Farther south, the Colorado River is a lifeline through arid lands, its flow engineered and contested as it sustains cities and farms and has carved dramatic geological monuments.

In Mexico and Central America, rivers are often shorter and steeper, descending quickly from highlands to the sea. They can be torrential in the wet season and diminished in the dry, shaping patterns of settlement, flood risk and agriculture. Panama's geography is uniquely defined by its narrowness and its linkage of two oceans, with water management forming the basis of the canal system that has reshaped global trade.

In the Caribbean, freshwater is more constrained and locally dependent. Larger islands may hold river valleys and interior watersheds, whilst low-lying islands rely heavily on rainfall, aquifers and careful management. Coastal wetlands, estuaries and mangrove forests—where land and sea interlock—serve as nurseries for fisheries and buffers against storm surges, linking ecological health directly to human security and survival.

Natural Resources and Biomes

This varied physical framework supports an exceptional range of ecosystems and vast natural wealth distributed unevenly across the continent. Across the far north, tundra gives way to a near-continuous belt of boreal forest, a major global store of carbon and freshwater. Southwards, mixed and deciduous forests cover much of the east, whilst the interior plains support temperate grasslands whose fertile soils have long underpinned one of the world's great agricultural heartlands.

The western mountains host stacked life zones: foothill woodlands, conifer forests, alpine meadows and glaciated peaks, acting as both biodiversity refuges and 'water towers' that store winter snowpack. In the south-west, deserts and semi-arid scrublands sustain life through precise adaptations, where water and shade are the currencies of survival.

Tropical ecosystems dominate in southern Mexico and Central America, ranging from lowland rainforest to cloud forest and mangrove coast. These regions are among the most biologically rich on Earth, yet also among the most vulnerable to deforestation, soil loss and changing rainfall patterns. The Caribbean adds a further dimension: coral reefs, seagrass beds and coastal lagoons that support fisheries, tourism and shoreline protection. These marine systems are highly productive but sensitive to warming seas, pollution and overuse.

Beneath this biological variety lies a deep geological endowment. The Canadian Shield holds major deposits of nickel, copper, gold and uranium. Sedimentary basins across the interior contain coal, oil and natural gas, shaping the economic histories of Canada and the United States and influencing Mexico's development along the Gulf coast. In Central America and the Caribbean, mineral resources vary widely, but fertile volcanic soils, forests and coastal fisheries have long been central to livelihoods, with tourism now a dominant economic force in many island states.

The distribution of resources—from prairie soils to timber belts, from hydrocarbon basins to mineral veins—has guided migration, investment and political power. It has also generated enduring tensions between exploitation and stewardship, as mining, logging, intensive farming and coastal development alter habitats and heighten exposure to hazards.

North America's continental framework is therefore not merely a scenic backdrop but the first architect of its human story. Mountains channel winds and movement; rivers connect basins and economies; climates decide what can be grown and where communities can endure. In the chapters that follow, the focus turns to how societies across Canada, the United States, Mexico, Central America and the Caribbean have adapted to, relied upon and been shaped by this formidable, varied setting over time.

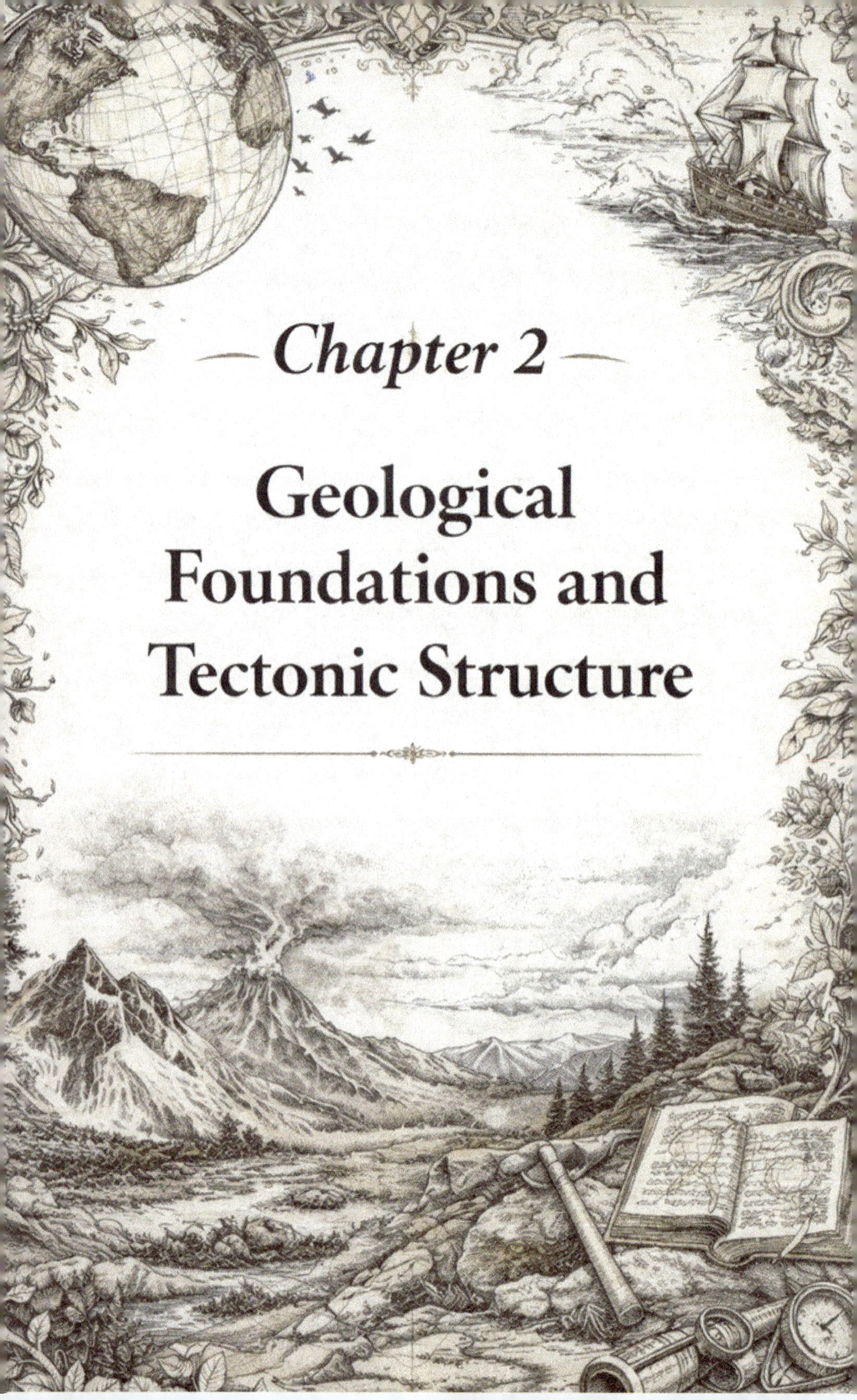

Chapter 2

Geological Foundations and Tectonic Structure

A Continent's Bedrock

To understand North America, one must begin with its immense geological age and extraordinary depth of time extending across billions of years of planetary history. The continent is not a single, uniform block but a mosaic assembled over billions of years through collision, separation and renewal driven by powerful tectonic forces. At its centre lies the Canadian Shield, a vast expanse of ancient igneous and metamorphic rock forming the continent's stable craton. This is exposed Precambrian bedrock, shaped less by rivers than by the grinding power of ice sheets that repeatedly advanced and retreated across immense distances and reshaped the surface over time.

These rocks preserve a record of Earth's early history—episodes of volcanism and mountain-building so ancient that erosion has long since reduced their heights. The Shield's thin soils and hard surfaces constrained agriculture but offered rich mineral seams, encouraging distinctive patterns of settlement and industry across Canada and influencing northern regions of the United States over centuries of development and extraction.

The Story of the Mountains

Much of the continent's dramatic relief is the product of collisions along its margins and prolonged tectonic struggle over deep geological time. The contrast between east and west reflects two distinct chapters in a long geological saga spanning hundreds of millions of years and multiple continental cycles of assembly.

In the east, the Appalachian Mountains are the worn remnants of violent ancient uplift. They formed during major mountain-building episodes associated with the assembly of the supercontinent Pangaea, when landmasses collided and the crust buckled into towering ranges. Over hundreds of millions of years, erosion lowered those heights into rounded ridges and valleys. The Appalachians' folded strata preserve extensive coal deposits and complex fault systems, shaping both the industrial history of the United States and regional development in Atlantic Canada over many generations.

The western mountains tell a younger, more active story marked by instability and renewal. Along the Pacific margin, oceanic plates have long been driven beneath the continental plate, a process that uplifts ranges, feeds volcanism and generates earthquakes. The Cordilleran systems—including the Rockies, Sierra Nevada, Cascades and Mexico's Sierra Madre—remain a region of ongoing geological dynamism. Volcanic chains continue through Mexico and Central America, where subduction fuels eruptions and earthquakes that have shaped landscapes, soils and settlement patterns from Guatemala to Costa Rica and Panama.

In this western realm, the continent is still being built and the hazards of tectonics remain a living fact of everyday geography and environmental risk for populations.

The Shaping Hand of Ice

If tectonics provided the framework, ice carved the surface with relentless force and continental scale across vast regions. During the Pleistocene, vast glaciers advanced from the north, covering much of Canada and reaching deep into the northern United States. Their impact was transformative and enduring across landscapes and ecosystems. They scoured rock, transported sediments and fundamentally reshaped drainage systems across entire regions and interconnected watersheds.

The basins of the Great Lakes were excavated and deepened by ice. Glacial deposits laid down fertile soils across parts of the interior, whilst leaving the Shield scraped and lake-studded. Retreating ice formed countless depressions that filled with water, creating the dense pattern of lakes that characterises large areas of Canada and the northern United States. Even today, the land continues a slow post-glacial rebound, subtly altering coastlines and drainage patterns over time and affecting modern environments and infrastructure.

Basins, Plains and the Modern Face

Between the ancient core and the young mountains lie the great interior basins and plains, underlain by thick layers of sedimentary rock deposited over millions of years by inland seas, rivers and eroding mountains. These strata store vast reserves of groundwater and fossil fuels and are fundamental to the agricultural and industrial strength of the interior regions today and their long-term productivity.

In the western interior, crustal stretching created basin-and-range landscapes of alternating ridges and valleys. Along the Gulf coast and parts of California, thick sediment accumulations became the porous reservoirs that trap oil and gas. These regions, formed by deposition as much as collision, became natural corridors for transport and concentrated settlement, supporting population growth and economic expansion across strategic areas of the continent.

In essence, every major feature of the continent is a chapter in deep time. The stable core offers permanence, the west reveals ongoing change and the ice-shaped surface explains much of modern water, soil and land use. Geology is not background scenery: it dictates mineral wealth, soil fertility, water availability and the geography of hazards, forming the most fundamental foundation of North America's human story and environmental constraints.

Chapter 3

Climate Regions and Weather Extremes

The Architecture of a Continent's Weather

The sheer scale of North America, stretching from the Arctic Ocean to the tropical seas of the Caribbean and Central America, creates one of the most complex climate systems on Earth today. This vast latitudinal reach places the continent beneath every major global circulation zone, from polar easterlies to tropical trade winds. Superimposed upon this atmospheric framework are the seasonal migration of the sun, the shifting positions of semi-permanent high- and low-pressure systems and, most decisively for day-to-day weather, the strength and path of the polar jet stream.

These forces operate across a dramatic physical landscape. Towering mountain chains running north–south, immense interior plains and warm bordering oceans all shape how air masses move, collide and transform over time. The result is a climate system characterised by sharp contrasts and rapid change. Calm conditions can give way to violent storms within hours and regions separated by only a few hundred kilometres may experience entirely different weather at the same moment.

Stability is therefore often fleeting. North America's geography encourages strong boundaries between air masses—cold, dry Arctic air; warm, moist tropical air; and hot, dry continental air—creating ideal conditions for atmospheric instability. This inherent volatility has made weather both a defining challenge and a central influence on settlement, agriculture and infrastructure across the continent for centuries.

Climates from Tropical to Polar

North America encompasses almost the full spectrum of global climate types found on Earth. In the far north, polar and subarctic climates dominate Alaska, northern Canada and the Arctic archipelagos. Here, winters are long, dark and severe, with temperatures remaining below freezing for much of the year. Summers are short and cool, limiting vegetation to tundra and boreal forest. Permafrost underlies much of this region, shaping ecosystems and placing constraints on construction, transport and resource development.

Southwards, humid continental climates prevail across much of southern Canada and the northern United States. These regions experience four distinct seasons: cold, snowy winters; warm to hot summers; and transitional spring and autumn periods marked by rapid weather changes. Large temperature differences between seasons reflect the continent's distance from moderating oceans and the ease with which air masses move across the open interior.

The south-eastern United States is largely humid subtropical. Long, hot and humid summers contrast with mild winters and rainfall is frequent throughout the year, often delivered by thunderstorms. Southern Florida, much of Central America and many Caribbean islands fall within tropical climate zones. Here, temperatures remain warm year-round and seasonal variation is defined more by rainfall than by temperature, with alternating wet and dry seasons shaping agriculture, water supply and ecosystems.

To the west of the interior plains, climates become progressively drier. Semi-arid steppe conditions dominate the Great Plains' western margins, giving way to true desert climates in the American Southwest and northern Mexico, including the Sonoran, Mojave and Chihuahuan Deserts. Along a narrow stretch of coastal California, a Mediterranean climate prevails, characterised by wet, mild winters and hot, dry summers—a rare climate type on the continent that has shaped distinctive agricultural systems and settlement patterns.

In contrast, the Pacific Northwest and coastal British Columbia experience temperate maritime climates. Moist air from the Pacific Ocean brings abundant rainfall, relatively mild temperatures and reduced seasonal extremes, supporting dense forests, productive fisheries and stable river systems.

Altitude adds a further layer of complexity. Mountain climates create cooler, wetter conditions at higher elevations, producing alpine environments above deserts, subtropical lowlands or temperate plains. Within a single watershed, climates may range from semi-arid foothills to snow-covered peaks, profoundly influencing water availability, hazard exposure and ecological diversity.

Seasonal Dynamics and Defining Phenomena

North America's climate is highly seasonal, with atmospheric circulation patterns shifting dramatically between summer and winter each year. During summer, the land heats rapidly, drawing warm, moisture-laden air northwards from the Gulf of Mexico and the Caribbean. This moisture fuels widespread humidity and frequent thunderstorms across the central and eastern regions of the continent. In the south and east, afternoon convection becomes a daily feature, while in the interior plains, the collision of air masses can produce severe weather.

In winter, the polar jet stream typically shifts southward, acting as a dynamic boundary between cold Arctic air and warmer southern air. Along this front, powerful mid-latitude cyclones develop, drawing energy from temperature contrasts. Depending on their track and intensity, these systems can produce heavy rain, freezing rain, blizzards or severe thunderstorms. Winter storms often travel long distances, affecting multiple regions over several days and disrupting transport, energy supply and commerce on a continental scale.

A distinctive seasonal feature of the south-western United States and northern Mexico is the North American Monsoon. Driven by intense summer heating over the Mexican Plateau and surrounding deserts, wind patterns shift to draw moisture northward from the Pacific Ocean and the Gulf of California. From mid-summer into early autumn, this moisture produces dramatic afternoon thunderstorms, delivering a significant proportion of annual rainfall to an otherwise arid region. The monsoon is highly variable, alternating between active periods of heavy rain and prolonged dry spells, adding uncertainty to water management, hazard planning and agriculture.

Weather Extremes

North America's climatic energy is most evident in its extreme weather events, which occur with a frequency and intensity unmatched in many other parts of the world today.

Tornadoes - The central United States remains the global epicentre of tornado activity. The continent's geography allows warm, moist air from the Gulf of Mexico to surge northwards, while cooler, drier air descends from Canada and hot, dry air flows eastward from the interior plateaux. When these air masses meet beneath strong upper-level winds, rotating supercell thunderstorms can develop, producing tornadoes of exceptional strength. Although forecasting and warning systems have improved dramatically, tornadoes remain a significant hazard, shaping building practices, emergency planning and public awareness across the plains and adjacent regions.

Hurricanes and Tropical Cyclones - From late spring through autumn, warm waters in the Atlantic Ocean, Gulf of Mexico and Caribbean provide the energy for tropical cyclones. These storms threaten the eastern and southern coasts of the United States, Mexico, Central America and the Caribbean islands. Their impacts extend beyond destructive winds to include torrential rainfall and storm surge, often the deadliest element. Slow-moving storms can cause catastrophic inland flooding, overwhelming river systems and infrastructure hundreds of kilometres from the coast and long after landfall.

Drought and Heatwaves - Large areas of the western interior are vulnerable to prolonged drought and extreme heat. Persistent high-pressure systems can trap hot air over regions for weeks, producing heatwaves that strain electricity grids, damage crops and threaten human health. Reduced snowpack and declining river flows compound water shortages, while dry conditions heighten the risk of wildfires. From the boreal forests of western Canada to the mountain ranges of Mexico, fire has become an increasingly prominent and disruptive feature of the landscape.

Winter Blizzards - In Canada and the northern United States, winter storms can combine heavy snowfall, strong winds and severe cold to create blizzard conditions. Visibility may drop to near zero, transport networks can be paralysed and communities isolated for days. Lake-effect snow adds another dimension, as cold air passing over relatively warm Great Lakes generates intense local snowfall that can bury towns under metres of snow in a single event.

Climate Change and the Future

These climatic phenomena are not peripheral to North American life. They shape where people live, how food is grown, how cities are built and how infrastructure is designed and maintained. In recent decades, human-driven climate change has begun to alter the background conditions under which these systems operate. Warmer air holds more moisture, intensifying rainfall and flooding. Heatwaves are becoming more frequent and severe, droughts more persistent and wildfire seasons longer. Shifts in jet stream behaviour may be changing storm tracks and seasonal patterns.

Understanding North America's climate is therefore no longer only a matter of description, but of necessity. As populations grow and environmental pressures increase, the continent's ability to adapt to a more volatile climate will be central to its future resilience, shaping economic planning, environmental policy and the daily lives of its people for generations.

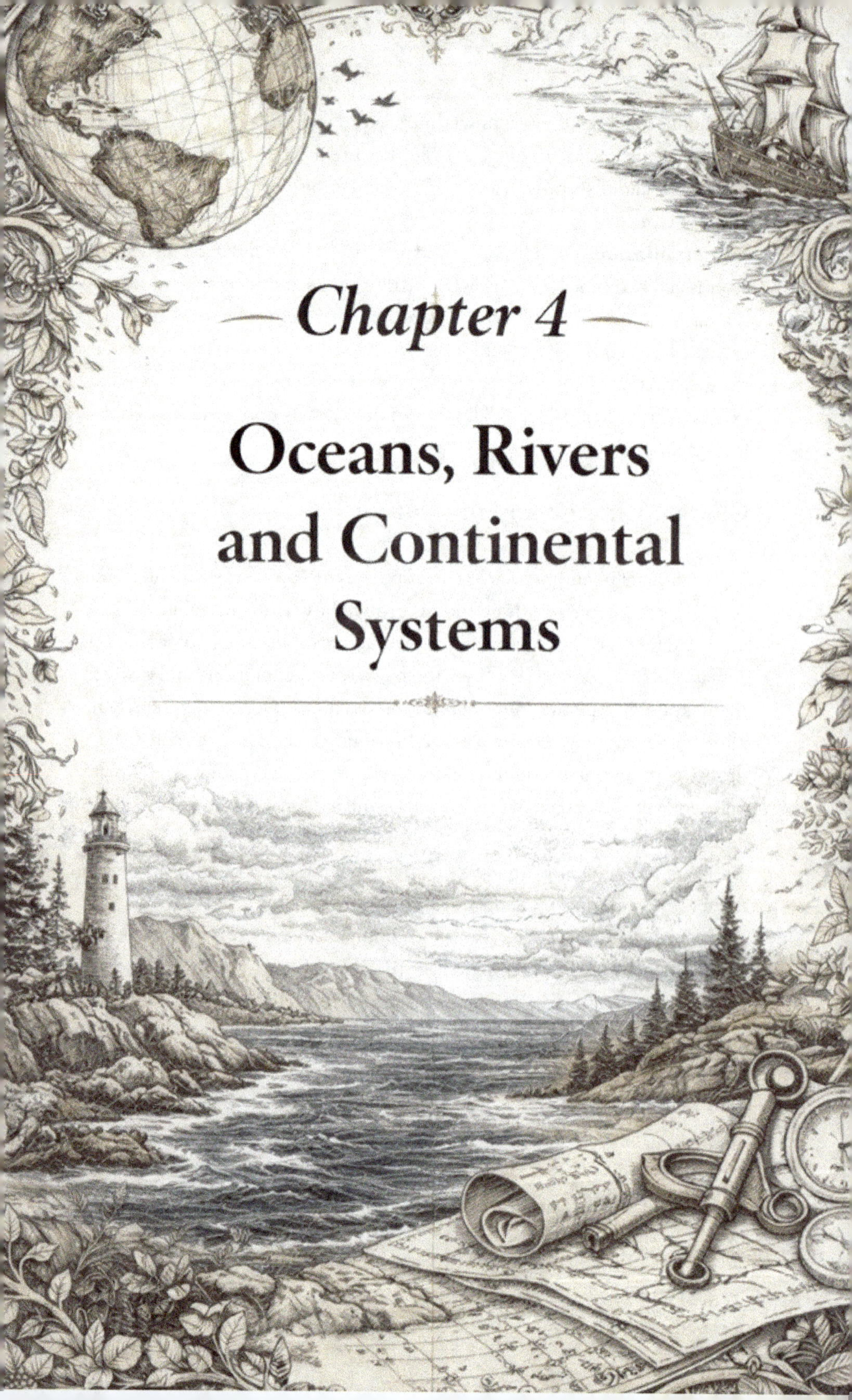

Chapter 4

Oceans, Rivers and Continental Systems

The Blue Framework of a Continent

While climate governs the atmosphere above North America, it is water that binds the continent together at the surface and beneath it in complex, interdependent ways across time. Oceans, rivers, lakes and underground aquifers form the circulatory system of the land, shaping ecosystems, enabling human settlement and linking distant regions into shared environmental and economic systems. From the frozen Arctic seas to the warm waters of the Caribbean and from glacier-fed mountain rivers to slow-moving lowland deltas, water is the primary agent through which the continent is connected, transformed and sustained over time and history.

North America's hydrological systems are inseparable from its physical geography and long geological evolution. Mountain chains direct rainfall and snowfall into vast drainage basins; plains allow rivers to meander and expand; and coastlines determine where fresh water meets salt in productive and fragile zones.

Over time, these systems have carved valleys, built floodplains and deltas and created corridors that guided migration, trade and empire. In the modern era, they have become engines of agriculture, industry, power generation and urban growth—while also emerging as focal points of environmental stress, resource depletion and political conflict across regions.

The Encircling Oceans

North America is bounded by three great oceans, each exerting a profound influence on climate, ecology and human activity across multiple scales and systems.

To the east lies the Atlantic Ocean, whose warm currents, particularly the Gulf Stream, moderate temperatures along the eastern seaboard. This ocean has historically been the continent's primary gateway to Europe and Africa, shaping early colonisation, trade and migration. Its continental shelf supports rich fisheries, while its warm waters fuel tropical cyclones that periodically strike the Gulf Coast, the Caribbean and the eastern United States. Rising sea levels and coastal erosion now threaten densely populated shorelines and low-lying islands, making the Atlantic margin one of the most vulnerable regions on the continent today and in coming decades.

To the west, the Pacific Ocean presents a sharply different character. Cold, nutrient-rich currents such as the California Current support highly productive marine ecosystems, including kelp forests and major fisheries. The Pacific coast is also a tectonically active margin, where earthquakes, tsunamis and volcanic activity reflect the ongoing movement of Earth's plates.

For centuries, the Pacific has connected North America to Asia, shaping trade networks, migration patterns and geopolitical strategy across the wider Pacific world and beyond.

To the north, the Arctic Ocean is both the smallest and most rapidly changing of the world's oceans. Sea ice has long defined its ecology and limited navigation, but accelerating warming is transforming this frozen frontier. Retreating ice is opening new shipping routes and access to resources, while profoundly disrupting Arctic ecosystems and Indigenous ways of life. The Arctic's transformation is one of the clearest indicators of global climate change, with implications far beyond the polar regions and into global systems.

Great River Systems and Drainage Basins

Between these oceans lies a continent organised around immense river systems and interconnected watersheds. North America's rivers are not isolated features, but components of vast drainage basins that collect precipitation from thousands of kilometres and deliver it to the sea through complex networks.

The largest of these is the Mississippi–Missouri–Ohio river system, which drains roughly two-fifths of the contiguous United States. Rising in the Rocky Mountains and the Appalachian highlands, its tributaries gather water across the Great Plains and Central Lowlands before emptying into the Gulf of Mexico. This system has been central to North American history: a transportation artery, an agricultural lifeline and a defining feature of regional identity. Its fertile floodplains underpin some of the world's most productive farmland, while its controlled channels and levees reveal humanity's long effort to manage, rather than adapt to, natural flow processes and seasonal variability.

To the north, the Mackenzie River system drains a vast portion of northwestern Canada into the Arctic Ocean. It is one of the world's great river systems by length and volume, yet remains sparsely populated along much of its course. Seasonal freezing and thawing define its rhythms and its watershed plays a crucial role in Arctic freshwater balance and ocean circulation patterns.

On the eastern side of the continent, the St Lawrence River forms a natural highway linking the Great Lakes to the Atlantic. Together, the St Lawrence–Great Lakes system constitutes the largest connected freshwater system on Earth by surface area. These waters have supported Indigenous societies for millennia and later became the industrial heartland of Canada and the United States, enabling inland navigation, manufacturing and sustained urban growth over generations.

Along the Pacific slope, rivers such as the Columbia, Fraser and Sacramento descend steeply from mountain headwaters to the sea. Their swift gradients make them ideal for hydroelectric power, while their seasonal flows support salmon runs that are central to both ecosystems and Indigenous cultures. Farther south, the Colorado River stands as one of the continent's most contested waterways. Rising in the Rockies and flowing through arid landscapes, it carved the Grand Canyon and sustains millions of people across the American Southwest and northern Mexico—yet its waters are now so heavily allocated that they rarely reach the sea.

In Mexico and Central America, river systems are generally shorter but more intense. Steep topography and tropical rainfall produce fast-flowing rivers prone to seasonal flooding. These waters sustain agriculture and hydroelectric generation but also pose hazards to settlements built along their banks. Panama's rivers, in particular, underpin the operation of the Panama Canal, one of the most strategically important waterways in the world, linking the Atlantic and Pacific Oceans through a carefully engineered freshwater system and controlled hydrology.

Lakes, Wetlands and Inland Seas

Beyond rivers, North America is distinguished by its abundance of lakes and wetlands across multiple climatic zones and landscapes. The Great Lakes—Superior, Michigan, Huron, Erie and Ontario—are inland seas in all but name. They store roughly one-fifth of the world's surface freshwater and influence climate, weather and economy across a vast region. Lake-effect snow, generated when cold air passes over warmer lake waters, can produce extreme local snowfall, while the lakes themselves have long served as trade corridors and industrial hubs.

Elsewhere, countless smaller lakes dot the landscapes of Canada and the northern United States, many formed by glacial action. These lakes regulate local climates, support fisheries and tourism and act as reservoirs within broader watersheds, buffering seasonal variations in water supply and temperature.

Wetlands are among the continent's most productive and threatened environments. The Florida Everglades, a slow-moving sheet of freshwater flowing southward, exemplifies the delicate balance between water, vegetation and wildlife. Along the Gulf Coast, the Mississippi Delta's wetlands buffer storms, nurture fisheries and trap sediments—yet they are rapidly eroding due to altered river flow, sea-level rise and sustained human intervention over decades.

In Central America and the Caribbean, mangroves and coastal lagoons perform similar roles, protecting shorelines, filtering pollutants and supporting marine life. Their loss exposes communities to storm surge and undermines local economies dependent on fishing, tourism and coastal stability.

Water, Climate and Human Systems

North America's water systems are deeply entwined with climate and human activity across all regions and scales. Snowpack in western mountains acts as a natural reservoir, releasing water gradually through spring and summer. Changes in snowfall and melt timing now threaten this balance, affecting agriculture, cities and ecosystems downstream. Aquifers beneath the Great Plains and other regions supply irrigation and drinking water, but over-extraction has lowered water tables and raised concerns about long-term sustainability and resilience.

Human engineering has profoundly altered natural flow. Dams regulate rivers for flood control, irrigation and power generation, while canals and diversions redirect water across watersheds and political boundaries.

These interventions have enabled large populations to thrive in otherwise inhospitable environments, but they have also disrupted sediment flows, blocked fish migration and intensified conflicts between upstream and downstream users across regions.

Water has therefore become a central political issue. Disputes over allocation, quality and access cross local, national and international boundaries, particularly where rivers and aquifers are shared. Climate change adds urgency to these tensions, as shifting precipitation patterns and rising temperatures place greater strain on already stressed systems and governance frameworks.

An Interconnected and Fragile System

Oceans, rivers, lakes and wetlands form a single, interconnected framework that sustains North America at every scale and level. They regulate climate, shape landscapes, support biodiversity and underpin economies. Yet this framework is increasingly fragile. Pollution, overuse, habitat loss and climate change threaten water quality and availability across the continent and its diverse regions.

Understanding North America's hydrological systems is therefore essential not only for interpreting its geography and history, but for confronting its future. As the pressures of population growth and environmental change intensify, the management of water—how it is shared, protected and restored—will be one of the defining challenges of the continent's next chapter and long-term resilience.

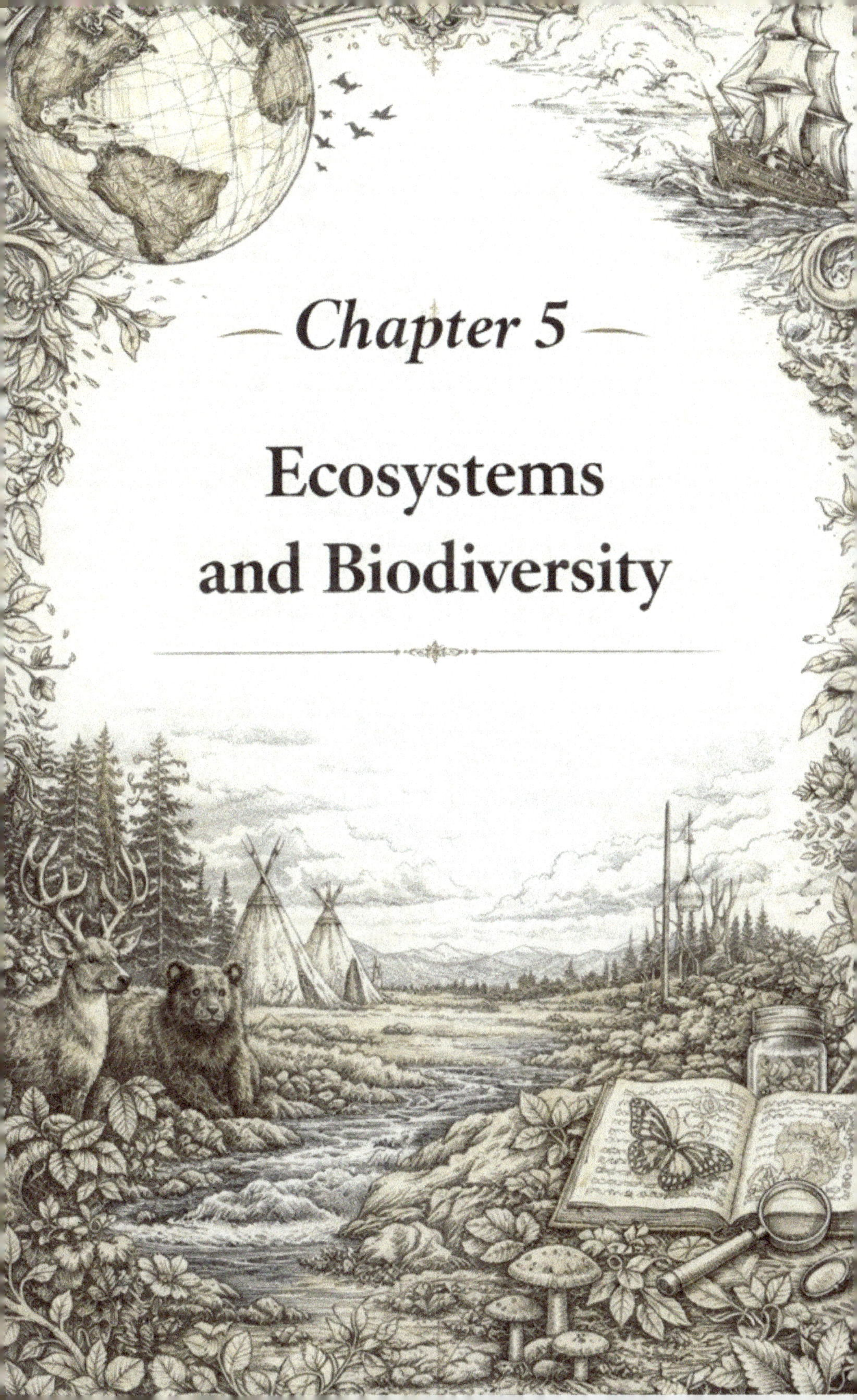

Chapter 5

Ecosystems and Biodiversity

A Continent of Living Worlds

North America's extraordinary physical range—from the icebound tundra of the far north to the warm, clear waters of tropical reefs—supports an equally varied abundance of life across immense distances. This chapter surveys the continent's principal ecosystems, or biomes: broad communities of plants and animals shaped by shared climate, soils and landform. These are not static landscapes but living systems—restless, interconnected and constantly reshaped by fire, flood, storm and seasonal change over time.

From the immense conifer forests of Canada to the tropical forests of Central America and from the grasslands of the interior to the island chains of the Caribbean, North America's biodiversity is the outcome of long evolutionary histories punctuated by geological upheaval and climatic swings. In more recent centuries, it has also been profoundly influenced by human settlement, land use and the movement of species. Together, these living worlds form a continental mangle, with threads that run across borders and seas, linking distant places through migration, currents and shared environmental pressures.

Tundra and Boreal Forest

At the northern edge of the continent lies the Arctic tundra: a treeless realm of permafrost, fierce winds and dramatic seasonal change. Life here is an exercise in endurance under extreme conditions. Vegetation stays low to the ground—mosses, lichens, sedges and dwarf shrubs—seizing the brief summer to grow, flower and set seed before cold returns. Animal life is equally specialised. Caribou undertake vast migrations across open landscapes; musk oxen survive blizzards in dense coats; and polar bears, dependent on sea ice, hunt seals along the shifting edge of the frozen ocean. The tundra is fragile, its thin surface easily disturbed and it is now among the regions most rapidly altered by warming temperatures and accelerating environmental change. Even modest shifts can thaw frozen soils, redirect drainage and rearrange the delicate pattern of plant life on which the food web depends.

South of the tundra spreads the boreal forest, or taiga: the largest terrestrial biome on Earth, sweeping across Alaska and Canada and reaching into the northern United States. It is a world of conifers—spruce, fir, pine and larch—adapted to long winters, short growing seasons and often acidic soils. Fire is a defining force here, clearing old stands, recycling nutrients and opening space for regeneration. The boreal forest supports a distinctive cast of wildlife: moose browsing in wetlands, snowshoe hares turning white with the seasons and predators such as lynx and great grey owls tracking cyclical prey populations. In summer it becomes a vast breeding ground for migratory birds that disperse across the continent and into the tropics.

Its scale can seem uniform, yet its ecology is finely balanced and small changes in temperature or fire regime can ripple across enormous distances.

Eastern Forests

Across much of eastern North America, from the Great Lakes to the Gulf Coast, lies the temperate deciduous forest. Defined by four clear seasons, it is shaped by winter cold, spring growth and the annual shedding of leaves in autumn. Broadleaf trees—oak, maple, hickory and beech—dominate, creating layered habitats in which spring wildflowers briefly flourish before the canopy closes. These forests support diverse animal life, including white-tailed deer, black bears, foxes, grey squirrels, wild turkeys and a remarkable variety of birds, many of which migrate between North America and the Caribbean or Central America each year.

Centuries of logging, farming and urban expansion have altered these forests profoundly, but old-growth fragments remain and extensive second-growth woodlands now cover many regions, forming a patchwork landscape of recovery and continued use. Their modern character is inseparable from human history, yet the underlying ecological processes—succession, soil formation and seasonal rhythms—remain enduring.

In the south-east, particularly along the Atlantic and Gulf Coastal Plain, warmer conditions support subtropical ecosystems. The Florida Everglades is the best known: a vast, slow-moving wetland often described as a 'river of grass', fed by freshwater flowing south from Lake Okeechobee. Sawgrass marshes, mangroves and tree islands create habitat for alligators, wading birds and rare species such as the Florida panther. This is a system balanced delicately on water quality and flow, vulnerable to drainage, pollution and saltwater intrusion.

Here, minor shifts in hydrology can trigger cascading change, transforming habitat structure and undermining entire food chains.

Grasslands and Prairies

At the centre of the continent lie the temperate grasslands, once a near-continuous expanse from the Canadian prairies through the Great Plains to the southern United States and into northern Mexico. These landscapes are shaped by semi-arid climates, fertile soils and recurring disturbance—fire, drought and grazing—that prevents woodland from taking hold. In the wetter east, tallgrass prairie once rose above head height but has been largely converted to cropland. In the drier west, shortgrass prairie remains more extensive, though fragmented by development and intensive land use.

Wind, fire and grazing interact to sustain open horizons, building some of the richest soils on Earth and making these regions among the world's great agricultural heartlands.

The prairies co-evolved with immense herds and the predators that followed them. The American bison was a keystone species, shaping vegetation through grazing and wallowing. Pronghorn, adapted for speed across open land and prairie dogs, whose burrow systems supported a host of other species, were central players in grassland ecology. The transformation of prairie into farmland ranks among the most dramatic ecological changes of the modern era, though conservation efforts increasingly focus on restoring remnant grasslands and the processes—fire regimes, native grazing patterns and connectivity—that once sustained them.

Restoration seeks not simply to preserve scenery, but to revive the living mechanics that make grasslands function.

Deserts, Mountains and Tropical Forests

The west of the continent is a region of stark contrasts and compressed ecological zones. Deserts such as the Mojave, Sonoran and Chihuahuan are not empty spaces but ecosystems of finely tuned adaptation. Plants store water, minimise loss through waxy coatings or reduced leaves and spread shallow roots to capture brief rains. Many animals avoid daylight heat, emerging at night; some, such as kangaroo rats, can survive without drinking, relying on metabolic water and moisture in food.

Life here depends on timing, efficiency and the ability to endure long intervals between brief pulses of abundance.

Rising above these arid basins, the western mountains form stacked bands of habitat. As elevation increases, foothill scrub gives way to conifer forest, then to alpine meadows and bare rock. The Rockies and Sierra Nevada support species such as grizzly bears, mountain goats and specialised birds like Clark's nutcracker, which caches seeds and shapes forest regeneration. These ranges also act as continental 'water towers', storing snowpack that feeds rivers far downstream.

As temperatures rise, many species shift upslope in search of suitable conditions, yet mountain environments offer refuge only to a point—the land eventually runs out.

Along the Pacific coast, from northern California into Canada and Alaska, temperate rainforests thrive where abundant rainfall and coastal fog sustain towering trees and lush understories. Here stand some of the largest and oldest organisms on Earth, including coast redwoods and giant sequoias.

The ecosystem is layered and moisture-rich, supporting ferns, mosses and a dense web of insects and birds, including species dependent on old-growth structure. In these forests, decay is as essential as growth, recycling vast biomass into continuously renewed soils and habitat.

Farther south, in Mexico and across Central America, tropical forests and cloud forests support extraordinary biodiversity. Warm temperatures, high rainfall and complex topography create habitats ranging from lowland rainforest to cool, misty highlands. These regions are rich in endemic species and vital for water regulation, yet they are also among the most pressured by deforestation, agricultural expansion and changing rainfall patterns.

In the tropics, forest loss does not merely remove trees; it can alter entire local climates, river flows and soil stability.

The Marine and Coastal Fringes

North America's marine environments are as varied as its inland biomes and equally vital to ecological health. Along the Pacific coast, cold, nutrient-rich waters support kelp forests—underwater habitats of immense productivity that shelter fish, invertebrates and marine mammals such as sea otters. In the Atlantic, Gulf of Mexico and Caribbean, warmer seas foster coral reefs and seagrass beds, including major reef systems off Mexico and Central America and around the islands of the Caribbean. These ecosystems support fisheries, protect shorelines and sustain tourism economies across many nations.

Currents link distant coasts, carrying larvae, nutrients and heat, ensuring that marine systems are connected even when shorelines are politically divided.

Where rivers meet the sea, estuaries, mangroves and salt marshes form some of the most productive ecosystems on the continent. They filter pollutants, buffer storm surges and serve as nurseries for fish and feeding grounds for birds. Sites such as the Chesapeake Bay and the Mississippi Delta illustrate both the power of these environments and their vulnerability to development, pollution and sea-level rise.

When these coastal fringes degrade, the consequences extend inland through fisheries collapse, reduced water quality and increased exposure to storms.

Forces of Change and Conservation

North America's biodiversity was shaped over deep time, yet the pace of change accelerated sharply with modern land use and industrial development. Habitat loss through agriculture, urbanisation and resource extraction remains the primary threat. Invasive species—such as zebra mussels in freshwater systems or feral pigs in forests—disrupt native ecological balances. Pollution, over-exploitation and the growing influence of climate change further intensify pressures by shifting species ranges, altering fire cycles and warming seas.

These forces rarely act in isolation; they compound one another, amplifying stress and reducing ecological resilience.

Yet the continent has also been central to the modern conservation movement. The creation of Yellowstone in 1872 set an early precedent for large-scale protection and a wider network of national parks, protected areas and wildlife refuges now safeguards representative habitats across many regions. Increasingly, conservation has expanded beyond preservation towards restoration: reintroducing key species, rebuilding wetlands, restoring seagrass beds and undertaking prairie recovery at landscape scales. Such efforts acknowledge that protection alone cannot repair damaged ecological relationships.

Conservation in the modern sense is as much about rebuilding function as it is about guarding boundaries.

North America's ecological story is therefore one of profound loss, remarkable persistence and ongoing negotiation between use and protection. Its biodiversity holds ecological, economic and cultural value and its living systems underpin the basic services—clean water, fertile soils, coastal protection and climate regulation—upon which societies depend. To safeguard these ecosystems is not simply to preserve nature, but to secure the foundations of life and livelihood for the continent's future generations.

PART II

HUMAN HISTORY AND DEVELOPMENT

Part Two of this guide explores the human narrative of North America.

Overview

Part Two of this guide turns from landscape to lived experience, tracing the human narrative of North America across deep time. While Part One established the physical stage of mountains, rivers, coastlines and climate zones, Part Two introduces the peoples who have inhabited, shaped and contested this vast region for millennia. The chapters that follow chart an arc from the earliest arrivals and the flourishing of Indigenous worlds, through the shattering transformations of European exploration and colonisation, to the industrial and political revolutions that forged the modern era.

This is not a neat, linear tale. North America's history is a dense and often painful weave of movement, innovation, exchange, conflict and adaptation. It unfolds across a continent that is both a single geographical whole and a patchwork of distinct regions: the northern forests and plains of Canada; the sprawling interior and coasts of the United States; the deserts, highlands and tropical lowlands of Mexico; the volcanic and forested bridge of Central America and the island nations of the Caribbean, from the Bahamas and Cuba to Haiti and the Dominican Republic, Jamaica, Barbados, Trinidad and Tobago and the smaller states of the Lesser Antilles, including Antigua and Barbuda, Dominica, Grenada, Saint Kitts and Nevis, Saint Lucia and Saint Vincent and the Grenadines. To understand the societies and challenges of today, one must first understand the long, layered human past that produced them.

Indigenous Flourishing

The story begins with the continent's first peoples, whose presence stretches back more than thirteen thousand years and likely earlier still. They were never a single civilisation, but a multitude of nations and cultures speaking hundreds of languages, adapting to environments that ranged from Arctic tundra and boreal forest to desert, prairie, rainforest and reef-fringed coasts.

Across what is now Canada and the United States, complex societies formed with distinctive economies and belief systems: coastal communities built wealth around fisheries and maritime trade; interior peoples shaped grassland and woodland environments through controlled burning and seasonal movement; and in the river valleys of the east and south, agricultural worlds emerged, supporting dense populations and monumental earthworks associated with the Hopewell and Mississippian traditions.

Farther south, in Mexico and Central America, Indigenous societies developed some of the most influential civilisations in the Americas. Powerful city-states, trade networks and intellectual traditions—expressed through architecture, mathematics, astronomy and writing—flourished across

Mesoamerica. These worlds were not isolated from the wider continent: they were connected through migration, exchange and shared ecological systems. This long era of Indigenous flourishing established deep relationships to land and water and it laid cultural, political and economic foundations that endure, despite centuries of disruption.

Exploration and Colonisation

A profound rupture began with the arrival of Europeans. Early Norse contact in the north was followed, more decisively, by transatlantic voyages after 1492. Exploration was driven by overlapping motives: the search for trade routes, the pursuit of wealth, imperial rivalry and the spread of Christianity. Yet what followed was far more than exploration. It was a sustained process of conquest, settlement and colonisation that reshaped the continent's demographic, political and ecological reality.

The collision between Old World ambitions and established Indigenous nations produced complex outcomes. There were alliances and exchanges as well as wars; trade brought new goods and technologies even as it altered economies and power balances; and, most catastrophically, disease swept through communities with devastating effect. Across the continent—from Canada's Atlantic seaboard to the interior plains, from the Pacific coast to the Mexican heartland and through Central America and the Caribbean—colonisation created new societies built upon displacement, forced labour and racial hierarchies, alongside new cultural forms forged through mixing, survival and resistance.

The Caribbean, in particular, became a focal point of imperial competition and plantation economies. The histories of Cuba, Haiti, the Dominican Republic, Jamaica, Barbados, the Bahamas, Trinidad and Tobago and the smaller island states are inseparable from the transatlantic slave trade, sugar production and maritime empires—forces that linked island shores to global markets and left legacies still felt in language, culture, land ownership and inequality.

Industrialisation and its Costs

The transformations of colonisation accelerated with the rise of industrialisation. Beginning in the late eighteenth century and expanding through the nineteenth and twentieth, the shift from agrarian economies to mechanised manufacturing and resource extraction remade North America's cities, transport networks and labour systems. Railways and ports tightened the bonds between interior and coast; new industries drew waves of migrants and reconfigured social life; and the continent's vast reserves of timber, minerals, oil and gas became engines of economic power.

Yet industrial progress carried heavy costs. Forests were cleared at unprecedented scale; rivers were dammed and diverted; mines and factories reshaped landscapes and polluted air and water; and fossil fuels became the foundation of modern economies. The consequences were not distributed evenly. Indigenous lands were further encroached upon, communities were displaced or marginalised and industrial wealth often grew alongside stark inequality.

From the coalfields and manufacturing belts of Canada and the United States to oil-producing regions and industrial corridors in Mexico and through export-oriented agriculture and extraction across parts of Central America and the Caribbean, industrialisation established a pattern of intensive resource use. It also marked the beginning of measurable human influence on climate, as rising emissions and widespread environmental change began to alter the conditions upon which societies depended.

Legacies and Challenges in Modern North America

These forces culminate in the complex portrait of contemporary North America: a region of immense economic weight and cultural dynamism, home to nearly six hundred million people, shaped by migration from every corner of the globe. It includes some of the world's largest economies and cities, as well as small island nations whose histories and futures are tightly bound to oceans, trade and climate.

Modern North America is defined by the long, often difficult legacies of its past: the resilience and sovereignty claims of Indigenous nations; the enduring structures and cultural identities formed through colonisation; the demographic and cultural consequences of slavery and forced labour; and the technological benefits and environmental burdens inherited from industrial society. Across Canada, the United States and Mexico and throughout Belize, Guatemala, El Salvador, Honduras, Nicaragua, Costa Rica, Panama and the Caribbean states—the modern era is marked by the need to address questions of sustainability, equality, governance and identity in an increasingly interconnected world.

In essence, Part Two provides the historical context for understanding why North America looks, feels and functions as it does. From the first footsteps on ancient ground to the networks of the twenty-first century, this is the story of how human ambition, ingenuity and encounter have shaped a continent—sometimes through creativity and cooperation, sometimes through violence and loss—and how those choices continue to echo in the present.

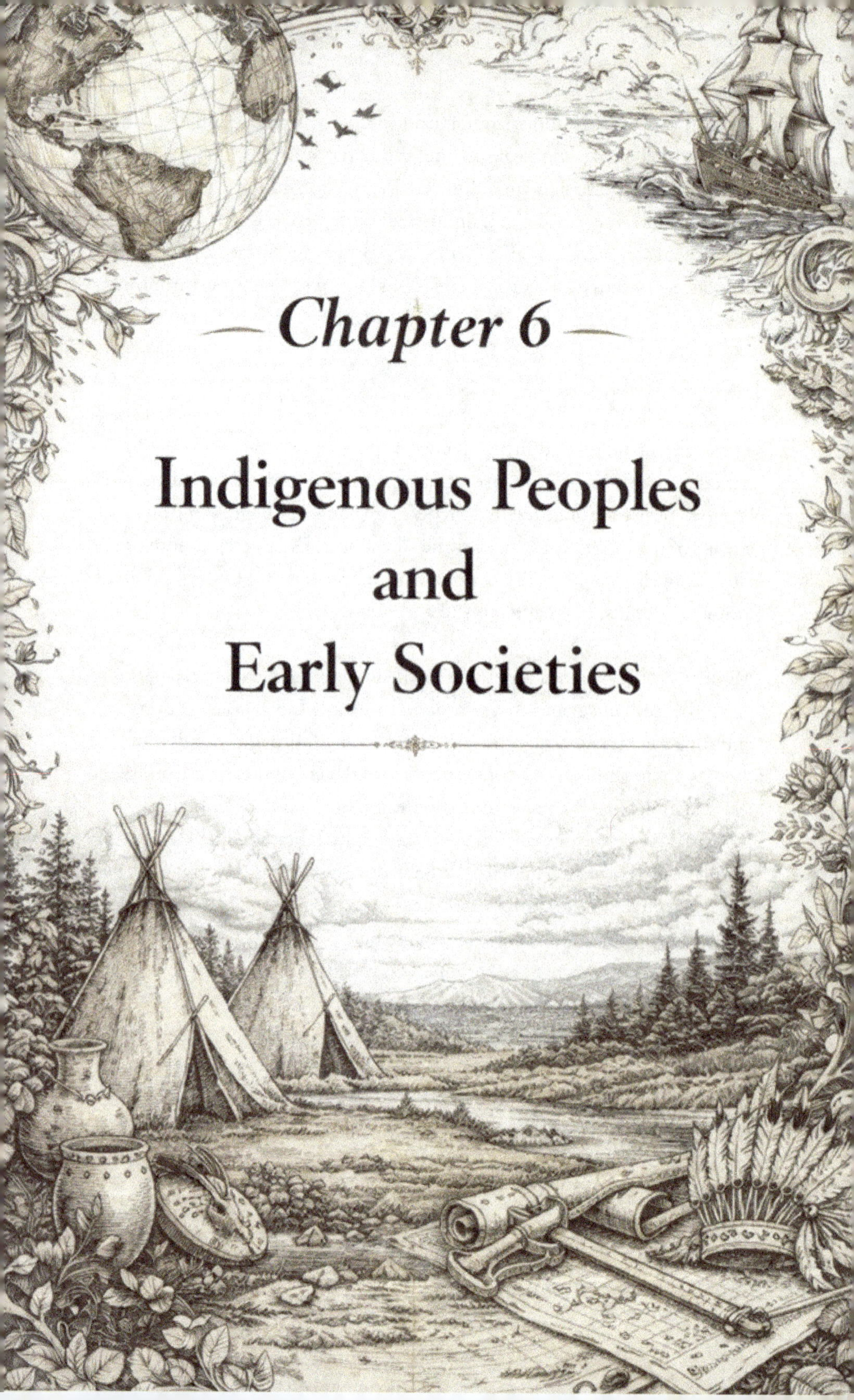

Chapter 6

Indigenous Peoples and Early Societies

Early Migrations and the Peopling of a Continent

The human story of North America does not begin with European arrival in 1492, but far earlier, with a series of remarkable migrations across a vast land bridge known as Beringia. During periods of lowered sea level in the last Ice Age, this broad expanse of tundra connected Siberia to Alaska, allowing people to move gradually into the Americas over generations. The precise timing of these migrations remains the subject of active scholarly debate. Some evidence suggests human presence as early as 40,000 years ago, while more conservative interpretations place initial settlement closer to 13,000 years ago. What is clear is that these first peoples dispersed widely, giving rise over time to hundreds of distinct nations, cultures and languages across the continent and its varied regions.

These early migrants carried more than tools for hunting and survival. They brought social structures, belief systems, oral traditions and ecological knowledge that would underpin human life in every North American environment. From the outset, settlement was not random but informed by careful observation of landscapes, animals and seasonal rhythms, laying the foundations for enduring relationships between people and place across centuries.

For much of the twentieth century, archaeological understanding was dominated by the 'Clovis First' model. This theory proposed that the earliest inhabitants of North America were associated with distinctive fluted stone spear points first identified near Clovis, New Mexico, dating to around 13,000 years ago. This view has since been fundamentally revised. Sites such as Meadowcroft Rockshelter in Pennsylvania have yielded clear evidence of human occupation—tools, hearths and habitation layers—dating back roughly 16,000 years. These findings demonstrate that people were present well before the emergence of Clovis technology and likely arrived by diverse routes and strategies that remain under investigation today.

Additional sites reinforce this picture of a deeper and more complex peopling process. Excavations at Buttermilk Creek in Texas and Bluefish Caves in the Yukon provide corroborating evidence of pre-Clovis occupation, suggesting that colonisation unfolded gradually rather than as a single wave. Together, these discoveries reveal a long and adaptive human presence that preceded the end of the Ice Age across multiple landscapes.

The descendants of these earliest peoples formed the roots of all later Indigenous societies. Initially, many lived as highly mobile hunters of Pleistocene megafauna such as mammoths and giant bison. As climates warmed and these animals declined, societies adapted in sophisticated ways. New technologies, including the spear-thrower or atlatl, improved hunting efficiency, while subsistence strategies diversified to include fishing, trapping and the gathering of wild plants. These adaptations fostered regional specialisation and cultural diversity, as communities learned to exploit rivers, forests, plains and coasts with increasing precision and knowledge.

The first enduring patterns of settlement, seasonal movement and resource management emerged during this formative period, shaping lifeways long afterwards.

Mound Builders and Confederacies

East of the Mississippi River, a succession of complex societies arose whose legacy remains etched into the landscape through thousands of earthen mounds across wide territories. Collectively known as the Mound Builders, these cultures constructed large-scale earthworks that served as ceremonial platforms, elite residences and burial sites. Their construction required coordinated labour, long-term planning and a sophisticated understanding of engineering and social organisation across generations.

Among the earliest were the Adena (c. 500 BCE–100 CE) and Hopewell (c. 100 BCE–500 CE) cultures of the Ohio River Valley. Rather than centralised states, these were expansive networks of communities linked by trade routes spanning much of the continent. Along these routes flowed copper from the Great Lakes, mica from the Appalachians, shells from the Gulf Coast and obsidian from the Rocky Mountains. The geometric earthworks and mound complexes they left behind were often aligned with celestial events, reflecting advanced astronomical knowledge and ceremonial life. Trade networks also facilitated the spread of ideas, rituals and agricultural practices, creating a broad cultural sphere across eastern North America over centuries.

This tradition reached its height with the Mississippian culture (c. 800–1600 CE), the most complex society north of Mexico before European contact. Its greatest centre, Cahokia, near present-day St Louis, was a vast urban settlement supported by intensive maize agriculture and governed by a powerful religious and political elite. At its peak around 1050 CE, Cahokia may have housed some 15,000 inhabitants and featured more than 120 mounds. Monks Mound, a massive ten-storey earthen structure, remains the largest prehistoric earthwork in the Americas.

Mississippian influence spread widely, visible in shared artistic styles, religious symbols and settlement patterns throughout the southeastern interior. The society also illustrates the close relationship between environment and culture, as its inhabitants carefully managed floodplains, forests and waterways to sustain dense populations over centuries and climatic fluctuations.

In the north-east, complex political alliances emerged that rivalled any contemporary systems elsewhere in the world. Foremost among these was the Haudenosaunee Confederacy, often known as the Iroquois Confederacy. According to oral tradition, the confederacy was founded by the Peacemaker, Deganawidah and his spokesman Hiawatha, perhaps as early as the twelfth century. It united five nations—the Mohawk, Oneida, Onondaga, Cayuga and Seneca—later joined by the Tuscarora. Their Great Law of Peace established a sophisticated form of representative governance that balanced the autonomy of individual nations with collective decision-making, conflict resolution and mutual defence. Emphasising consensus, accountability and diplomacy, the confederacy demonstrates that complex political theory developed independently in North America and later influenced European and colonial thinking about governance and law.

Pueblos, Canals and Cliff Dwellings

In the arid landscapes of the American Southwest, Indigenous societies developed ingenious adaptations to a challenging environment of heat, scarcity and unpredictability. The Ancestral Puebloans, alongside neighbouring cultures such as the Hohokam and Mogollon, built enduring communities based on advanced dryland farming. Their agricultural systems incorporated crop diversification, storage techniques and water management strategies that reflected deep ecological knowledge and long-term planning across difficult terrain.

The Hohokam, centred in what is now southern Arizona, constructed the most extensive irrigation network in pre-Columbian North America. Hundreds of miles of canals diverted water from the Salt and Gila Rivers to irrigate fields of maize, beans and cotton. Maintaining this system required careful coordination, social cooperation and technical expertise, allowing sizeable populations to flourish in an otherwise inhospitable desert environment for centuries.

The Ancestral Puebloans, whose heartland lay in the Four Corners region, are renowned for their architectural achievements. Over time, they evolved from pit-houses to above-ground masonry structures and eventually to the iconic cliff dwellings built into canyon alcoves. Sites such as Mesa Verde in Colorado and Chaco Canyon in New Mexico testify to remarkable engineering skill and social complexity. Chaco Canyon, in particular, functioned as a major ceremonial and economic centre, linked to distant communities by a network of straight roads. Its buildings were carefully aligned with solar and lunar cycles, revealing advanced astronomical understanding and cosmological belief systems that reinforced social cohesion and shared identity.

Around 1300 CE, prolonged drought and likely social stresses led to the abandonment of many major centres. Yet these peoples did not disappear. Their descendants migrated and reorganised into the historic Pueblo communities of the Rio Grande valley and the Hopi mesas. Acoma Pueblo, known as 'Sky City', has been continuously occupied since at least 1150 CE, making it one of the oldest inhabited settlements in what is now the United States. These communities continue to maintain languages, ceremonial practices and social traditions that connect the present directly to the deep past and ancestral landscapes.

The Pacific Coast, Plains and Subarctic

Across North America, societies developed in close dialogue with their environments, adapting with precision to local opportunities and limits. On the Northwest Coast, from northern California through British Columbia to Alaska, abundant marine and forest resources supported dense, sedentary populations without agriculture. Nations such as the Tlingit, Haida, Kwakwaka'wakw and Chinook lived in large plank-house villages and developed highly stratified societies. Their cultures are renowned for monumental art—totem poles, carved masks and painted house fronts—and for the potlatch, a ceremonial institution that redistributed wealth, affirmed status and preserved historical memory through ritual and storytelling across generations.

On the Great Plains, Indigenous life was transformed by technological change and expanding interregional exchange. Prior to European contact, many Plains societies combined limited farming in river valleys with seasonal bison hunting on foot. This changed dramatically in the seventeenth and eighteenth centuries with the spread of the horse from Spanish settlements and the acquisition of firearms through trade. Mounted hunting revolutionised mobility, warfare and trade, enabling nations such as the Lakota, Cheyenne and Comanche to follow bison herds across vast distances and to resist colonial expansion with formidable effectiveness. The emergence of horse culture reshaped political and social organisation across the plains, creating fluid and dynamic power relationships and new strategic frontiers.

In the Subarctic regions of Canada and Alaska, nations including the Cree, Dene and Gwich'in lived in smaller, highly mobile groups. Survival depended on intimate knowledge of seasonal cycles and animal behaviour, particularly of caribou and moose. Technologies such as the canoe, snowshoe and toboggan were perfectly adapted to movement across forest, river and snow. Knowledge was transmitted through oral tradition and apprenticeship, ensuring continuity in demanding environments where misjudgement could be fatal and resources scarce.

Legacies and the Confrontation with History

The arrival of Europeans unleashed a catastrophe of unprecedented scale across much of the continent. While conflict and disease were not unknown in pre-contact societies, the introduction of Old World pathogens—smallpox, measles and influenza—to populations with no prior exposure proved devastating. Epidemics often spread far in advance of direct contact, sometimes destroying entire communities and severing cultural continuity before Europeans arrived. In some regions, mortality rates reached 70 to 90 per cent, collapsing social structures and creating conditions that facilitated colonial domination and dispossession.

This demographic collapse was followed by centuries of warfare, displacement, land seizure and forced assimilation. Yet the idea that Indigenous peoples belong only to the past is a profound misunderstanding. Despite immense loss, Native nations endured through adaptation, resistance and negotiation. Today, more than 570 federally recognised tribes in the United States and over 630 First Nations communities in Canada remain sovereign political entities with distinct cultures, languages and governing traditions, and continuing legal rights.

The early societies of North America were not merely precursors to European expansion. They were complex, innovative civilisations in their own right—builders of cities, managers of landscapes, creators of extensive trade networks and developers of sophisticated political and philosophical systems. Their history is not a prelude but the foundation and continuation of the continent's human story. To understand North America fully, one must recognise the depth, diversity and enduring presence of its first peoples, whose ingenuity and resilience shaped a continent long before—and long after—European arrival and continuing change.

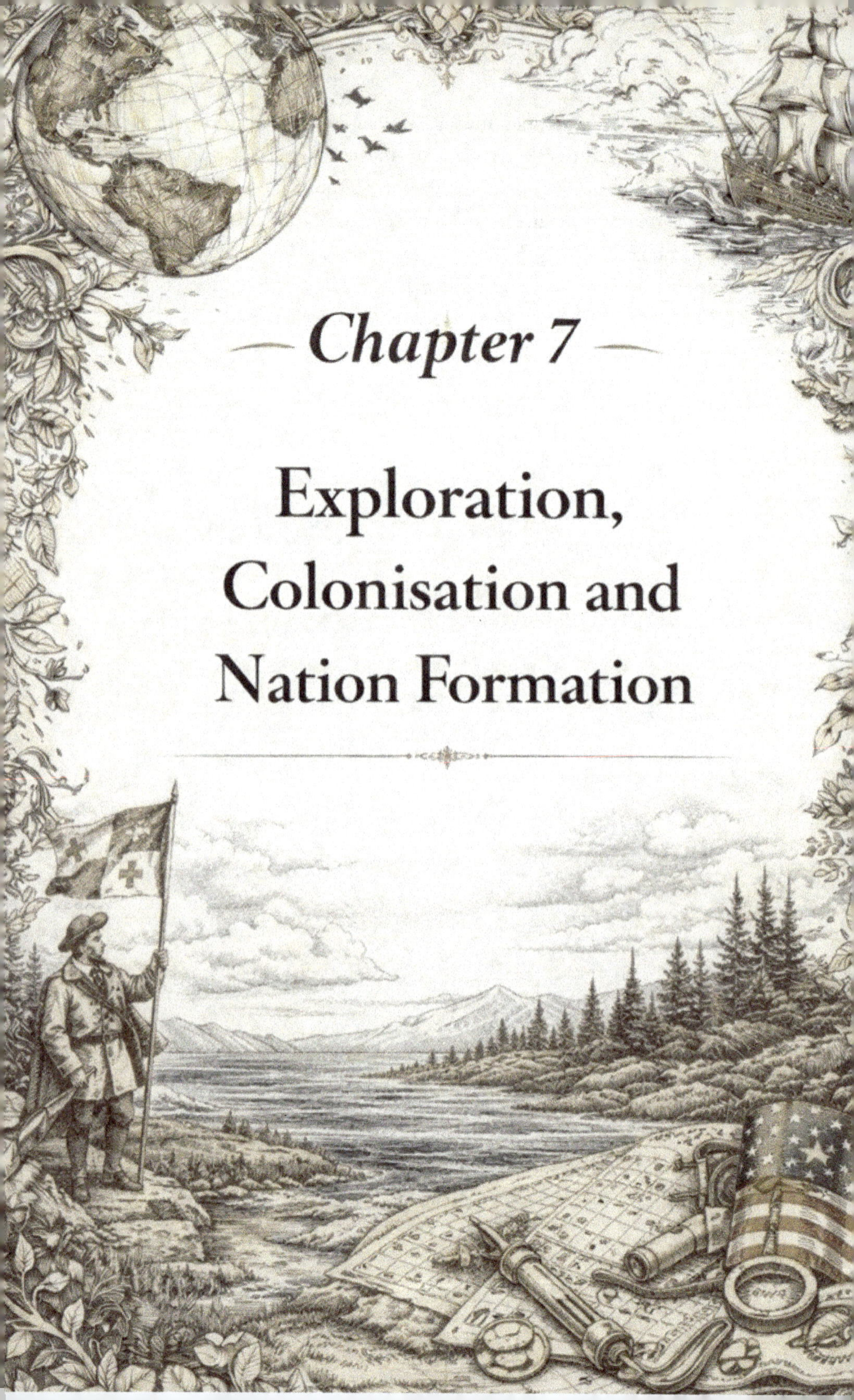

Chapter 7

Exploration, Colonisation and Nation Formation

The Old World's Imperatives

For thousands of years after the first peoples settled North America, the continent developed largely apart from the political and economic systems of Europe, Africa and Asia. This relative isolation ended not because of a sudden European fascination with distant lands, but as the result of a powerful convergence of forces within Western Europe during the late fifteenth century. Political ambition, commercial pressure and religious zeal combined with new intellectual currents to propel Europeans outward across the oceans and into unfamiliar worlds.

The Renaissance fostered renewed interest in classical knowledge, geography and science, while advances in cartography and seamanship expanded the practical limits of travel. Exploration became conceivable not merely as adventure, but as a means to acquire wealth, prestige and spiritual authority. At the heart of this drive lay trade. European elites sought direct access to the lucrative markets of Asia—spices, silks and porcelains—that reached Europe through long and costly overland routes controlled by Muslim and Italian intermediaries. The Ottoman capture of Constantinople in 1453 further constricted these routes, raising prices and sharpening the incentive to find alternatives, especially by sea.

At the same time, technological innovation transformed maritime possibility. The caravel, a light and manoeuvrable sailing vessel and navigational instruments such as the astrolabe and magnetic compass made long ocean crossings more feasible. Emerging centralised monarchies—most notably Spain and Portugal, soon followed by France and England—possessed both the financial resources and political motivation to sponsor voyages of exploration. This commercial ambition was inseparable from a powerful religious ideology. The crusading spirit that had animated the Reconquista of the Iberian Peninsula was readily transferred to overseas expansion, framing exploration as a divine mission to spread Christianity alongside empire and profit across continents.

Royal patronage combined with private investment, turning exploration into both a personal gamble for fame and fortune and a calculated strategy to extend imperial power and outmanoeuvre rival states in Europe.

Spanish and Portuguese Encounters

Europe's first sustained encounters with the Americas were, in many respects, accidental and shaped by misunderstanding. In 1492, the Genoese navigator Christopher Columbus, sailing under the Spanish crown, reached the Caribbean islands while seeking a westward route to Asia. Though mistaken in his geography, his voyages initiated permanent transatlantic contact and triggered a rapid escalation of European activity. Reports of fertile land and precious metals fuelled Spanish ambition and ushered in an era of expansion whose consequences would be global and enduring.

This process is now understood as the Columbian Exchange: a vast and unprecedented transfer of crops, animals, diseases, peoples and ideas between the Old and New Worlds. Maize, potatoes and tomatoes travelled east; horses, cattle and wheat travelled west; pathogens such as smallpox accompanied them, with devastating effects on Indigenous populations. Ecologies, economies and societies on both sides of the Atlantic were transformed in ways that still shape the modern world.

Spanish expansion was swift and often brutal, driven by a conquistador ethos that fused martial violence, religious conviction and the pursuit of wealth. In the early sixteenth century, Hernán Cortés dismantled the Aztec Empire in Mexico, while Francisco Pizarro destroyed the Inca Empire in South America. Although these conquests lay south of North America proper, their implications were felt across the continent, altering imperial expectations and Indigenous diplomacy.

Expeditions pushed northwards in search of wealth and territory. Figures such as Pánfilo de Narváez and Hernando de Soto moved through the south-eastern interior, leaving trails of destruction, disease and upheaval. Francisco Vázquez de Coronado's expedition of 1540–1542 penetrated deep into the American Southwest, encountering Pueblo societies but failing to locate the fabled cities of gold, despite vast hardship.

Spain's most enduring legacy in North America took shape through permanent settlements and the mission system, particularly in Florida, the Southwest and California. St Augustine, founded in 1565, became the oldest continuously occupied European settlement in the continental United States. Spanish influence shaped language, religion, agriculture and legal traditions that remain embedded in large parts of the continent and its regional identities.

Portugal's formal claim to the Americas, secured by the Treaty of Tordesillas in 1494, lay primarily in South America. Its influence on North America was nevertheless profound. Portuguese traders became central to the emerging transatlantic slave trade, a system soon adopted by other European powers to sustain colonial economies. Portuguese advances in navigation and cartography also circulated widely, indirectly supporting later exploration of North American coasts and Atlantic routes.

French, Dutch and English Models

As Spanish and Portuguese dominance waned, other European powers pursued colonisation according to distinct priorities and social models, shaped by geography and competition.

New France developed as a vast but thinly populated domain centred on the St Lawrence River, the Great Lakes and the Mississippi basin. Its economic foundation was the fur trade, particularly beaver pelts, which depended on cooperation with Indigenous hunters and trading partners. As a result, French colonisation often emphasised alliances rather than mass settlement. Jesuit missionaries sought conversion, while traders known as coureurs des bois frequently lived among Indigenous communities, forging kinship ties through marriage and shared economic interests. Although conflict existed, French expansion initially disrupted Indigenous land use less aggressively than English settlement in many areas.

French colonial society thus evolved as a hybrid system shaped by mobility, diplomacy and adaptation to local environments, creating networks of mutual dependence that stretched across much of the continent's interior over generations.

The Dutch presence was shorter-lived but influential. New Netherland, centred on New Amsterdam, was established by the Dutch West India Company as a commercial venture. It became a cosmopolitan trading hub characterised by relative religious tolerance and legal pluralism. However, its emphasis on commerce rather than large-scale settlement left it militarily vulnerable. In 1664, it was absorbed by England and renamed New York, though its mercantile and multicultural legacy would endure in urban life.

It was England that developed the colonial model with the most far-reaching consequences for eastern North America. English colonies varied widely in origin and purpose. Virginia, founded in 1607 at Jamestown, began as a profit-seeking corporate venture and struggled for survival.

New England colonies, such as Plymouth (1620) and Massachusetts Bay (1630), were settled largely by religious dissenters seeking to build godly communities. Despite their differences, English colonies shared a defining characteristic: the establishment of permanent agricultural settlements intended to replace existing land use and assert lasting control.

English concepts of land ownership—fenced farms, fixed boundaries and private property—clashed fundamentally with Indigenous systems based on shared and seasonal use. The result was persistent and often devastating conflict, including the wars with the Powhatan Confederacy in Virginia and King Philip's War in New England. Over time, English colonies developed codified legal systems, representative assemblies and market-oriented agriculture, creating enduring social hierarchies and strong regional identities that shaped later politics.

Colonial Societies and the Path to Revolution

By the eighteenth century, North America's colonies had matured into distinct regional societies with entrenched economic interests. In the southern colonies, plantation agriculture reliant on enslaved African labour produced tobacco, rice and later cotton, generating immense wealth for a small elite while entrenching racialised systems of exploitation. New England developed a more diversified economy based on small farms, fishing, shipbuilding and trade, underpinned by strong local governance and religious traditions. The middle colonies, including New York and Pennsylvania, became productive agricultural regions and cultural crossroads shaped by migration and diversity, often marked by pragmatic tolerance.

All these colonies were embedded in transatlantic networks that moved goods, people and ideas, tying North America to a global system of commerce and empire. Imperial rivalry repeatedly drew them into European wars, culminating in the Seven Years' War (1754–1763). Britain's victory eliminated France as a continental rival and transferred vast territories to British control, but the cost of war left Britain heavily indebted and politically impatient.

In response, Parliament imposed new taxes and regulations on the Thirteen Colonies, provoking a crisis over sovereignty and representation. Colonial resistance drew on Enlightenment ideas, local traditions of self-government and long-standing grievances. Out of this tension emerged a revolutionary movement that blended economic, political and philosophical demands, and increasingly embraced organised mobilisation.

The American Revolution (1775–1783) was both a war for independence and a civil conflict that divided colonial society. With decisive French support, the colonies secured independence in 1783 and established a republic grounded in Enlightenment principles, even as it remained deeply compromised by the institution of slavery. The revolution also reshaped the north: tens of thousands of loyalists migrated to British North America, reinforcing a distinct political and cultural path that would later define Canada. The ideological impact of the revolution extended far beyond the continent, influencing subsequent democratic movements and constitutional experiments around the world for decades.

Nation Formation in the North and South

The late eighteenth and early nineteenth centuries marked an era of rapid nation-building and accelerating territorial change. The United States, under its new Constitution, embarked on aggressive territorial expansion. Justified by the ideology of Manifest Destiny, this process included the Louisiana Purchase of 1803, war with Mexico in 1846–1848 and the steady advance of settlement across Indigenous lands. Treaties were routinely broken and forced removals culminated in tragedies such as the Trail of Tears, which displaced the Cherokee and other south-eastern nations in the 1830s with immense suffering.

Expansion relied on military force, legal manipulation and settler migration, permanently transforming political boundaries and ecosystems across the continent and reshaping regional economies.

To the north, fears of American expansion and internal division encouraged British colonies to unite. Through negotiation rather than revolution, the Dominion of Canada was formed in 1867.

Confederation established a federal system designed to balance regional interests and accommodate linguistic and cultural diversity, particularly between English- and French-speaking populations, while maintaining ties to Britain.

In the south, Mexico emerged from a long and turbulent war of independence from Spain between 1810 and 1821. Its early national history was marked by instability, internal divisions and the loss of vast northern territories to the United States. By the mid-nineteenth century, the divergent trajectories of the United States and Mexico were clear: one expanding rapidly and industrialising, the other struggling to reconcile regional autonomy, Indigenous communities and central authority amid repeated foreign interventions and shifting regimes.

Freedom and Coercion

This era of exploration, colonisation and nation-building is defined by a central and painful paradox at its core. European settlers in North America constructed societies founded on ideals of liberty, self-government and opportunity. Yet these societies were made possible through systems of profound coercion: the dispossession and subjugation of Indigenous peoples and the enslavement of millions of Africans across generations.

The wealth and power of emerging nations rested on these injustices. As a result, the societies forged during this period carried within them deep contradictions between proclaimed ideals and lived realities. These tensions shaped subsequent history, contributing to the American Civil War and continuing struggles over civil rights, Indigenous sovereignty and historical redress in many forms.

The legacies of this era remain inseparable from the present. Modern debates over inequality, identity, reparations and reconciliation are rooted in the choices and structures established during the age of European expansion and imperial competition.

Understanding this period is therefore essential to understanding North America itself—not only as a place of opportunity and innovation, but as a continent whose history is marked by enduring conflict between freedom and coercion, and the continuing work of justice.

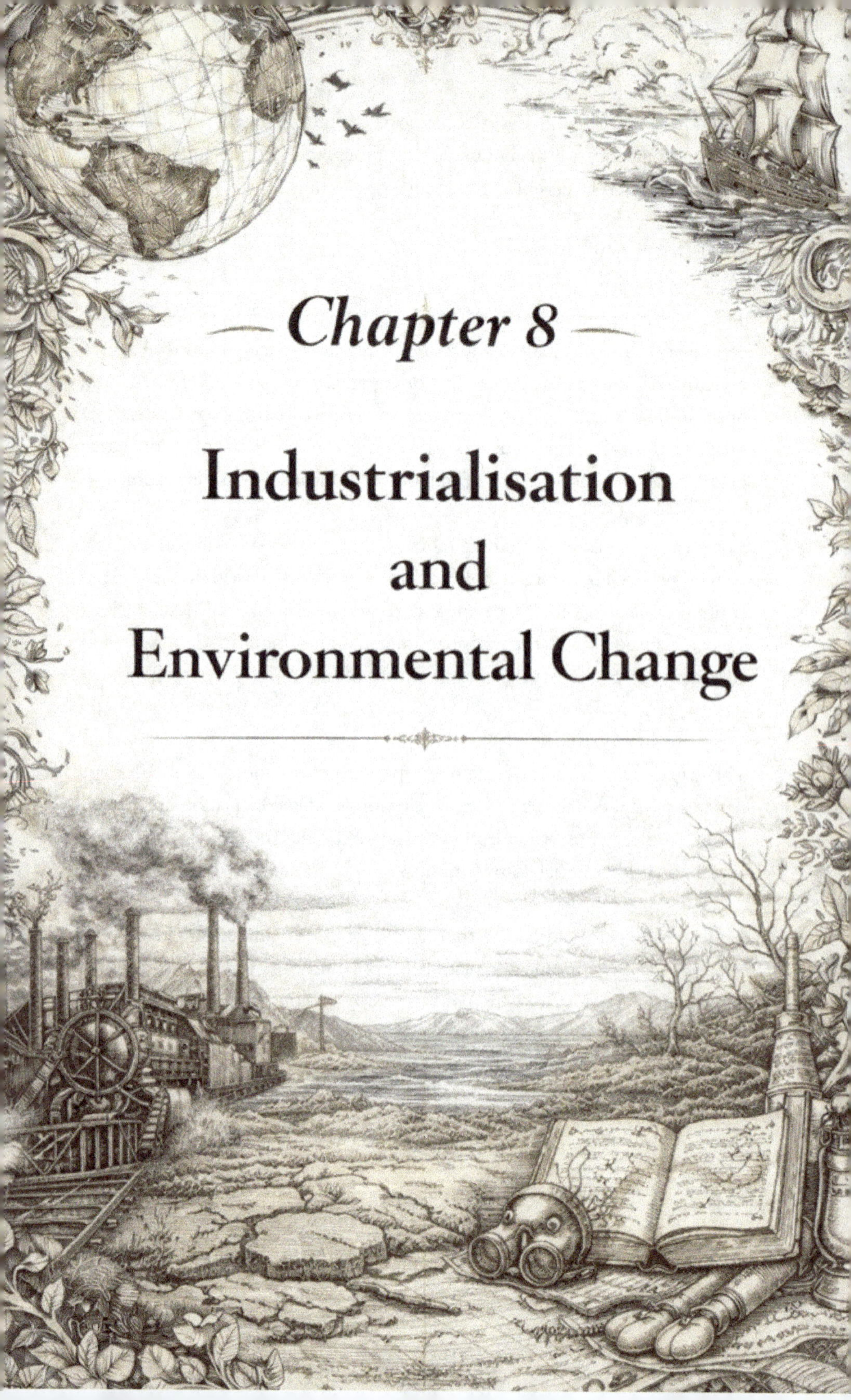

Chapter 8

Industrialisation and Environmental Change

A Continental Transformation

The decades following the mid-eighteenth century brought the most rapid and far-reaching reshaping of North American life since the first rise of agriculture. This was the age of industrialisation: a process that began in Britain and spread unevenly but relentlessly across the United States, Canada and, later, Mexico, drawing the wider region—Central America and the Caribbean—into new circuits of capital, labour and extraction. It altered far more than economies. It changed how people understood time, work and distance and it reordered the relationship between society and the natural world in lasting ways.

Steam, coal and mechanised production delivered astonishing increases in output and wealth, along with a vast shift from rural life to towns and cities. Yet these achievements carried costs that were often ignored, displaced or deliberately obscured. Forests fell at unprecedented scale, rivers were harnessed and polluted, wildlife was commodified and ecosystems simplified into resource frontiers. Industrialisation also coincided with the early detectable imprint of human activity in the climate record: rising atmospheric carbon dioxide and a measurable warming signal emerging during the nineteenth century. The modern North American landscape—its transport corridors, industrial cities, agricultural belts and environmental burdens—was forged in this period, alongside an ecological transformation whose consequences still define political and moral debate across societies.

The transformation was not merely material. Family structures, labour patterns, gender roles and even the very idea of a working day were recast, generating both new opportunities and deep social tensions that would reverberate for generations and shape modern identity.

Technology and the 'Market Revolution'

Industrial change arrived not simply through factories, but through a continent-wide reorganisation of exchange often described as the 'Market Revolution'. Between the American Revolution and the Civil War, a world of local subsistence and slow circulation gave way to a more commercial, interconnected economy. This reorientation was driven by three reinforcing revolutions: transportation, communication and manufacturing, each feeding the others with accelerating force. It also fostered a new culture of credit, speculation and entrepreneurial risk. Banking, investment and the expansion of consumer markets bound local economies into regional systems and, increasingly, into global trade, making prosperity and crisis travel faster than ever before and reshaping expectations.

Transportation was the first great engine of change. Early roads and turnpikes were soon eclipsed by canals, most famously the Erie Canal completed in 1825. By linking the Hudson River to the Great Lakes, it cut transport costs dramatically, transformed New York City into a dominant commercial centre and opened the interior to market agriculture. Within a few decades, canals were overtaken by railways. The first steam locomotives of the 1830s triggered a boom in track-building that redrew the map. In 1869, the First Transcontinental Railroad joined the Atlantic and Pacific at Promontory Summit, Utah, compressing a continent into a timetable. Railways did not merely move goods; they moved people, accelerated settlement, stimulated the extraction of timber, coal and ore and standardised time itself through the creation of time zones and shared schedules.

Communication was revolutionised in parallel. In 1844, Samuel Morse's first telegraph message travelled from Washington to Baltimore, severing information from the pace of physical transport. Prices, news and business orders could be transmitted almost instantly, knitting distant markets into a single system and transforming political coordination, journalism and financial speculation. The modern sense of a national public—sharing the same headlines and reacting to the same events—began to take shape in wires strung across fields and along railway lines and into towns.

Manufacturing completed the triad. In New England, textile mills drew power from rivers such as the Merrimack, concentrating production under one roof and dividing labour into repetitive tasks. The factory system created a new social order: scheduled shifts, hierarchical management and discipline enforced by clocks rather than seasons. Early mills recruited young women from rural households; later, swelling immigrant populations filled industrial jobs as cities expanded. The development of interchangeable parts—demonstrated with particular force in the arms industry—laid the groundwork for mass production, enabling quicker assembly, repair and standardisation across expanding markets and widening consumer demand.

Factories thus remade daily life. Work was no longer integrated into household rhythms but separated, regimented and timed—an innovation as culturally disruptive as it was economically powerful and socially divisive.

Urbanisation and Social Stratification

These changes fuelled a demographic upheaval: mass urbanisation on a scale previously unknown. Cities such as New York, Philadelphia, Chicago, Boston, Montreal and Toronto expanded at extraordinary speed. They drew in rural populations seeking wages and possibility and they absorbed waves of migrants from Europe, particularly from Ireland and Germany, driven by famine, poverty and political unrest. Cities became centres of finance, culture and invention, but also places where deprivation and overcrowding were concentrated and made visible, often in stark proximity.

Urban growth regularly outpaced infrastructure. Water supplies were inadequate, sanitation systems incomplete, housing crowded and poorly ventilated. Epidemics—cholera and typhoid among them—became grim features of nineteenth-century city life. The new industrial order was written into the cityscape: affluent districts of wide streets and private gardens contrasted with dense tenements where working families lived close to factories and docks. In workplaces, long hours, low pay and dangerous machinery produced injury and early death as routine costs of production, often borne silently.

Out of these conditions emerged the first sustained labour movements. Workers organised unions, staged strikes and demanded shorter hours, safer conditions and fair wages, meeting fierce resistance from employers and, at times, the state. The struggle over work—who controlled it, who profited from it and what price should be paid in human health—became one of the defining conflicts of industrial society and mass politics.

In the United States, industrial modernity was also entwined with a darker intensification. The global demand for cotton, fuelled by British and northern textile manufacturing, expanded the plantation system across the American South. The cotton gin, invented in 1793, made short-staple cotton hugely profitable. The result was a 'Cotton Kingdom' built on enslaved African labour, sustained by a brutal internal slave trade that forced the movement of enslaved people into newly cleared lands. Northern industrial growth and southern plantation wealth were not separate stories but connected parts of the same economic machine—an interdependence that sharpened sectional conflict and fed the path to civil war with gathering force.

The Environmental Reckoning

Industrialisation marked a profound shift in energy and in the scale of human impact. Societies moved from renewable flows—wind, water and wood—to the mining and burning of fossil stocks, first coal and later oil. This change granted immense power, enabling larger cities, faster transport and constant manufacturing. It also inaugurated an ecological transformation whose costs were initially localised, then cumulative and finally global, unfolding over generations.

Resource extraction expanded at industrial scale. Forests were cleared for timber and fuel; waterways were dammed for power and navigation; mines scarred landscapes and released toxic runoff. In the Upper Midwest, the great white pine forests of Michigan and Wisconsin were stripped within decades. Wildlife was harvested for profit with devastating effect: the near-destruction of the American bison on the plains and the collapse of passenger pigeon populations became defining symbols of abundance turned to loss, and of ecological simplification.

Air and water were treated as waste sinks. Coal smoke blackened urban skies; sulphur and soot choked industrial centres; rivers received untreated chemical waste and sewage. The image of the smokestack became a badge of progress even as it signalled environmental degradation and public health crisis. Over time, public awareness grew—through journalism, photography and the accumulation of scientific evidence—prompting early reform efforts and the first steps towards regulation and municipal responsibility.

From this damage, however, emerged the beginnings of modern environmental consciousness. Writers and thinkers associated with American Transcendentalism, including Henry David Thoreau and Ralph Waldo Emerson, argued for wilderness as a moral and spiritual counterweight to industrial utility. Their influence merged with the power of landscape art and expedition reports to shape policy. The United States created national parks, beginning with Yellowstone in 1872 and later Yosemite in 1890. A conservation movement formed with internal tensions: John Muir argued for preservation of wilderness; Gifford Pinchot promoted 'wise use' and managed exploitation. The debate between extraction and stewardship—between private profit and public responsibility—would become a permanent feature of North American politics and public culture.

These early efforts also raised enduring questions about whose interests conservation served and how the creation of protected lands intersected with the dispossession of Indigenous peoples who had long lived in and managed those landscapes and watersheds.

The Canadian, Mexican, Central American and Caribbean Experiences

Industrialisation did not spread evenly across the region and its forms differed sharply by place, timing and power.

In Canada, industrial development was more gradual and closely tied to resource extraction—timber, minerals and wheat—within an economy shaped first by Britain and increasingly by the United States. The Canadian Pacific Railway, completed in 1885, was a national project of consolidation and expansion, binding the country east to west and opening the prairies to settlement in a manner broadly comparable to the American transcontinental railway. Canadian cities grew, labour movements emerged and immigration reshaped society, while environmental pressures followed the same familiar lines: logging, mining and the transformation of prairie ecosystems into export agriculture and extensive settlement.

In Mexico, the nineteenth century's political instability after independence slowed industrial growth. When large-scale development accelerated under Porfirio Díaz in the late nineteenth century, it relied heavily on foreign capital and technology, with railways and mining expanding rapidly. The benefits were concentrated among elites and foreign investors, while rural communities faced dispossession and deepening inequality—conditions that fed directly into the Mexican Revolution of 1910. Industrial nodes developed unevenly, often tied to mines, rail corridors and export routes, reinforcing regional disparities that the state struggled to manage and legitimise.

Across Central America, the industrial era often arrived through export economies rather than heavy manufacturing. Railways and ports were built less to integrate national interiors than to move specific commodities—coffee, sugar, bananas and timber—to overseas markets. Foreign companies and investment frequently shaped infrastructure and politics, producing growth alongside dependency and social tension. Panama's position as a geographical hinge gave it a distinctive trajectory: the ambition to control a passage between oceans turned water, engineering and global power into central themes of its modern history and state formation.

The Caribbean experienced its own industrial-era transformation, deeply tied to plantation economies and the afterlives of slavery. Sugar, rum and later other export commodities structured the economies of islands such as Barbados, Jamaica, Cuba and the Bahamas, while Haiti and the Dominican Republic carried the heavy legacies of revolution, occupation and external pressure. The region's economies were often organised around global demand and shipping routes, with wealth concentrated and labour extracted under harsh conditions. As the nineteenth century turned into the twentieth, new extractive industries added layers to this pattern: Trinidad and Tobago's oil and asphalt industries, bauxite extraction in Jamaica and large-scale agriculture and mining in other territories. For smaller island states, economic life was constrained by limited land, fragile soils and dependence on trade, making them acutely vulnerable to shifts in commodity prices and to hurricanes that could undo years of growth in a single storm and season.

Across the continent and islands alike, industrialisation intensified older inequalities while creating new ones: between town and countryside, capital and labour, exporter and consumer, owner and dispossessed, and between environment and economy.

The New Era

By the opening of the twentieth century, North America had been wired, railed and increasingly fuelled by fossil energy on a continental scale. The foundations of the consumer economy were in place and the region stood at the threshold of a second industrial revolution driven by electricity, petroleum and the internal combustion engine. Environmental impacts that had often seemed regional—smoke over a city, a polluted river, a logged forest—were poised to become continental and, ultimately, global, as industrial capacity and consumption expanded.

Industrialisation changed not only what people produced and how they lived. The soot-stained streets, clear-cut forests and engineered rivers of the nineteenth century were not a completed story but an opening chapter in an age increasingly defined by human power over climate and ecosystems. Patterns of consumption, technological dependency and environmental alteration established became the default settings of the twentieth century—embedding industrial life into the social fabric of North America and into the ecological dilemmas that now shape its future and political choices.

Chapter 9

North America in the Contemporary World

The 21st Century Continent

As North America entered the twenty-first century, it did so at a moment of extraordinary capability and equally profound strain. The continent—anchored by Canada, the United States and Mexico and extending through Central America and the Caribbean—has become a global centre of economic power, cultural production and technological innovation. Yet the modern era is not one of uncomplicated dominance. It is marked by introspection, adaptation and frequent conflict: a reassessment of historical narratives, sharpening debates over identity and inequality, the mounting pressures of a changing climate and a continual renegotiation of the continent's place within a more crowded and competitive world order and shifting alliances.

This period is also defined by the rapid acceleration of digital life. Connectivity, automation and artificial intelligence are transforming work, communication and governance, even as they raise increasingly urgent questions about surveillance, privacy, misinformation and who benefits from technological change and concentrated platform power.

The Economic and Social Landscape

Economically, the late twentieth and early twenty-first centuries have been shaped by the formal integration of the continental economy. Agreements such as NAFTA and its successor, the USMCA, tightened supply chains across Canada, the United States and Mexico, creating one of the world's largest trading blocs. The modern automobile is emblematic: components may cross borders multiple times before assembly is complete. This integration expanded trade and deepened interdependence, but its benefits were uneven. Certain industrial regions in the United States and parts of Canada experienced painful job losses and long-term decline, while Mexico saw the growth of export-oriented manufacturing along the border and in key industrial corridors, often without comparable gains in wages, worker protection or environmental standards for many communities.

Globalisation intensified this pattern outsourcing, financialisation and relentless competition created new openings for multinational firms and high-skilled sectors, but also hollowed out older industrial communities and fed a sense of insecurity. In many places, the promise of stable work gave way to precarious employment, weakening local tax bases and eroding public services. The result has been a geography of winners and losers written across the continent, shaping politics and daily life.

These economic shifts unfolded alongside major demographic change. The United States has continued to diversify rapidly; Canada's immigration system has made major cities such as Toronto and Vancouver among the most multicultural in the world; and Mexico has seen sustained internal migration towards urban centres. Central America has experienced both urban growth and outward migration shaped by violence, economic constraint and climate stress. In the Caribbean, population change is closely tied to tourism economies, diaspora networks and the vulnerabilities of small-island life and limited resources.

Across the region, generational change has accelerated cultural transformation. Younger populations adopt different social norms and digital identities and they often hold more transnational ties through migration, education and online communities. This dynamism has sparked creativity and renewal, but it has also sharpened intergenerational tensions over values, belonging and the meaning of citizenship in fast-changing societies.

Rising inequality has become one of the defining conditions of contemporary North America. Wealth has concentrated at the top, amplified by technological change, policy choices and the outsized influence of finance and platform-based economies. This economic divide overlaps with long-standing racial and social disparities, visible in gaps in health outcomes, education, housing security and encounters with policing and justice systems. The continent's social contract—its implied promise of fairness and upward mobility—has come under strain, contributing to political polarisation and the growth of movements demanding systemic change and broader accountability.

Polarisation, Populism and Democratic Stress

Politically, the early twenty-first century has been an era of heightened volatility and institutional testing. In the United States, partisanship has hardened into an ideological chasm that shapes legislation, courts, media ecosystems and even everyday social life. Successive presidencies have been accompanied by intense cultural conflict over healthcare, immigration, climate policy, the boundaries of rights and the role of government itself. Public trust in institutions has weakened and the spread of misinformation, amplified by social platforms, has further eroded the possibility of shared factual ground and civic confidence.

Across the continent, a broader rise in populist politics has challenged established norms. Populism frames politics as a struggle between a virtuous 'people' and a corrupt 'elite' and it draws strength from economic insecurity, regional neglect and cultural anxiety. It has taken different forms: nationalist rhetoric and anti-establishment movements in the United States, protest mobilisations in Canada and polarised debates in Mexico over the balance between presidential authority and independent institutions. In Central America and parts of the Caribbean, democratic stability has often been tested by corruption, insecurity, economic dependence and the pressures of migration, sometimes producing cycles of protest, repression and institutional fragility and contested legitimacy.

Questions of democratic resilience have therefore moved to the centre of public life. Disputes over electoral legitimacy, the influence of money in politics, the independence of courts and the health of civic discourse now shape the political atmosphere. The continent's democracies are not simply threatened by dramatic crises, but by slower erosion: the normalisation of distrust, the weakening of accountability and the replacement of compromise with permanent mobilisation and antagonism.

The Climate Crisis

No issue defines the continent's contemporary challenge more clearly than climate change and its compounding effects. North America is a major contributor to historical greenhouse gas emissions and increasingly exposed to their consequences. The evidence is visible in extremes: hotter and longer heatwaves, deepening droughts and water scarcity in the west; catastrophic wildfires from California to British Columbia; stronger hurricanes and intensified rainfall events along the Gulf and Atlantic coasts; and rising seas that threaten low-lying cities and islands alike, including critical infrastructure.

These impacts are not evenly distributed. Communities with fewer resources—often marginalised by race, class or geography—are hit first and recover last. In the Caribbean, sea-level rise and intensifying storms pose an existential challenge to small island states whose economies depend heavily on coastal infrastructure and tourism. In Central America, shifts in rainfall and temperature threaten agriculture and heighten migration pressures. In Mexico, the United States and Canada, the transition away from fossil fuels threatens powerful industries and the livelihoods of regions built around coal, oil and gas, creating political resistance even as ecological urgency grows and costs mount.

Adaptation is underway—renewable energy infrastructure, redesigned urban planning, disaster preparedness networks, water management reforms—but progress remains uneven and contested. Climate change forces a confrontation not only with physics, but with politics: how to balance short-term economic interests against long-term habitability and how to share burdens and benefits fairly across regions and generations in practice.

Reckoning with History and Identity

A defining cultural current of the contemporary era is a renewed and often contentious reckoning with the past and its living legacies. In the United

States, movements confronting systemic racism and police violence have forced a re-examination of the legacies of slavery, segregation and exclusion. This has reshaped public debate over monuments, school curricula and the stories nations tell about themselves and the meanings attached to citizenship.

Across the continent, there is also a deepening recognition of the historical and ongoing injustices inflicted upon Indigenous peoples. In Canada, revelations about the legacy of residential schools intensified national attention on a long-standing system of forced assimilation. In the United States and Mexico, debates over sovereignty, treaty obligations and land rights have gained renewed urgency. In Central America, Indigenous and Afro-descendant communities continue to press for recognition, autonomy and protection of ancestral territories. This is not merely a question of symbolic acknowledgement. It also concerns language revitalisation, cultural continuity, land stewardship and the practical power to govern community futures and resources.

These reckonings feed into a wider 'culture war' over identity, history and social values. Disputes over what should be taught, whose experiences are centred and what equality requires have become defining features of public life. Digital platforms intensify these struggles: they elevate marginalised voices and accelerate activism, but they also amplify outrage, misinformation and ideological sorting, turning historical memory into a contested political battlefield with real consequences.

North America in a Multipolar World

The continent's global role is evolving as the post–Cold War moment of American primacy gives way to a more complex world order. Strategic competition—particularly with China—has increasingly shaped economic policy, technology development and security priorities, while global shocks have exposed vulnerabilities in supply chains, public health and cyber-security. The pandemic era, in particular, underscored how deeply interdependent modern societies are and how quickly disruption can cascade across borders, institutions and everyday life.

Internal continental relationships remain crucial but not frictionless. Canada and the United States and the United States and Mexico are bound by trade, migration and shared environmental systems, yet they regularly clash over tariffs, border policy, energy, water and regulatory standards. Central America sits at the heart of regional migration dynamics and is often caught between the gravitational pull of larger economies and the internal pressures of violence, poverty and climate stress. The Caribbean's states, though smaller in population, occupy strategic maritime space and face acute exposure to global economic shifts and environmental hazards and debt pressures.

The continent therefore confronts problems no country can solve alone: migration, climate change, pandemic preparedness, organised crime networks and cyber threats. Cooperation is both necessary and difficult, requiring trust and long-term planning in political environments increasingly shaped by short-term conflict, polarisation and crisis management.

In summary, twenty-first-century North America is a continent of paradoxes: immense innovation alongside entrenched inequity; deep integration alongside sharp division; global influence alongside internal fragility. Its trajectory will be determined by how it navigates the interlocking challenges of ecological sustainability, social cohesion and democratic governance. The century now demands that the oldest societies and the newest nations of North America—Canada, the United States, Mexico, the states of Central America and the island nations of the Caribbean—find ways to build a future that carries the full weight of the past while meeting the urgent realities of a rapidly changing world and uncertain global conditions.

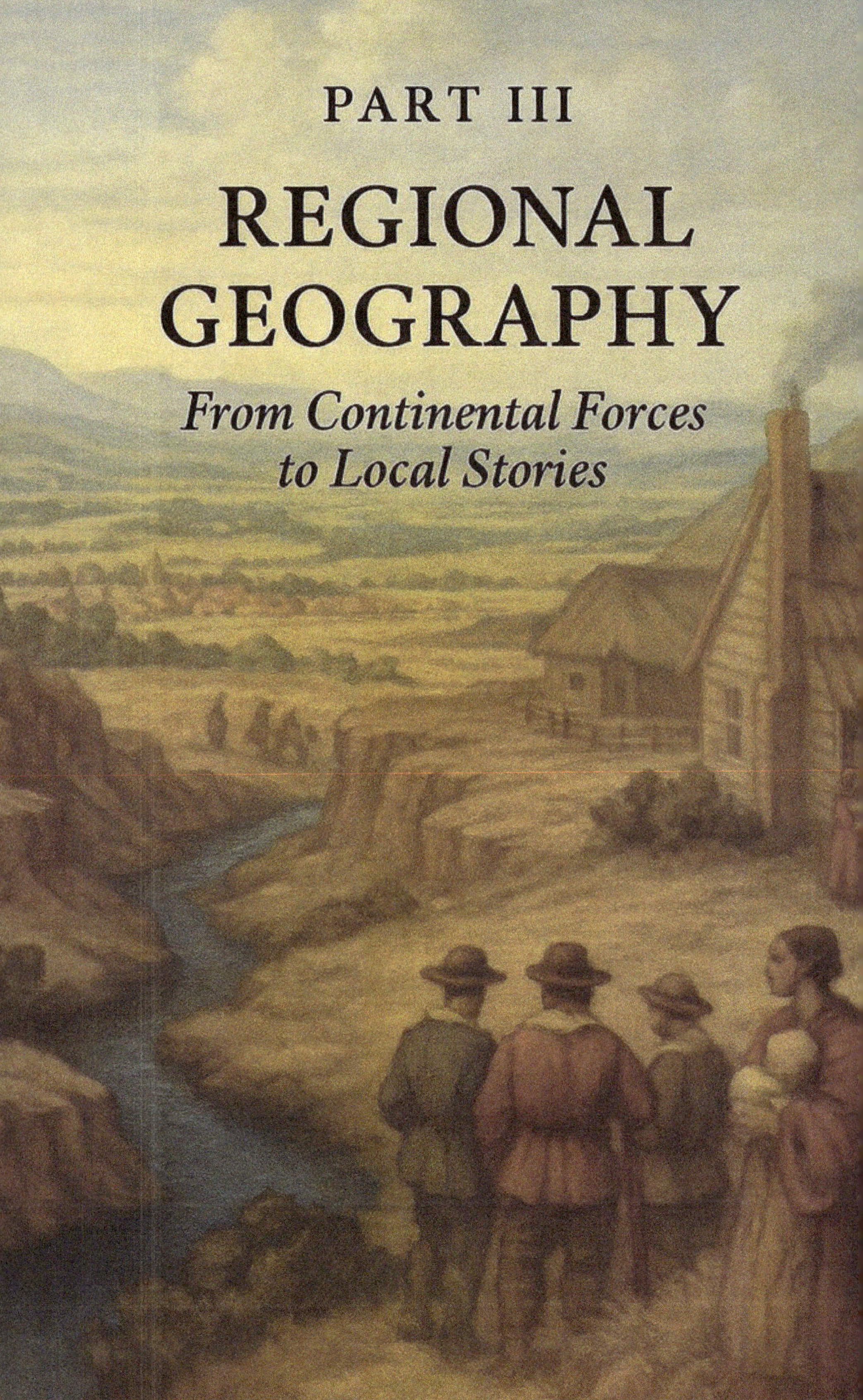

PART III

REGIONAL GEOGRAPHY

From Continental Forces to Local Stories

From Continental Forces to Local Stories

Part I established the immense physical framework of North America, from its ancient geological foundations to the powerful climatic systems that continue to shape life across the continent. Part II traced the long human story that unfolded upon that stage, following the movement of peoples, ideas and power across millennia. In Part III, *Regional Geography*, the focus now shifts from the continental scale to the local and regional. This section undertakes a detailed examination of the individual countries and territories that together form modern North America.

Here, the emphasis moves from broad forces to lived places. The aim is to understand how shared continental processes—geology, climate, colonisation, industrialisation and globalisation—have been interpreted, adapted and transformed within specific environments and histories.

Unity in Diversity

North America is not a single, uniform entity, but a complex mosaic of regions. Each possesses its own distinctive combination of landscape, historical experience, cultural expression and contemporary challenge. A river valley in central Mexico, a coastal community in Atlantic Canada, a rapidly expanding city in the American Sunbelt and a volcanic highland in Central America may share a continent, yet their stories diverge sharply.

This section seeks to uncover those differences without losing sight of the connections between them. By examining regions individually, we can see how universal forces have been refracted through local conditions to produce one of the world's most politically, economically and culturally diverse continents. The task is not simply to describe places, but to understand how environment and history interact to shape everyday life and long-term trajectories.

Canada and Greenland

The journey begins in the far north with Canada, a country defined by scale and contrast. Its vast boreal forests, extensive freshwater systems and Arctic frontiers coexist with densely populated urban corridors and a highly globalised economy. Canada's identity has been shaped by its Indigenous foundations, its dual English and French colonial heritage and its evolution into a multicultural federal state.

Alongside Canada, we consider Greenland: geographically immense, environmentally extreme and sparsely populated. Although politically linked to Europe, Greenland is physically and culturally part of the North American world. Its Inuit heritage, Arctic environment and growing strategic significance place it at the intersection of Indigenous continuity, climate change and global geopolitics.

The United States of America

The focus then turns to the United States, the continent's largest population centre and economic power. The United States encompasses extraordinary regional diversity: the historic industrial heartlands of the Northeast, the agricultural expanses of the Midwest, the rapidly growing cities of the South and West, the deserts of the Southwest and the temperate Pacific coast.

This section explores how such diversity is held together within a federal political system and how national identity, economic power and global influence coexist with deep regional inequalities and social tensions. Understanding the United States requires attention not only to its scale, but to the contrasts that define its internal geography.

Mexico

In Mexico, physical and cultural landscapes are inseparable from a deep historical inheritance. Ancient Mesoamerican civilisations left enduring marks on settlement patterns, agriculture and belief systems, particularly across the central plateau and southern highlands. Spanish colonisation added new layers of language, religion and governance, producing a society shaped by convergence rather than replacement.

Mexico's geography is dramatic and varied: high plateaux, rugged mountain chains, fertile valleys and extensive coastlines on two oceans. These features continue to influence economic activity, regional identity and political relationships, including Mexico's complex and vital connection with its northern neighbour.

Central America

South of Mexico lies Central America: Belize, Guatemala, Honduras, El Salvador, Nicaragua, Costa Rica and Panama. This narrow isthmus functions both as a land bridge between continents and as a biological corridor of exceptional richness. Volcanic ranges, tropical forests and dual coastlines create environments of striking intensity and vulnerability.

Historically linked by shared Indigenous heritage and Spanish colonisation, the Central American states followed divergent paths after independence. This section examines how geography, colonial legacies, external influence and internal political struggles have produced a region of both common challenges and distinct national identities, each navigating its own balance between resilience and instability.

The Caribbean

The final regional focus is the Caribbean, an island world forming the continent's south-eastern arc. From the large islands of Cuba, Jamaica and Hispaniola—shared by Haiti and the Dominican Republic—to the smaller states of the Lesser Antilles, including Barbados, Saint Lucia and Trinidad and Tobago, the sea is the unifying force.

Caribbean history has been profoundly shaped by plantation economies, European rivalry and the transatlantic slave trade, leaving legacies of cultural creativity alongside enduring inequality. Today, the region is a global cultural influence, exporting music, language and ideas far beyond its shores. Its contemporary challenges revolve around economic diversification, political sovereignty and exceptional exposure to climatic extremes, demanding high levels of adaptation and resilience.

Summary

Through this regional exploration, Part III seeks to present North America in all its specificity and complexity. It recognises that understanding the continent requires attention not only to what unites its regions, but to the distinctive character of each place. By examining how environment shapes economy, how history informs identity and how local realities interact with global forces, this section traces a continuous conversation stretching from the Arctic Circle to the Darién Gap.

To know North America, in other words, is to understand both the continent as a whole and the particular genius of its many parts.

NORTH AMERICA

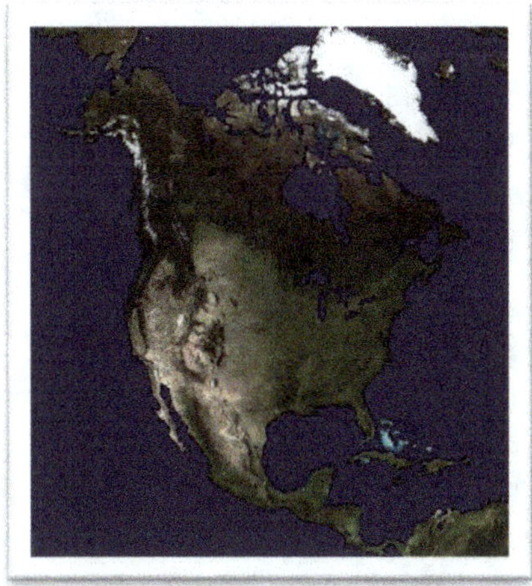

North America is a continent defined by its immense geographic scale and profound historical transformations, encompassing nations including Canada, the United States, Mexico and numerous Indigenous nations. Its vast forests, plains, mountain ranges and coastlines have sustained diverse societies intimately connected to the land and to evolving transcontinental networks. Historically, the region was shaped by powerful pre-Columbian civilisations, the disruptive forces of European colonisation and the rise of modern nation-states, playing a pivotal role in global movements of goods, people and ideologies through Atlantic trade and continental expansion. Following centuries of colonial rivalry and internal conflict, the modern era has seen these countries forge distinct political identities while engaging in deep economic integration through frameworks such as the USMCA, all while grappling with the complex legacies of industrialisation, migration and environmental stewardship. The cliff dwellings of Mesa Verde, the Federalist Papers, the murals of Diego Rivera and the engineering marvel of the Panama Canal underscore North America's enduring influence on global culture, governance and connectivity. This chapter examines the continent's foundational heritage, its ongoing quest for equitable societies and its significant role in shaping the modern world's political and economic architecture.

GREENLAND

Greenland, known in Greenlandic as Kalaallit Nunaat, is the world's largest island, located between the Arctic and Atlantic Oceans to the north-east of North America and east of the Canadian Arctic. It is an autonomous territory within the Kingdom of Denmark. The national. With an estimated population of around 56,000 people, the capital and largest city is Nuuk, which serves as the political, economic and cultural centre. Greenlandic (Kalaallisut) is the official language, while Danish is also widely used. The Danish krone is the official currency. Shaped by Inuit civilisation, Norse settlement and Danish influence, Greenland blends deep Indigenous traditions with modern governance. Its vast Arctic environment, strategic location and natural resources contribute to its growing international significance. This balance between ancient heritage and contemporary development defines the identity of Greenland.

Geography

Greenland spans a massive Arctic landscape dominated by ice and natural features. Approximately 80 per cent of the island is part of the Greenland Ice Sheet, the second-largest body of ice in the world. The coastline is deeply indented with fjords, cliffs and islands, while ice-free coastal regions support tundra vegetation. Mountain ranges rise sharply from the coast, particularly in the east. Glaciers flow into the sea, creating icebergs that drift through surrounding waters. The climate is predominantly Arctic, with long, cold winters and short, cool summers, though conditions vary by region. Natural hazards include avalanches, glacial movement and impacts of climate change, which is rapidly altering ice coverage and ecosystems. Greenland hosts unique Arctic wildlife, including polar bears, seals and whales, making environmental protection a critical concern.

History

The history of Greenland extends back over 4,000 years with the arrival of Paleo-Inuit peoples, followed by the ancestors of today's Inuit population. Norse settlers from Iceland established colonies in the south around the 10th century, though these later disappeared. From the early 18th century, Greenland came under Danish colonial rule, shaping its political and economic development. In the 20th century, Greenland's strategic importance increased, particularly during the Second World War and the Cold War. Home rule was established in 1979, followed by self-government in 2009, granting Greenland extensive autonomy while Denmark retains responsibility for defence and foreign affairs. Modern Greenland continues to navigate the legacy of colonialism while strengthening Indigenous identity and political self-determination.

Government and Politics

Greenland operates as a self-governing territory within the Kingdom of Denmark, with its own parliament, the Inatsisartut and government, the Naalakkersuisut. The head of government is the Premier, while Denmark's monarch remains head of state. Greenland manages most domestic affairs, including education, healthcare and natural resources, while defence and foreign policy are coordinated with Denmark. Political life reflects debates over economic development, environmental protection, social welfare and the long-term prospect of full independence. Democratic institutions, regular elections and strong community engagement underpin political stability in a small and closely connected society.

Economy

Greenland's economy is small but strategically important, characterised by a mixed system with significant public sector involvement. Fishing and seafood exports, particularly shrimp and halibut, form the backbone of the economy. Denmark provides substantial financial support through annual subsidies. In recent years, interest has grown in mineral resources, including rare earth elements, as well as tourism and renewable energy. Climate change is opening new economic opportunities while also posing risks to traditional livelihoods. Challenges include economic diversification, dependence on imports and balancing development with environmental and cultural preservation. Sustainable growth remains a central economic objective.

Demographics and Society

With a population of approximately 56,000, Greenland is one of the least densely populated regions in the world. Most residents are Inuit, with a significant minority of Danish and other European backgrounds. The population is concentrated in coastal towns and settlements, as the interior is largely uninhabitable. Greenlandic culture emphasises community, connection to nature and resilience in harsh environments. While living standards have improved, challenges include limited access to services in remote areas, health disparities and social change. Language, cultural revitalisation and youth engagement play key roles in shaping modern Greenlandic society.

Culture

Greenlandic culture is deeply rooted in Inuit traditions, shaped by centuries of adaptation to Arctic conditions. Oral storytelling, drum dancing and traditional hunting practices remain culturally significant. Modern cultural expression includes music, visual arts and literature that blend Indigenous heritage with contemporary themes. Festivals and community events reinforce social bonds and cultural identity. While influenced by Nordic and global culture, Greenland maintains a distinct artistic voice that reflects themes of nature, survival and identity in a changing Arctic world.

Education and Healthcare

Education in Greenland is publicly funded and overseen by the autonomous government. Schooling is provided in both Greenlandic and Danish, with efforts to strengthen Indigenous language instruction. Higher education opportunities are limited domestically, leading many students to study abroad, particularly in Denmark. Healthcare is publicly funded and aims to provide universal access, though geographic isolation creates challenges in service delivery. Telemedicine and regional clinics play an important role. Public health priorities include mental health, substance misuse and improving outcomes in remote communities.

Infrastructure

Greenland's infrastructure reflects its extreme geography and sparse population. There are no roads connecting towns; transport relies on boats, aircraft and helicopters. Airports and harbours are essential lifelines for trade and travel. Digital connectivity has improved, though remote areas still face limitations. Energy production increasingly focuses on hydropower, reducing reliance on imported fossil fuels. Climate change is placing new demands on infrastructure resilience, particularly in coastal settlements affected by erosion and thawing permafrost.

Tourism

Tourism is a growing sector in Greenland, attracting visitors seeking Arctic landscapes and cultural experiences. Key attractions include glaciers, fjords, the Northern Lights and wildlife such as whales and musk oxen. Activities range from dog sledding and hiking to cultural tourism in Inuit communities. Nuuk and Ilulissat serve as major tourism hubs. Sustainable tourism is emphasised to protect fragile ecosystems and respect local culture while supporting economic development.

Current Issues and Future Outlook

Greenland faces both significant challenges and emerging opportunities. Climate change is transforming the environment, affecting traditional ways of life while increasing global interest in Arctic resources and shipping routes. Economic diversification, social wellbeing and the question of full independence remain central political issues. At the same time, Greenland benefits from strong cultural identity, growing international attention and increasing self-governance. The future will depend on balancing development with environmental stewardship and cultural preservation.

Overview

Greenland is a land defined by vast space, resilience and cultural continuity. Rooted in Inuit heritage and shaped by centuries of external influence, it is forging a distinct modern identity within the Arctic. Its dramatic geography presents both challenges and opportunities, demanding careful management and sustainable vision. As Greenland looks ahead, strengthening autonomy, protecting the environment and supporting community wellbeing will be central to ensuring a stable and prosperous future for the island and its people.

DID YOU KNOW...?

Greenland is home to Camp Century, a secret Cold War–era US military installation built beneath the ice cap in north-west Greenland. Constructed in 1959, the base was part of a classified project known as *Project Iceworm*, which explored the feasibility of deploying nuclear missiles under the Arctic ice. Camp Century consisted of a network of tunnels carved directly into the ice, covering several kilometres and housing around 200 personnel. It included living quarters, laboratories, a hospital, a chapel and the world's first portable nuclear reactor used to generate power in such an extreme environment. Persistent ice movement eventually rendered the base unstable, leading to its abandonment in 1967. Today, it lies buried beneath the ice, serving as a striking reminder of Cold War ambition, Arctic engineering ingenuity and the long-term environmental legacy of military experimentation in one of the world's most remote regions.

KEY FACTS AND FIGURES

Geography & Environment

• Total area: 2.16 million km² (world's largest island).

• Coastline: Over 44,000 km (highly indented Arctic coastline).

• Ice coverage: ≈80% covered by the Greenland Ice Sheet.

• Highest point: Gunnbjørn Fjeld (3,694 m).

• Major features: Greenland Ice Sheet, Ilulissat Icefjord, extensive fjords and glaciers.

• Wildlife: Polar bears, Arctic foxes, musk oxen, seals, whales.

• 3 UNESCO World Heritage sites.

Population & Society

• Population: ≈56,000 (2024 estimate).

• Density: 0.03 persons/km² (among the lowest in the world).

• Urbanisation: ≈90% (population concentrated in coastal towns).

• Ethnicity:

o Inuit (Kalaallit): ≈88%

o Danish and other European: ≈12%

• Languages: Greenlandic (Kalaallisut – official), Danish.

• Religion: Christian (predominantly Lutheran): ≈96%.

• Literacy: ≈99%.

• Life expectancy: ≈72 years.

Economy

• GDP (nominal): ≈£2.5 billion.

• GDP per capita (PPP): ≈£40,000.

• Key industries:

o Fishing and seafood processing

o Public administration and services

o Tourism

o Mining and mineral exploration

• Major exports: Fish and seafood (shrimp, halibut), minerals.

• Currency: Danish krone (DKK; £1 ≈ 8.6 DKK).

Government

- Self-governing territory within the Kingdom of Denmark.
- System: Parliamentary democracy with extensive autonomy.
- Head of State: King Frederik X of Denmark.
- Head of Government: Premier of Greenland.
- Parliament: Inatsisartut (31 members).

Infrastructure

- Transport: No intercity road network; travel by air and sea.
- Major airports: Nuuk Airport, Kangerlussuaq Airport.
- Energy mix: Predominantly hydropower, with limited fossil fuel use.
- Digital connectivity: Well developed in towns; limited in remote settlements.

Major Urban Centres

- Nuuk: ≈19,000 – Capital and administrative centre.
- Sisimiut: ≈5,500 – Major fishing and industrial town.
- Ilulissat: ≈4,800 – Tourism hub near UNESCO-listed icefjord.
- Aasiaat: ≈3,000 – Regional transport and education centre.

NUUK - GREENLANDS CAPITAL AND ADMINISTRATIVE CENTRE

The National Flag

The national flag of Greenland, known as 'Erfalasorput' ('our flag'), features a design of two equal horizontal bands: white on the top and red on the bottom. A large circle, slightly offset towards the hoist, is divided along these colours, with the red half in the white field and the white half in the red field. The white colour symbolises the ice cap and glaciers that cover much of the island, while the red represents the ocean and the radiant midnight sun. The circle's position evokes the sun setting over the horizon and its division echoes the stark, contrasting landscapes of ice and sea. Adopted on 21 June 1985, the flag is a distinctive emblem of Greenland's unique Arctic environment and its political autonomy within the Kingdom of Denmark.

KEY PEOPLE AND PLACES

PEOPLE

Knud Rasmussen (1879–1933) A Greenlandic-Danish explorer and anthropologist, Rasmussen is widely celebrated for his Arctic expeditions and studies of Inuit culture. His work documented traditional ways of life, contributed to Arctic exploration and preserved Greenlandic heritage for future generations.

Hans Egede (1686–1758) A Norwegian-Danish missionary known as the 'Apostle of Greenland,' Egede established the first permanent mission in Greenland in 1721. He played a key role in the spread of Christianity and European cultural influence while interacting with Greenlandic communities.

Jonathan Motzfeldt (1938–2010) The first Prime Minister of Greenland, serving from 1979 to 1991 and again from 1997 to 2002. He oversaw the establishment of home rule, promoted political development, economic planning and the recognition of Greenlandic autonomy within the Kingdom of Denmark.

Vibeke Grøn (b. 1963) A prominent Greenlandic politician and advocate for sustainable development, Grøn has focused on education, environmental protection and local governance. Her work highlights the importance of preserving Greenland's culture and natural resources amid social and economic change.

Jens Frederik Motzfeldt (1770–1842) An early political figure and civil servant, he played a significant role in Greenlandic administration under Danish rule, contributing to the integration of Greenlandic communities into the Danish kingdom while supporting education and missionary efforts.

PLACES

Nuuk (founded 1728) The capital and largest city of Greenland, located on the southwest coast. Nuuk serves as the political, cultural and economic centre, featuring government institutions, universities, museums, ports and vibrant Greenlandic cultural life, blending traditional Inuit and modern influences.

Ilulissat A coastal town in western Greenland, famous for the Ilulissat Icefjord, a UNESCO World Heritage site. It is renowned for dramatic icebergs, Arctic landscapes and cultural tourism, attracting visitors for scientific research, photography and eco-tourism adventures.

Sisimiut Greenland's second-largest town, Sisimiut is a hub for fishing, industry and education. Located on the west coast, it preserves Inuit traditions while supporting modern economic development, community life and outdoor activities such as dog sledding and hiking.

Qaqortoq A town in southern Greenland known for its colourful buildings, colonial architecture and cultural events. Qaqortoq serves as a centre for art, history, tourism and local commerce, highlighting the blend of Greenlandic traditions and European influences.

Kangerlussuaq A settlement in western Greenland notable for its international airport, Arctic research facilities and access to natural landscapes. Kangerlussuaq plays a key role in scientific exploration, tourism and transportation while offering views of glaciers, tundra and polar wildlife.

Disko Island An island off western Greenland, famous for glaciers, volcanic formations and Arctic biodiversity. Disko Island is a major site for scientific research, eco-tourism and cultural exploration, highlighting Greenland's natural heritage and geological significance.

TIMELINE OF EVENTS

c. 2500 BCE: First Indigenous Settlements: Early Inuit cultures, including Saqqaq then the Dorset peoples, settled Greenland, adapting to the Arctic through hunting, fishing and traditions before European contact.

c. 985: Norse Settlement of Greenland: Norse explorer Erik the Red established European settlements in southern Greenland, linking the island to the Viking world of the North Atlantic.

1126: Establishment of the Bishopric of Gardar: The creation of a bishopric reflected Norse Greenland's integration into medieval Christian Europe and strengthened political ties with Norway.

c. 1400–1500: Disappearance of Norse Settlements: The Norse colonies gradually vanished, likely due to climate change, isolation and shifting trade patterns.

1500s: Continued Inuit Presence: Inuit societies thrived across Greenland, maintaining sustainable lifeways and networks despite the absence of European settlements.

1721: Danish-Norwegian Colonisation Begins: Missionary Hans Egede founded a settlement near modern Nuuk, marking renewed European presence and Danish-Norwegian control.

1776: Royal Greenland Trading Department Established: Denmark formalised its trade monopoly, shaping Greenland's economy and relations with Inuit communities.

1814: Treaty of Kiel: Greenland remained under Danish control after the Denmark–Norway union ended, becoming tied to the Danish crown.

1911: Introduction of Local Councils: Denmark introduced advisory councils, allowing limited participation in governance for Greenlanders.

1941: Second World War and Allied Presence: During the war, the United States established military bases, increasing Greenland's strategic importance.

1951: Thule Air Base Agreement: A defence agreement between Denmark and the United States led to Thule Air Base, affecting communities and geopolitics.

1953: Integration into the Danish Realm: Greenland ceased to be a colony and became part of Denmark, with Greenlanders gaining citizenship.

1979: Home Rule Established: Greenland achieved Home Rule, gaining control over domestic affairs and increased political autonomy.

1985: Withdrawal from the European Communities: Greenland left the European Communities after a referendum, reflecting concerns over fisheries and control.

2009: Self-Government Act: Greenland gained expanded self-government, including control over natural resources and recognition as a distinct people.

2010: Increased Focus on Climate Change: Melting ice drew global attention to Greenland's role in climate research and Arctic politics.

2014: Expansion of International Diplomacy: Greenland increased its presence in Arctic and global forums, asserting environmental and economic interests.

2018: Interest in Mineral Resources: International focus turned to Greenland's mineral and energy potential, raising sustainability debates.

2020: COVID-19 Pandemic Impact: The pandemic affected travel, public health and economy, highlighting Greenland's isolation and resolve.

CANADA

Canada occupies a vast expanse of northern North America, bordered by three oceans: the Atlantic, Pacific and Arctic. With an estimated population of around 40 million people, the capital city is Ottawa, while metropolitan centres such as Toronto, Montréal and Vancouver exert major cultural, economic and political influence. English and French are the two official national languages, with a multitude of Indigenous and immigrant languages spoken across the country. The Canadian Dollar serves as the national currency. Shaped by millennia of Indigenous civilisations, French and British colonisation and successive waves of immigration, the nation blends deep historical roots with deliberate modern development. Its immense resources, commitment to multilateralism and high quality of life contribute significantly to its international stature and domestic prosperity. This combination of historical depth and contemporary stability defines the identity of Canada.

Geography

Spanning an immense and varied landscape, Canada features extraordinary geographical diversity. It includes vast boreal forests, expansive prairies, rugged mountain systems such as the Rockies and the Coast Mountains and the vast Canadian Shield. The northern territories encompass dramatic Arctic tundra and glaciers, while coastal regions offer fertile valleys and fjords. Major waterways include the Great Lakes-St. Lawrence system, the Mackenzie River and countless other lakes and rivers. The climate ranges from Arctic to temperate, with significant seasonal variation across the country. Natural hazards such as winter storms, wildfires, permafrost thaw and coastal erosion significantly shape regional life. The country hosts remarkable biodiversity, though ecosystems face pressure from resource extraction, urbanisation and climate change. Conservation efforts and sustainable land management remain central to preserving the nation's diverse natural heritage.

History

The history of Canada begins thousands of years before European contact with the diverse and advanced cultures of First Nations, Inuit and Métis peoples. European exploration and settlement began in the late 15th and 16th centuries, leading to French and British colonies. The rivalry between these powers culminated in British victory, though the distinctive culture of New France endured. Following Confederation in 1867, the 19th and 20th centuries saw westward expansion, industrialisation and the nation's emergence from colonial status to full sovereignty. Canada's participation in two world wars and its role in founding international institutions shaped its modern identity. The latter half of the 20th century was marked by official bilingualism, the patriation of the constitution with a Charter of Rights and Freedoms and ongoing processes of truth and reconciliation with Indigenous peoples. Modern Canada continues to navigate its complex past while reaffirming its role as a cooperative and diverse society.

Government and Politics

Canada is a federal parliamentary democracy and a constitutional monarchy, with the British monarch as the ceremonial head of state represented by the Governor General. Government authority is divided between the federal level, ten provinces and three territories. The federal system comprises three branches: executive, legislative and judicial. Executive power is vested in the Prime Minister and the Cabinet, drawn from the elected House of Commons. Legislative power rests with the bicameral Parliament, consisting of the elected House of Commons and the appointed Senate. The Supreme Court of Canada heads the judiciary. Regular elections, a robust charter of rights and an independent judiciary underpin political stability. Political life is characterised by multiple national parties, with the Liberals and Conservatives traditionally dominant. Domestically, debates centre on healthcare, federal-provincial relations, climate policy and Indigenous reconciliation, while internationally Canada maintains a strong commitment to multilateralism, peacekeeping and humanitarian engagement.

Economy

Canada possesses one of the world's largest and most stable economies, characterised as a mixed-market system with a significant resource base. Key sectors include natural resources (energy, mining, forestry), manufacturing, technology, finance and agriculture. The nation is a global leader in sectors such as aerospace, artificial intelligence and clean technology. Agriculture remains highly productive, exporting crops such as wheat, canola and pulses. Despite its economic strength, challenges include regional economic disparities, productivity gaps, infrastructure needs and managing the transition to a low-carbon economy. The Canadian Dollar is a major global currency and the economy is deeply integrated with that of the United States through the USMCA. Continued investment in innovation, sustainable resource development and trade diversification is viewed as essential for sustaining long-term prosperity.

Demographics and Society

With a population of approximately 40 million, Canada is one of the most sparsely populated and culturally diverse developed nations. The population is highly urbanised, concentrated in metropolitan regions near the southern border. Canadian society is fundamentally shaped by a policy of multiculturalism, resulting in a complex mosaic of ethnic, cultural and religious identities. Significant population groups include people of European, Asian, Indigenous, African and Middle Eastern descent. While English and French dominate public life, over 200 languages are reported as mother tongues. High living standards and social safety nets coexist with challenges, including the cost of housing, healthcare wait times and addressing the legacy of colonialism towards Indigenous peoples. The concepts of pluralism, tolerance and social cohesion remain central to the national ethos.

Culture

Canadian culture has achieved distinct global recognition, shaped by its diverse population, geography and history as a bilingual nation. Indigenous traditions, French-Canadian heritage and immigrant influences form essential cultural foundations. Literature, film, music and visual arts from Canada enjoy international acclaim, from iconic musicians and authors to a vibrant film festival scene. Sport plays a major role in national life, particularly ice hockey, lacrosse (the national summer sport) and Canadian football. Cultural expression frequently explores themes of identity, nature, survival and community. While deeply influenced by global trends and its southern neighbour, Canadian culture continues to evolve with a focus on inclusivity and public broadcasting support, reflecting ongoing debates about sovereignty, diversity and national purpose.

Education and Healthcare

Canada maintains a highly regarded education system, encompassing public and private institutions at primary, secondary and tertiary levels. It is home to many world-leading universities and research centres, attracting a high number of international students. Education is primarily managed at the provincial level, ensuring high standards with some regional variation. Healthcare operates through a publicly funded, universal system (Medicare), though administration is provincial. While access to essential medical care is guaranteed, challenges include wait times for certain procedures, mental health service availability and integrating dental and pharmacare. Policy debates focus on sustaining the public system, improving long-term and elder care and addressing public health issues in a vast country.

Infrastructure

Infrastructure across Canada reflects both immense geographic challenges and significant investment. Extensive road and railway networks support mobility and commerce across great distances, though much of the north is only accessible by air or seasonal roads. Major ports on three coasts and international airports facilitate global trade. Digital infrastructure is generally robust in urban centres, though disparities in broadband access persist in rural, remote and northern communities. Energy systems are diverse, with significant hydroelectric, oil, gas, nuclear and growing renewable capacity. Infrastructure priorities include public transit expansion, climate-resilient design and bridging the infrastructure gap in Indigenous communities. Balancing connectivity, sustainability and resilience remains a national priority.

Tourism

Tourism is a significant contributor to the Canadian economy, offering extraordinary diversity of attractions. Natural landmarks include the Rocky Mountains, Niagara Falls, the Bay of Fundy and the vast wilderness of the national parks system. Iconic cities such as Vancouver, Toronto, Montréal and Québec City provide world-renowned cultural, historical and culinary experiences. Outdoor activities like skiing, hiking and wildlife viewing attract millions of visitors annually. Indigenous cultural tourism and historic sites from the colonial and fur trade eras offer insight into the nation's complex past. Sustainable tourism initiatives increasingly aim to protect fragile ecosystems and support local and Indigenous economies.

Current Issues and Future Outlook

Canada faces significant challenges alongside considerable strengths. Climate change and biodiversity loss, national unity and regional alienation, housing affordability and achieving meaningful reconciliation with Indigenous peoples remain central national concerns. Internationally, navigating an increasingly complex relationship with the United States and asserting sovereignty in the Arctic require careful diplomatic and strategic engagement. At the same time, the country benefits from strong democratic institutions, a resilient economy, immense natural resources and a respected global brand. The future outlook depends on fostering intergenerational fairness, managing demographic shifts, investing in a green transition and upholding inclusive democratic norms. How effectively these issues are managed will shape Canada's global role and domestic cohesion in the decades ahead.

Overview

Canada is a nation defined by its geography, diversity and commitment to peaceful governance. Rooted in Indigenous heritage and shaped by a distinct colonial past, immigration and a tradition of compromise, it has emerged as a respected international actor. Its vast geography presents both immense resource wealth and profound environmental responsibility. Moving forward, the nation seeks to reconcile its aspirational values with persistent social and economic challenges while sustaining its quality of life and democratic institutions. Continued innovation, inclusion and principled leadership remain key to ensuring a resilient and prosperous future for Canada.

DID YOU KNOW...?

Canada is home to the Diefenbunker, one of the world's most extensive Cold War-era nuclear fallout shelters, located just outside Ottawa. Constructed between 1959 and 1961, it was designed to house over 500 key government officials, including the Prime Minister, for up to 30 days in the event of a nuclear attack. The four-storey, 100,000-square-foot underground facility included a CBC radio studio, a vault for the Bank of Canada's gold reserves and an emergency government centre. Decommissioned in 1994, it now operates as a museum. This monumental concrete structure stands as a stark symbol of Cold War anxiety, technological preparation and the enduring human preoccupation with survival.

KEY FACTS AND FIGURES

Geography & Environment

• Total area: 9.98 million km².

• Coastline: Over 243,000 km (longest coastline in the world; Pacific, Atlantic, Arctic Oceans).

• Highest point: Mount Logan (5,959 m).

• Major rivers: Mackenzie, Saint Lawrence, Yukon.

• Diverse wildlife: Beaver, moose, polar bear, bald eagles, grizzly bears.

• 22 UNESCO World Heritage sites.

Population & Society

• Population: 40 million (2024 estimate).

• Density: 4 persons/km².

• Urbanisation: 83%.

• Ethnicity:

o European descent: ≈69%

o Asian: ≈20%

o Indigenous (First Nations, Métis, Inuit): ≈5%

o African Canadian: ≈4%

o Other/Mixed: ≈2%

• Languages: English and French (official).

• Religion: Christian (53%), Unaffiliated (37%), Other (10%).

• Literacy: 99%.

• Life expectancy: 82 years.

Economy

• GDP (nominal): £1.8 trillion.

• GDP per capita (PPP): ≈£52,000.

• Key industries:

o Natural resources (energy, mining, forestry)

o Manufacturing and technology

o Finance and services

• Major exports: Energy products, motor vehicles, minerals, forestry products, agricultural commodities.

• Currency: Canadian Dollar (CAD; £1 ≈ 1.71 CAD).

Government

• Federal parliamentary constitutional monarchy.
• Head of State: King Charles III (represented by the Governor General).
• Head of Government: Prime Minister of Canada.
• Prime Minister: Justin Trudeau (2025).

Infrastructure

• Major airport: Toronto Pearson International (over 40 million passengers/year).
• Energy mix: Hydroelectric dominant; fossil fuels, nuclear and other renewables significant.

Major Urban Centres

• Toronto (ON): 6.8m – Financial and business capital.
• Montréal (QC): 4.0m – Cultural and linguistic hub.
• Vancouver (BC): 2.6m – Pacific trade and gateway city.
• Calgary (AB): 1.6m – Energy sector centre.
• Ottawa (ON): 1.1m – National capital.

TORONTO - CANADA'S FINANCIAL AND BUSINESS CAPITAL

The National Flag

The national flag of Canada, known as the Maple Leaf, features a vertical triband of red, white and red. The central white square is twice the width of each red band and bears a stylised, 11-pointed red maple leaf. The red colour symbolises the sacrifices made during the First and Second World Wars, as well as the country's fortitude, while the white represents peace, tranquillity and the snowy northern landscape. The single, prominent maple leaf is a long-standing national emblem, recognised worldwide as a symbol of Canada's natural heritage, unity and independence. The flag, adopted on 15 February 1965, replaced the Canadian Red Ensign and serves as a definitive emblem of the nation's sovereignty and distinctive identity.

KEY PEOPLE AND PLACES

PEOPLE

Mathieu da Costa (c. 1589–c. 1619) A multilingual interpreter of African and likely Portuguese descent, he is the first recorded free Black person in Canada and was a crucial intermediary between European explorers and Mi'kmaq communities.

Alexander Mackenzie (1764–1820) Explorer and fur trader who led the first recorded European expeditions to reach the Arctic Ocean and, later, the Pacific Ocean by land across North America, profoundly expanding geographical knowledge.

Vilhjalmur Stefansson (1879–1962) Prominent Arctic explorer and ethnologist who led the landmark Canadian Arctic Expedition, which asserted sovereignty and documented the culture and geography of the western Arctic.

Taqulittuq (Tookoolito) (c. 1838–1876) An Inuk translator and guide from Cumberland Sound who, with her husband Ipirvik, was indispensable to several 19th-century Arctic expeditions, providing essential survival skills and cultural knowledge.

Bob Bartlett (1875–1946) Celebrated Newfoundland-born Arctic Sea captain and explorer who navigated the perilous northern waters for decades and famously led survivors to safety after the loss of the ship *Karluk*.

Leonard Marchand (1933–2016) A member of the Syilx (Okanagan) Nation who became the first Status Indian elected to the Parliament of Canada and served as a pioneering cabinet minister and senator.

Madeleine Redfern (b. 1964) An Inuk lawyer, former Mayor of Iqaluit and prominent public administrator known for her advocacy on issues of northern governance, justice and infrastructure development.

PLACES

L'Anse aux Meadows (occupied c. 1000 CE) A UNESCO World Heritage Site on Newfoundland's coast, representing the only confirmed Norse settlement in North America and evidence of the first European presence on the continent.

Quebec City (founded 1608) One of North America's oldest European settlements, founded by Samuel de Champlain as the capital of New France; its historic fortifications and old town are a UNESCO site.

Red River Colony (established 1812) The first permanent European settlement in the Prairie West, which became the nucleus of the Métis Nation and the site of the pivotal Red River Resistance led by Louis Riel.

Athabasca Pass (discovered 1811) A vital travel corridor through the Rocky Mountains that became a key segment of the 19th-century fur trade route, linking the interior to the Pacific watershed.

Churchill, Manitoba (key site from 1717) A strategically important port on Hudson Bay, historically central to the fur trade and Arctic exploration, now a global hub for polar bear and beluga whale observation.

Sverdrup Islands (claimed 1902–1903) An archipelago in the High Arctic discovered by Norwegian explorer Otto Sverdrup; their formal transfer to Canada in 1930 was a critical event in defining Canada's Arctic sovereignty.

Voyageur Canoe Routes (peak use 18th–early 19th c.) The extensive network of rivers and portages across the Canadian Shield that formed the primary transportation and trade arteries for the continental fur trade for centuries.

TIMELINE OF EVENTS

c. 12,000 BCE: First Indigenous Settlements: Indigenous peoples settled across what is now Canada, developing diverse nations, cultures and complex trade networks long before European contact.

1497: John Cabot Reaches Newfoundland: John Cabot's voyage for England marked one of the earliest European explorations of the Canadian coastline.

1534: Jacques Cartier Explores the St Lawrence: French explorer Jacques Cartier claimed land for France, beginning sustained French interest in Canada.

1608: Founding of Quebec City: Samuel de Champlain established Quebec City, becoming the centre of New France and French colonial administration.

1670: Hudson's Bay Company Established: The company was granted control over vast territories, shaping trade, exploration and Indigenous relations through the fur trade.

1759: Battle of the Plains of Abraham: British forces defeated the French near Quebec City, leading to British control of Canada.

1763: Treaty of Paris: France formally ceded most of its North American territories to Britain, confirming British rule over Canada.

1791: Constitutional Act: Canada was divided into Upper and Lower Canada, establishing separate political systems for English- and French-speaking populations.

1867: Confederation: The British North America Act united Ontario, Quebec, Nova Scotia and New Brunswick to form the Dominion of Canada.

1885: Completion of the Canadian Pacific Railway: The railway connected Canada from coast to coast, promoting settlement, trade and national unity.

1914: First World War Begins: Canada entered the war as part of the British Empire, contributing significantly to the Allied war effort.

1917: Battle of Vimy Ridge: Canadian forces achieved a decisive victory, strengthening Canada's national identity and international reputation.

1931: Statute of Westminster: Canada gained full legislative independence from Britain, except for constitutional amendments.

1939: Second World War Begins: Canada entered the war independently, emerging as a strong middle power with a growing global role.

1949: Newfoundland Joins Confederation: Newfoundland became Canada's tenth province, completing the modern political map of the country.

1960: Voting Rights Extended to Indigenous Peoples: Status First Nations people gained the right to vote in federal elections without losing treaty status.

1982: Patriation of the Constitution: Canada gained full constitutional independence and adopted the Charter of Rights and Freedoms.

2010: Vancouver Winter Olympics: Canada hosted the Olympic Games, achieving a record medal performance and global recognition.

2020: COVID-19 Pandemic Impact: The pandemic caused widespread health, economic and social disruption, significantly affecting daily life across Canada.

THE UNITED STATES OF AMERICA

The United States of America (USA), commonly known as the United States, occupies a vast portion of North America, bordered by the Atlantic and Pacific Oceans. With an estimated population of around 335 million people, the capital city is Washington, D.C., while cities such as New York, Los Angeles and Chicago exert major cultural, economic and political influence. English is the predominant national language, though many languages are spoken across the country. The United States Dollar serves as the national currency. Shaped by Indigenous civilisations, European colonisation and successive waves of immigration, the nation blends deep historical roots with rapid modern development. Its vast resources, technological innovation and global reach contribute significantly to its economic power and international influence. This combination of historical depth and contemporary dynamism defines the identity of the United States.

Geography

Spanning an immense and varied landscape, the United States features extraordinary geographical diversity. It includes vast plains, fertile river valleys, rugged mountain systems such as the Rocky Mountains and Appalachians, extensive deserts in the south-west and dense forests in the Pacific north-west and east. Alaska adds dramatic Arctic landscapes, while Hawaii contributes volcanic islands in the Pacific. Major waterways include the Mississippi–Missouri river system, the Colorado River and the Great Lakes, the largest group of freshwater lakes in the world. The climate ranges from Arctic to tropical, with temperate zones dominating much of the mainland. Natural hazards such as hurricanes, tornadoes, earthquakes, wildfires and droughts significantly shape regional life. The country hosts remarkable biodiversity, though ecosystems face pressure from urbanisation, pollution and climate change. Conservation efforts and environmental regulation remain central to preserving the nation's diverse natural heritage.

History

The history of the United States begins thousands of years before European contact with the advanced cultures of Native American peoples. European exploration and settlement began in the late 15th and early 16th centuries, eventually leading to British, Spanish, French and Dutch colonies. Tensions between the British Crown and thirteen colonies culminated in the American Revolution (1775–1783), resulting in independence in 1776. The 19th century saw territorial expansion, industrialisation and the devastating Civil War (1861–1865), which ended slavery but left lasting social divisions. The 20th century marked the rise of the United States as a global power through involvement in world wars, economic leadership and technological innovation. Civil rights movements reshaped society, expanding democracy and equality. Modern America continues to grapple with its complex past while redefining its role in an interconnected world.

Government and Politics

The United States is a federal constitutional republic founded on the principle of separation of powers. Government authority is divided between the federal level and fifty states. The federal system comprises three branches: executive, legislative and judicial. The President serves as both head of state and government, while legislative power rests with a bicameral Congress consisting of the House of Representatives and the Senate. The Supreme Court heads the judiciary, interpreting the Constitution. Regular elections, a strong constitution and an independent judiciary underpin political stability. Political life is dominated by two major parties, the Democrats and Republicans. Domestically, debates centre on healthcare, taxation, civil rights, gun laws and immigration, while internationally the United States maintains extensive alliances and plays a leading role in global diplomacy and security.

Economy

The United States possesses the world's largest economy, characterised by a mixed-market system driven by private enterprise and innovation. Key sectors include finance, technology, manufacturing, agriculture, energy and entertainment. The nation is a global leader in technological development, hosting major corporations in computing, aerospace, pharmaceuticals and artificial intelligence. Agriculture remains highly productive, exporting crops such as maize, soybeans and wheat. Despite its economic strength, challenges include income inequality, national debt, infrastructure ageing and economic adjustment to automation and climate change. The US Dollar functions as the world's primary reserve currency, reinforcing global economic influence. Continued investment in research, infrastructure and workforce development is viewed as essential for sustaining long-term competitiveness.

Demographics and Society

With a population of approximately 335 million, the United States is one of the most populous and culturally diverse nations in the world. The population is largely urban, concentrated in metropolitan regions along the coasts and major river systems. American society reflects centuries of immigration, resulting in a complex mosaic of ethnic, cultural and religious identities. Significant population groups include people of European, African, Hispanic, Asian and Indigenous descent. While English dominates public life, Spanish and many other languages are widely spoken. High living standards coexist with social challenges, including inequality, healthcare access, racial justice and regional disparities. The concept of individual freedom, opportunity and civic participation remains central to the national ethos.

Culture

American culture has had a profound global impact, shaped by its diverse population, frontier history and emphasis on individual expression. Indigenous traditions, African American culture and immigrant influences form essential cultural foundations. Literature, film, music and visual arts from the United States enjoy worldwide reach, from jazz and rock to Hollywood cinema and contemporary digital media. Sport plays a major role in national life, particularly American football, basketball, baseball and ice hockey. Cultural expression frequently explores themes of freedom, identity, ambition and social change. While deeply influenced by global trends, American culture continues to evolve, reflecting ongoing debates about history, values and national purpose.

Education and Healthcare

The United States maintains an extensive education system, encompassing public and private institutions at primary, secondary and tertiary levels. It is home to many of the world's leading universities and research centres, attracting international students and scholars. Education policy is primarily managed at state and local levels, resulting in variation in quality and access. Healthcare operates through a predominantly private system supplemented by public programmes such as Medicare and Medicaid. While medical innovation and specialist care are world-leading, access and affordability remain significant challenges. Policy debates focus on expanding coverage, controlling costs and addressing public health issues including obesity, mental health and ageing populations.

Infrastructure

Infrastructure across the United States reflects both vast scale and uneven development. Extensive road and highway networks support mobility and commerce, while rail infrastructure varies significantly by region. Major ports and airports facilitate global trade and travel. Digital infrastructure underpins the modern economy, though disparities persist between urban and rural areas. Energy systems include significant oil, gas, nuclear and renewable capacity, with growing investment in wind and solar power. Water management, ageing transport systems and climate resilience drive major infrastructure initiatives. Balancing modernisation with sustainability remains a national priority.

Tourism

Tourism is a major contributor to the US economy, offering extraordinary diversity of attractions. Natural landmarks include the Grand Canyon, Yellowstone National Park, Yosemite and Alaska's wilderness. Iconic cities such as New York, Los Angeles, San Francisco and New Orleans provide world-renowned cultural, historical and entertainment experiences. Theme parks, music heritage, culinary tourism and sporting events attract millions of visitors annually. Indigenous heritage sites and historic landmarks offer insight into the nation's complex past. Sustainable tourism initiatives increasingly aim to protect fragile ecosystems and cultural sites while supporting local economies.

Current Issues and Future Outlook

The United States faces significant challenges alongside considerable strengths. Climate change, political polarisation, economic inequality, healthcare reform and racial justice remain central national concerns. Internationally, shifting geopolitical dynamics require careful diplomatic and strategic engagement. At the same time, the country benefits from strong institutions, a highly innovative economy, abundant resources and cultural influence. The future outlook depends on fostering social cohesion, addressing environmental pressures, investing in education and infrastructure and maintaining democratic norms. How effectively these issues are managed will shape America's global role and domestic stability in the decades ahead.

Overview

The United States of America is a nation defined by diversity, ambition and continual reinvention. Rooted in Indigenous heritage and shaped by revolutionary ideals, immigration and expansion, it has emerged as a central global power. Its vast geography offers immense opportunity alongside environmental responsibility. Moving forward, the nation seeks to reconcile its ideals with social realities while sustaining economic vitality and democratic governance. Continued innovation, inclusion and responsible leadership remain key to ensuring a resilient and prosperous future for the United States.

DID YOU KNOW...?

The United States is home to Area 51, one of the world's most secretive military facilities, located in Nevada's remote desert. Established during the Cold War, it was instrumental in the development of experimental aircraft such as the U-2 spy plane and stealth technology. Long shrouded in secrecy, the site has fuelled widespread speculation about unidentified flying objects and government cover-ups. Declassified documents later confirmed its role in advanced aerospace testing, though many details remain restricted. The surrounding exclusion zone and abandoned test structures stand as symbols of Cold War secrecy, technological ambition and enduring public fascination.

KEY FACTS AND FIGURES

Geography & Environment

• Total area: 9.83 million km².
• Coastline: Over 19,900 km (Atlantic, Pacific, Arctic Oceans).
• Highest point: Denali (6,190 m).
• Major rivers: Mississippi–Missouri, Colorado, Columbia.
• Diverse wildlife: Bald eagles, bison, bears, alligators.
• 25 UNESCO World Heritage sites.

Population & Society

• Population: 335 million (2024 estimate).
• Density: 36 persons/km².
• Urbanisation: 83%.
• Ethnicity:
o European descent: ≈58%
o Hispanic/Latino: ≈19%
o African American: ≈13%
o Asian: ≈6%
o Native American: ≈1.3%
• Language: English (de facto).
• Religion: Christian (63%), Unaffiliated (29%).
• Literacy: 99%.
• Life expectancy: 77 years.

Economy

• GDP (nominal): £21 trillion.
• GDP per capita (PPP): ≈£63,000.
• Key industries:
o Technology and innovation
o Finance and services
o Manufacturing and agriculture
• Major exports: Machinery, aircraft, pharmaceuticals, agricultural products.
• Currency: United States Dollar (USD; £1 ≈ 1.27 USD).

Government

- Federal constitutional republic.
- Head of State and Government: President of the United States.
- President: Joe Biden (2025).

Infrastructure

- Major airport: Atlanta (over 90 million passengers/year).
- Energy mix: Fossil fuels dominant; renewables expanding.

Major Urban Centres

- New York City (NY): 8.5m – Financial and cultural capital.
- Los Angeles (CA): 3.9m – Entertainment and trade hub.
- Chicago (IL): 2.7m – Industry and transport centre.
- Houston (TX): 2.3m – Energy sector hub.
- Washington, D.C.: 700,000 – Capital city.

WASHINGTON - USA'S CAPITAL CITY

The National Flag

The national flag of the United States of America, known as 'The Stars and Stripes,' features a blue rectangle, known as the union or canton, in its upper left corner against a field of thirteen alternating red and white stripes. These thirteen horizontal stripes, seven red and six white, represent the original thirteen colonies that declared independence from Great Britain. The union contains fifty small, white, five-pointed stars arranged in rows, symbolising the fifty states that comprise the union. The red in the flag symbolises hardiness and valour, the white signifies purity and innocence and the blue represents vigilance, perseverance and justice. The design, with its stars and stripes, embodies the nation's history, federal structure and the enduring ideals of unity and freedom.

KEY PEOPLE AND PLACES

PEOPLE

Christopher Columbus (c. 1451–1506) Genoese explorer whose 1492 voyage across the Atlantic under Spanish sponsorship initiated lasting European exploration of the Americas.

George Washington (1732–1799) First President of the United States and commanding general of the Continental Army during the American Revolution.

Daniel Boone (1734–1820) Legendary pioneer and frontiersman who blazed the Wilderness Road through the Cumberland Gap into Kentucky.

Thomas Jefferson (1743–1826) Third President and principal author of the Declaration of Independence, which articulated the foundational ideals of American democracy.

Meriwether Lewis (1774–1809) & William Clark (1770–1838) Leaders of the Corps of Discovery Expedition, commissioned to explore the newly acquired Louisiana Territory and reach the Pacific.

Abraham Lincoln (1809–1865) Sixteenth President who preserved the Union during the Civil War and issued the Emancipation Proclamation.

Martin Luther King Jr. (1929–1968) Civil rights leader whose advocacy of nonviolent protest was instrumental in advancing racial equality.

Neil Armstrong (1930–2012) Astronaut and commander of Apollo 11 who became the first person to walk on the Moon.

PLACES

Jamestown Settlement (founded 1607) The first permanent English colony in North America, located in present-day Virginia.

Independence Hall (completed 1753) The Philadelphia building where both the Declaration of Independence and the United States Constitution were adopted.

Statue of Liberty (dedicated 1886) Colossal sculpture in New York Harbor, a universal symbol of freedom and a historic beacon to millions of immigrants.

Yellowstone National Park (established 1872) The world's first national park, renowned for its geothermal features and dramatic landscapes.

Grand Canyon National Park (established 1919) A vast, awe-inspiring gorge carved by the Colorado River in Arizona, a significant natural wonder.

National Mall and Memorial Parks (established 1965) The iconic national park in Washington, D.C., encompassing monuments to American presidents and heroes.

Mount Rushmore National Memorial (dedicated 1941)
Sculpture in South Dakota featuring the faces of Presidents Washington, Jefferson, Theodore Roosevelt and Lincoln.

TIMELINE OF EVENTS

c. 12,000 BCE: First Indigenous Settlements: Indigenous peoples migrated into North America and developed diverse cultures, societies and trade networks long before European contact.

1492: Columbus Reaches the Americas: Christopher Columbus's voyage marked the beginning of sustained European exploration and colonisation, with devastating consequences for Indigenous populations.

1607: Founding of Jamestown: Jamestown, Virginia, became the first permanent English settlement in North America, surviving early hardship through tobacco cultivation.

1620: Pilgrims Arrive at Plymouth Rock: English Pilgrims settled in present-day Massachusetts in search of religious freedom and established early forms of self-government.

1775: American Revolutionary War Begins: Armed conflict broke out between the American colonies and Great Britain over taxation, representation and political authority.

1776: Declaration of Independence: The colonies formally declared independence from Britain, promoting ideals of liberty, equality and self-rule.

1787: U.S. Constitution Signed: Delegates drafted and signed the Constitution, establishing a federal system of government with checks and balances.

1803: Louisiana Purchase: The United States doubled its territory by purchasing land from France, accelerating westward expansion.

1861: American Civil War Begins: Southern states seceded from the Union, leading to a civil war largely centred on slavery, states' rights and national unity.

1865: End of Civil War: The Union victory preserved the nation and led to the abolition of slavery through the Thirteenth Amendment.

1890: Wounded Knee Massacre: U.S. troops killed hundreds of Lakota Sioux, marking the tragic end of major armed Native American resistance.

1920: Women Gain the Right to Vote: The Nineteenth Amendment granted women the right to vote nationwide following decades of campaigning.

1929: Great Depression Begins: The stock market crash triggered a severe economic depression, resulting in widespread unemployment and poverty.

1941: Entry into the Second World War: Following the attack on Pearl Harbour, the United States entered the war and emerged as a major global power.

1954: Brown v. Board of Education Decision: The Supreme Court ruled that racial segregation in public schools was unconstitutional, strengthening the Civil Rights Movement.

1969: Apollo 11 Moon Landing: The United States successfully landed the first humans on the Moon, demonstrating significant scientific and technological achievement.

2001: September 11 Attacks: Terrorist attacks in New York and Washington, D.C., killed thousands and reshaped U.S. domestic and foreign policy.

2008: Election of Barack Obama: Barack Obama became the first African American president, representing a milestone in American political history.

2020: COVID-19 Pandemic Impact: The pandemic caused widespread health, economic and social disruption, significantly affecting daily life across the country.

UNITED MEXICAN STATES (MEXICO)

The United Mexican States, commonly known as Mexico, occupies the southern portion of North America, bordered by the United States to the north and Belize and Guatemala to the southeast. With an estimated population of approximately 129 million people, the capital and largest city is Mexico City, a sprawling metropolis of immense cultural and political influence. Other major urban centres such as Guadalajara, Monterrey and Puebla shape the nation's economic and social landscape. Spanish is the de facto national language, with over 60 Indigenous languages also officially recognised. The Mexican Peso serves as the national currency. Shaped by millennia of advanced Indigenous civilisations, a transformative Spanish colonial era and a defining revolutionary history, the nation is a profound fusion of deep historical roots and dynamic modern development. Its strategic location, rich biodiversity and cultural vitality contribute to its role as a major economic and political force in the Americas.

Geography

Mexico's landscape is one of the world's most geographically diverse. The country is dominated by the vast Mexican Plateau, flanked by two major mountain ranges: the Sierra Madre Occidental to the west and the Sierra Madre Oriental to the east. This central plateau tilts upward from north to south and hosts the country's major population centres. The landscape is punctuated by the dramatic Trans-Mexican Volcanic Belt, home to towering peaks like Pico de Orizaba, the nation's highest point and the frequently active Popocatépetl. Coastal plains fringe the country along the Pacific Ocean, the Gulf of Mexico and the Caribbean Sea. To the southeast, the flat, limestone-based Yucatán Peninsula features unique cenotes and underground river systems. Mexico's climate ranges from arid deserts in the north to dense tropical rainforests in the south and southeast. This varied terrain hosts exceptional biodiversity, making Mexico one of the world's 'megadiverse' countries. However, ecosystems face significant pressure from urbanisation, deforestation and water stress.

History

The history of Mexico begins with the rise of sophisticated Mesoamerican civilisations, including the Olmec, Maya, Teotihuacan, Toltec and ultimately the vast Aztec Empire. The Spanish conquest, led by Hernán Cortés in the early 16th century, initiated nearly 300 years of colonial rule as the Viceroyalty of New Spain, a period that radically restructured society. A prolonged war for independence, beginning in 1810 and led by figures like Miguel Hidalgo and José María Morelos, culminated in sovereignty in 1821. The 19th century was marked by political instability, the loss of vast northern territories to the United States and the French Intervention. The early 20th century was defined by the Mexican Revolution, a profound social and political upheaval that produced the Constitution of 1917 and shaped the modern state. The subsequent century saw the establishment of a dominant political party, periods of economic transformation and an ongoing struggle to reconcile modernity with deep-seated social inequalities and Indigenous rights.

Government and Politics

Mexico is a federal presidential representative democratic republic. Political authority is divided between the federal union, 31 states and Mexico City as the capital with state-like prerogatives. The federal government is composed of three independent branches: the executive, headed by the President; the legislative, a bicameral Congress consisting of the Senate and the Chamber of Deputies; and the judicial, headed by the Supreme Court of Justice. The President is directly elected for a single six-year term. Historically dominated by the Institutional Revolutionary Party for much of the 20th century, Mexican politics have evolved into a more competitive multi-party system. Major domestic issues include security and organised crime, corruption, economic inequality and energy policy. In foreign affairs, Mexico maintains an active and independent diplomacy, emphasising principles of non-intervention and championing international cooperation, particularly within Latin America.

Economy

Mexico possesses one of the world's largest economies and is classified as an upper-middle-income country with a mixed economic system. It is a major exporter, heavily integrated into global supply chains, particularly with the United States and Canada under the USMCA trade agreement. Key economic sectors include manufacturing, especially automotive and aerospace; petroleum, though production has declined; tourism; and agriculture, with exports like avocados, tomatoes and beer. Remittances from citizens working abroad constitute a vital source of national income. Despite its economic strength and macroeconomic stability, the country faces persistent challenges, including a large informal economy, pronounced income disparity, regional underdevelopment and the need for broader innovation-driven growth. Sustaining competitiveness requires continued investment in infrastructure, education and legal certainty.

Demographics and Society

With a population of approximately 129 million, Mexico is the most populous Spanish-speaking country in the world and the second-most populous in Latin America. The population is predominantly urban, with a significant concentration in the centre of the country. Mexican society is the product of widespread 'mestizaje'—the mixing of Indigenous and European ancestries—creating a complex mosaic where Indigenous identity remains a powerful cultural and political force for millions. While overwhelmingly Roman Catholic, religious diversity has grown. Significant internal and international migration shapes demographic trends. Mexican society is characterised by strong familial and communal ties. It faces enduring social challenges, including addressing poverty, improving access to quality education and healthcare across regions and ensuring the rights and inclusion of its Indigenous peoples.

Culture

Mexican culture is a vibrant and syncretic makeup, globally renowned for its depth and colour. It is a profound fusion of Indigenous Mesoamerican and Spanish traditions, with subsequent influences from Africa, Asia and beyond. This heritage is expressed in a rich literary tradition, monumental muralism, distinctive architecture and a world-famous culinary tradition recognised by UNESCO. Music, from mariachi and 'ranchera' to contemporary genres and dance are central to national identity. Religious and secular festivals, such as Día de los Muertos, are spectacular displays of communal belief and artistic expression. Mexican cinema, television and visual arts continue to gain international acclaim. The culture is deeply intertwined with a historical consciousness that frequently explores themes of identity, revolution, death and celebration.

Education and Healthcare

Education in Mexico is structured into basic, upper-secondary and higher education levels. Public education is free and secular and attendance is compulsory up to the upper-secondary level. While significant progress has been made in enrolment rates, the system contends with challenges of quality, equity and high dropout rates, particularly in rural and impoverished areas. The country boasts several prestigious public universities, such as the National Autonomous University of Mexico. Healthcare is provided through a multi-tiered system, including public institutions like the Mexican Institute of Social Security, services for government employees and a public healthcare scheme for the uninsured. Private healthcare is also widely available. Key public health challenges include combating obesity and diabetes, improving maternal health and ensuring equitable access to medical services across the nation.

Infrastructure

Mexico's infrastructure reflects its level of development, with modern facilities coexisting with areas of significant need. The country has an extensive and improving network of highways and toll roads, particularly connecting major cities and industrial corridors. The railway system is primarily dedicated to freight. Major seaports on both the Pacific and Gulf coasts handle substantial international trade. Aviation infrastructure is robust, with Mexico City's airport being a major hub. Telecommunications networks are well-developed in urban centres. The energy sector is in a state of transition, with significant state-owned oil production but increasing investment in renewable sources like wind and solar. Critical infrastructure challenges include expanding and modernising water treatment and distribution systems, improving public transportation in cities and enhancing digital connectivity in rural areas.

Tourism

Tourism is a cornerstone of the Mexican economy and a vital source of foreign currency. The country offers an unparalleled diversity of attractions, drawing millions of visitors annually. Its appeal includes thousands of kilometres of coastline featuring world-class beach resorts like Cancún, Los Cabos and Puerto Vallarta. It is a treasure trove of cultural heritage, hosting numerous UNESCO World Heritage sites such as the ancient Maya city of Chichén Itzá, the historic centres of Mexico City and Oaxaca and the pre-Hispanic city of Teotihuacán. Ecotourism and adventure travel thrive in its diverse biosphere reserves, deserts and coral reefs. Gastronomic tourism, based on its famed cuisine and 'Pueblo Mágico' programmes highlighting picturesque towns further enrich the visitor experience. The sector continuously balances promotion with the sustainable management of natural and cultural assets.

Current Issues and Future Outlook

Mexico faces a complex array of contemporary challenges. Foremost among these are public security and the power of organised crime syndicates, which impact daily life and economic development. Corruption at various levels of government and business remains a pervasive obstacle. Deep social and economic inequalities persist, alongside the need to fully realise human rights and strengthen the rule of law. Environmentally, the country grapples with water scarcity, pollution and climate vulnerability. However, Mexico possesses formidable strengths: a young and growing workforce, strategic geographic and trade advantages, immense cultural capital and a resilient civil society. The nation's future trajectory will hinge on its ability to foster inclusive economic growth, strengthen its institutions, harness its demographic dividend and navigate a complex relationship with its northern neighbour. Success will define its role as a leading regional power and global partner.

Overview

The United Mexican States is a nation of profound contrasts and enduring vitality. Forged in the crucible of ancient civilisations and colonial encounter and defined by a revolutionary spirit, it has emerged as a modern powerhouse. Its identity is a rich synthesis of the Indigenous and the imported, the traditional and the innovative. While confronting significant social, economic and political challenges, Mexico's dynamic culture, strategic economic position and human potential provide a strong foundation. Its ongoing journey involves reconciling its storied past with the demands of the future, seeking a path toward greater equity, security and prosperity for all its people and solidifying its influential role on the world stage.

DID YOU KNOW...?

Beneath the streets of modern Mexico City lies a hidden, shimmering testament to its ancient past: the subsoil of the capital is studded with vast, glittering sheets of obsidian. This volcanic glass, forged in the fire of the volcanoes that ring the Valley of Mexico, was one of the most crucial and valuable materials for the Mesoamerican civilisations that flourished here, particularly the Aztecs. They prized obsidian for its sharpness, using it to craft lethal weapons like the 'macuahuitl' (a wooden sword edged with razor-sharp obsidian blades), exquisite ritual knives for sacrifice, mirrors for divination and intricate jewellery and art. This abundant local resource was a key to Aztec military and ritual power and its enduring presence under the modern metropolis serves as a powerful, tangible link to the formidable empire upon whose ruins the city was built.

KEY FACTS AND FIGURES

Geography & Environment

• Total area: 1.96 million km².

• Coastline: Over 9,300 km (Pacific Ocean, Gulf of Mexico, Caribbean Sea).

• Highest point: Pico de Orizaba (5,636 m).

• Major rivers: Rio Grande (Río Bravo), Grijalva, Usumacinta.

• Diverse wildlife: Jaguars, ocelots, grey whales, monarch butterflies.

• 35 UNESCO World Heritage sites.

Population & Society

• Population: 129 million (2024 estimate).

• Density: 66 persons/km².

• Urbanisation: 81%.

• Ethnicity:

o Mestizo (mixed Indigenous and European): ≈62%

o Indigenous peoples: ≈21%

o European descent: ≈15%

o Other: ≈2%

• Language: Spanish (official).

• Religion: Christian (≈78%, predominantly Roman Catholic).

• Literacy: 95%.

• Life expectancy: 75 years.

Economy

• GDP (nominal): £1.3 trillion.

• GDP per capita (PPP): ≈£18,000.

• Key industries:

o Manufacturing (automotive, electronics)

o Oil and energy

o Tourism and services

• Major exports: Vehicles, machinery, petroleum, agricultural products.

• Currency: Mexican Peso (MXN; £1 ≈ 21 MXN).

Government

• Federal presidential republic.
• Head of State and Government: President of Mexico.
• President: Claudia Sheinbaum (2025).

Infrastructure

• Major airport: Mexico City International Airport (over 45 million passengers/year).
• Energy mix: Oil and gas dominant; renewables growing.

Major Urban Centres

• Mexico City: 9.2m – Political, economic and cultural capital.
• Guadalajara: 1.5m – Technology and manufacturing hub.
• Monterrey: 1.4m – Industrial and business centre.
• Puebla: 1.7m – Manufacturing and colonial heritage city.
• Tijuana: 1.9m – Border trade and manufacturing hub.

MEXICO CITY - MEXICO'S POLITICAL, ECONOMIC AND CULTURAL CAPITAL

The National Flag

The national flag of Mexico consists of three vertical bands of green, white and red, with the national coat of arms centred on the white band. The green band symbolises hope and independence, the white represents unity and peace and the red signifies the blood of those who fought for the nation. The coat of arms, depicting an eagle holding a serpent while perched on a cactus, reflects an ancient Aztec legend and represents strength, resilience and Mexico's national identity.

KEY PEOPLE AND PLACES

PEOPLE

Hernán Cortés (c. 1485–1547) Spanish conquistador who led the expedition that captured the Aztec capital of Tenochtitlan in 1521, initiating over 300 years of Spanish rule.

Miguel Hidalgo y Costilla (1753–1811) Roman Catholic priest who initiated the Mexican War of Independence with the *Grito de Dolores* (Cry of Dolores) on September 16, 1810.

Antonio López de Santa Anna (1794–1876) A dominant political figure who served as president on eleven non-consecutive times and led Mexican forces during the Texas Revolution and the Mexican-American War.

Benito Juárez (1806–1872) A national hero and liberal reformer who served as president, championed the separation of church and state and is remembered for his defence of Mexican sovereignty.

Porfirio Díaz (1830–1915) General who served as president for over 30 years, a period of modernisation and foreign investment that also led to political repression and the Mexican Revolution.

Francisco 'Pancho' Villa (1878–1923) A leading general and folk hero of the Mexican Revolution, commanding the División del Norte against the federal government.

Emiliano Zapata (1879–1919) A revolutionary leader who fought for social justice and land reform for peasants, symbolised by his slogan 'Tierra y Libertad' (Land and Liberty).

Frida Kahlo (1907–1954) One of Mexico's most celebrated artists, known for her profound and often autobiographical paintings that explore identity, pain and Mexican culture.

PLACES

Teotihuacán (peak c. 450 CE) An ancient Mesoamerican city located northeast of modern Mexico City, renowned for its massive pyramids, the Pyramid of the Sun and the Pyramid of the Moon.

Historic Centre of Mexico City (founded 1325) Built atop the ruins of the Aztec capital Tenochtitlan, a UNESCO World Heritage site containing the Zócalo, Metropolitan Cathedral and Templo Mayor.

Chichen Itza (peak c. 600–1200 CE) A major city of the Maya civilisation in Yucatán, a UNESCO site famous for the stepped pyramid El Castillo (Temple of Kukulcán).

Historic Centre of Oaxaca (founded 1529) A colonial city and UNESCO site in southern Mexico, known for its well-preserved architecture and proximity to the Monte Albán archaeological site.

Historic Town of Guanajuato (founded 1548) A former silver mining town and UNESCO World Heritage site, famous for its colonial architecture, underground streets and the annual Cervantino Festival.

Pre-Hispanic City of Palenque (peak c. 500–700 CE) A Maya city state in Chiapas, a UNESCO site celebrated for its exquisite architecture, sculptures and bas-relief carvings set in a jungle landscape.

Copper Canyon (Barrancas del Cobre) A group of canyons in the Sierra Madre Occidental in Chihuahua, larger and deeper than the Grand Canyon, traversed by the Chihuahua al Pacífico railway.

TIMELINE OF EVENTS

c. 15,000–10,000 BCE: First Indigenous Settlements: Early Indigenous peoples settled across what is now Mexico, laying the foundations for complex civilisations, agriculture and trade networks.

c. 1200–400 BCE: Olmec Civilisation: Often regarded as Mesoamerica's first major civilisation, the Olmecs developed early writing, art and religious traditions.

c. 250–900 CE: Maya Classical Period: The Maya civilisation flourished, producing advanced achievements in astronomy, mathematics, architecture and writing.

1325: Founding of Tenochtitlán: The Mexica (Aztecs) founded their capital on Lake Texcoco, which later became Mexico City.

1519: Hernán Cortés Arrives: Spanish conquistador Hernán Cortés landed on the Gulf coast, beginning the Spanish conquest of Mexico.

1521: Fall of Tenochtitlán: Spanish forces defeated the Aztec Empire, marking the start of nearly three centuries of colonial rule.

1535: Viceroyalty of New Spain Established: Mexico became the centre of Spanish administration in North America, playing a key role in imperial trade and governance.

1810: Start of the War of Independence: Miguel Hidalgo issued the *Grito de Dolores*, launching the struggle against Spanish rule.

1821: Independence Achieved: Mexico gained independence from Spain and emerged as a sovereign nation.

1846–1848: Mexican–American War: The conflict resulted in Mexico losing large northern territories to the United States.

1857: Liberal Constitution Adopted: A new constitution limited Church and military power, reshaping the Mexican state.

1864–1867: French Intervention: France installed Emperor Maximilian I, but republican forces eventually restored the republic.

1876–1911: Porfiriato: Porfirio Díaz ruled Mexico, promoting economic modernisation while deepening social inequality.

1910–1920: Mexican Revolution: A major armed conflict transformed Mexico's political system and addressed land and labour issues.

1917: Constitution of 1917: A new constitution established social rights and remains the foundation of Mexico's political system.

1940s–1970s: Mexican Economic Miracle: Rapid industrialisation and economic growth significantly expanded the middle class.

1985: Mexico City Earthquake: A devastating earthquake caused widespread destruction and prompted major civil and political reforms.

1994: NAFTA Comes into Force: The North American Free Trade Agreement reshaped Mexico's economy and global trade role.

2000: End of One-Party Rule: The election of Vicente Fox ended over 70 years of single-party dominance.

2020: COVID-19 Pandemic Impact: The pandemic caused major health, economic and social challenges across Mexico.

CENTRAL AMERICA

Central America is a region defined by its compact geographic scale and profound historical transformations, encompassing nations including Guatemala, Honduras, El Salvador, Nicaragua, Costa Rica, Panama and Belize, alongside numerous Indigenous peoples. Its volcanic highlands, dense rainforests, coastal mangroves and narrow isthmian corridor have sustained diverse societies intimately connected to the land and to evolving transoceanic networks. Historically, the region was shaped by powerful pre-Columbian civilisations, the disruptive forces of Spanish conquest and the turbulent birth of modern republics, playing a pivotal role in global movements of goods and capital through its strategic position linking Atlantic and Pacific trade. Following centuries of colonial rule and internal strife, the modern era has seen these countries forge distinct political identities while engaging in regional integration through frameworks such as the Central American Integration System, all while grappling with the complex legacies of agrarian conflict, migration and biodiversity conservation. The Maya temples of Tikal, the literary works of Rubén Darío, the revolutionary theology of Archbishop Romero and the engineering marvel of the Panama Canal underscore Central America's enduring influence on global culture, political thought and connectivity. This chapter examines the region's foundational heritage, its ongoing quest for equitable societies and its significant role in shaping the modern world's political and economic architecture.

BELIZE

The United States of Belize, commonly known as Belize, occupies a small but strategically significant portion of Central America, bordered by Mexico to the north, Guatemala to the west and south and the Caribbean Sea to the east. Formerly known as British Honduras, Belize is the only Central American nation with English as its official language, a legacy of its colonial past. With an estimated population of approximately 410,000 people, Belize is one of the least populous nations in the Americas. The capital is Belmopan, while Belize City remains the largest urban centre and commercial hub. The Belize Dollar, pegged to the United States Dollar, serves as the national currency. Shaped by ancient Maya civilisations, British colonial rule and a peaceful transition to independence in 1981, Belize is a distinctive fusion of Caribbean, Central American and Anglo traditions. Its rich natural environment, cultural diversity and strategic location contribute to its growing regional importance.

Geography

Belize's geography is remarkably diverse for its compact size. The northern lowlands consist largely of flat, fertile plains, while the southern region rises into the forested Maya Mountains, home to the country's highest point, Doyle's Delight. Along the eastern coast stretches the Belize Barrier Reef, the second-largest coral reef system in the world and a treasured UNESCO site, supporting extraordinary marine biodiversity. Offshore lie numerous picturesque cayes, low coral islands central to both tourism and the fishing industry. Inland, dense tropical rainforests, vast savannahs, winding rivers and extensive wetlands dominate the undulating landscape. The country's tropical climate features a pronounced wet and dry season, yet it remains vulnerable to destructive hurricanes and severe flooding. Belize's ecosystems host exceptional biological richness, firmly placing it among the planet's vital biodiversity hotspots, though deforestation, coastal erosion and climate change pose relentless and ongoing threats to this natural heritage.

History

Belize's deep history begins with the flourishing of advanced Maya civilisations, which constructed impressive cities such as Caracol, leaving behind monumental architecture and sophisticated knowledge systems. From the 16th century, the region became hotly contested territory, with British loggers establishing camps to exploit valuable hardwoods like mahogany. Unlike much of Central America, Belize never formally became a Spanish colony, instead evolving into the distinctive British possession recognised as British Honduras. The gradual development of self-government culminated in a peaceful independence achieved in 1981. A persistent territorial claim by Guatemala has significantly shaped modern diplomacy, fostering Belize's strong emphasis on international law and diligent multilateral engagement throughout its existence.

Government and Politics

Belize is a stable parliamentary constitutional monarchy, recognising the British monarch as its ceremonial head of state, represented locally by a Governor-General. Executive power is exercised by an elected Prime

Minister and their Cabinet, while legislative authority rests with a bicameral National Assembly. The country is divided into six administrative districts for local governance purposes. National politics are dominated by two major parties, with peaceful electoral transitions forming a core part of the nation's democratic identity. Key domestic political issues consistently include economic diversification, managing public debt, crime prevention and crucial environmental protection. In foreign affairs, Belize maintains especially close ties with the Caribbean Community (CARICOM), its Central American neighbours and the wider Commonwealth network.

Economy

Belize has a small, open, upper-middle-income economy that relies heavily on a notably narrow range of export sectors. Tourism stands as the leading economic driver, closely complemented by agriculture, particularly sugar, bananas and citrus production. Offshore financial services and some light manufacturing also contribute to the national income. The country's long-standing currency peg to the US Dollar provides essential monetary stability, though economic growth remains vulnerable to external shocks and global market fluctuations. Structural challenges include a high public debt burden, limited industrial diversification and a deep dependence on imported goods. Long-term economic resilience will fundamentally depend on sustainable tourism, agricultural innovation and substantial investment in human capital development.

Demographics and Society

Belize is celebrated as one of the most ethnically and culturally diverse societies in the entire region. Its population comprises Mestizo, Creole, Maya, Garifuna, East Indian, Mennonite, Chinese and other distinct communities, each contributing richly to the national network. While English is the sole official language, Spanish, Kriol, Garifuna and various Maya languages are all widely spoken in daily life. The population is relatively young and is becoming increasingly urbanised, though many traditional communities remain rural and closely tied to the land. Belizean society places a strong emphasis on community, extended family and vibrant cultural heritage, while concurrently facing challenges related to income inequality, youth employment and equitable access to public services.

Culture

Belizean culture is a wonderfully distinctive blend of Caribbean rhythm, Central American tradition and subtle British institutional influence. Music and dance, including energetic punta and soulful brukdown, are central to cultural expression and celebration. The vibrant Garifuna Settlement Day festivities and annual Carnival are key manifestations of collective national identity. The nation's cuisine reflects its multicultural roots, combining fresh seafood, tropical produce and beloved staples like rice and beans. Storytelling, oral history and lively communal celebrations all play a vital role in actively preserving this unique heritage. Ultimately, Belize's cultural life remains deeply connected to its breathtaking natural environment and its layered historical consciousness.

Education and Healthcare

Education in Belize follows a structure inherited from the British system, encompassing primary, secondary and tertiary levels. While primary education is legally compulsory, access and quality can vary considerably, particularly in rural and remote areas. The country hosts several teacher-training colleges and a national university offering local degrees. Healthcare is delivered through a mixed system of public and private services, with government clinics providing basic care nationwide. Significant challenges include limited specialised medical services, recurring workforce shortages and the pressing need for improved maternal and preventative healthcare, particularly in underserved indigenous and rural regions across the country.

Infrastructure

Belize's infrastructure reflects both measurable progress and persistent limitation across the nation. The main road network adequately connects major towns but remains less developed in rural districts, where seasonal weather frequently disrupts transport. Ports and marine infrastructure are absolutely vital for both international trade and the crucial tourism industry. Air travel plays an equally crucial role, with international and domestic airports providing essential links. Telecommunications have improved significantly in recent years, though digital access remains noticeably uneven nationally. Energy generation still relies largely on imported fossil fuels and some hydropower, with growing interest in investing in renewable sources for the future. Strengthening overall resilience to climate-related damage remains a key and ongoing priority for development.

Tourism

Tourism is the undeniable cornerstone of Belize's modern economy and its global profile. The country is rightly celebrated for its pristine natural attractions, including the magnificent Belize Barrier Reef, the awe-inspiring Great Blue Hole and vast protected rainforests. Archaeological tourism centred on majestic Maya sites perfectly complements world-class eco- and adventure activities like diving, snorkelling and jungle exploration. Community-based and sustainable tourism initiatives are becoming increasingly prominent, aiming to carefully balance economic growth with essential environmental conservation and genuine cultural preservation efforts for future generations.

Current Issues and Future Outlook

Belize undeniably faces a range of serious contemporary challenges, including economic vulnerability, crime, climate change and environmental degradation. Rising sea levels and extreme weather events pose genuine existential risks to vulnerable coastal communities and fragile ecosystems. However, Belize also possesses significant inherent strengths: enduring political stability, remarkable cultural cohesion, abundant natural capital and a demonstrated commitment to conservation. Its future prospects will fundamentally rest on pursuing sustainable development, achieving improved education and healthcare outcomes and continuing its proactive regional and international cooperation on shared goals.

Overview

The nation of Belize is a land of striking contrasts and quiet resilience. Rooted in ancient Maya civilisation and shaped by a unique colonial legacy, it has forged a peacefully pluralistic modern identity. While confronting substantial economic and environmental challenges, Belize's profound cultural richness, breathtaking natural beauty and steady democratic traditions provide a solid foundation for progress. Its ongoing national journey seeks to harmonise sensible development with urgent conservation, honour its multifaceted multicultural heritage and secure a sustainable, inclusive future for all of its people.

DID YOU KNOW...?

Hidden beneath the lush jungles and rolling hills of Belize lies an extraordinary legacy of the ancient Maya: vast networks of limestone caves, many of which were considered sacred gateways to the underworld, or *Xibalba*. These caves were not merely geological features but central to Maya cosmology and ritual life. Archaeological discoveries have revealed ceremonial chambers deep underground, containing pottery, tools and human remains used in offerings to the gods. Some caves preserve ancient footprints and soot marks from torches, frozen in time for over a millennium. Today, these subterranean worlds remain powerful reminders of the profound spiritual relationship between the Maya civilisation and the land, linking modern Belize directly to its ancient past.

KEY FACTS AND FIGURES

Geography & Environment

• Total area: 22,966 km².

• Coastline: Approximately 386 km (Caribbean Sea).

• Highest point: Doyle's Delight (1,124 m).

• Major rivers: Belize River, New River, Hondo River, Sarstoon River.

• Diverse wildlife: Jaguars, tapirs, howler monkeys, manatees, scarlet macaws.

• 1 UNESCO World Heritage site (Belize Barrier Reef Reserve System).

Population & Society

• Population: Approximately 410,000 (2024 estimate).

• Density: 18 persons/km².

• Urbanisation: 46%.

• Ethnicity:

o Mestizo: ≈52%

o Creole: ≈25%

o Maya peoples: ≈11%

o Garifuna: ≈6%

o Other (including Mennonite, East Indian, Chinese, European): ≈6%

• Language: English (official); Spanish, Belizean Kriol, Garifuna and Maya languages widely spoken.

• Religion: Christian (≈80%, predominantly Roman Catholic and Protestant).

• Literacy: 82%.

• Life expectancy: 75 years.

Economy

• GDP (nominal): ≈£2.2 billion.

• GDP per capita (PPP): ≈£8,500.

• Key industries:

o Tourism

o Agriculture (sugar, bananas, citrus, seafood)

o Financial and offshore services

• Major exports: Sugar, bananas, citrus products, seafood.
• Currency: Belize Dollar (BZD; fixed at BZ$2 = £0.80 approx. / US$1).

Government

• Parliamentary constitutional monarchy.
• Head of State: King Charles III (represented by a Governor-General).
• Head of Government: Prime Minister of Belize.
• Prime Minister: Johnny Briceño (2025).

Infrastructure

• Major airport: Philip S. W. Goldson International Airport (approx. 1 million passengers/year).
• Energy mix: Imported fossil fuels and hydropower; renewables expanding.

Major Urban Centres

• Belize City: ≈70,000 – Largest city and commercial hub.
• Belmopan: ≈25,000 – Capital and administrative centre.
• San Ignacio / Santa Elena: ≈20,000 – Tourism and agricultural centre.
• Orange Walk Town: ≈18,000 – Sugar-producing region.
• San Pedro (Ambergris Caye): ≈17,000 – Tourism centre.

BELIZE CITY – BELIZE'S LARGEST CITY AND COMMERCIAL HUB.

The National Flag

The national flag of Belize features a royal blue field with narrow red stripes at the top and bottom and a large white disc at the centre bearing the national coat of arms. The blue symbolises the People's United Party and national unity, while the red represents the United Democratic Party, together reflecting political harmony. The coat of arms depicts two woodcutters standing beside a mahogany tree, framed by a wreath of fifty leaves, symbolising the nation's historical reliance on the timber industry and commemorating the year 1950, when the struggle for self-government began. The flag as a whole represents Belize's history, resilience and peaceful path to independence.

KEY PEOPLE AND PLACES

PEOPLE

Rt. Hon. George Cadle Price (1919–2011) Widely regarded as the 'Father of the Nation,' he was the first Premier and Prime Minister of Belize, leading the country to independence from British colonial rule in 1981.

Philip Goldson (1923–2001) A key political figure, journalist, an advocate for press freedom who founded *The Belize Billboard* newspaper and was a prominent voice for labour rights and education.

Antonio Soberanis Gómez (1897–1975) Considered the father of the Belizean labour movement, leading the Laborers and Unemployed Association in the 1930s to advocate for workers' rights during economic hardship.

Sir Colville Norbert Young (b. 1932) Belize's Governor-General from 1993 to 2021 and a noted linguist, educator and cultural figure who contributed to the preservation and study of Belizean Creole.

Thomas Vincent Ramos (1887–1955) A civil rights activist who fought for the recognition and rights of the Garifuna people in Belize, with his efforts leading to the establishment of Garifuna Settlement Day on November 19th.

Andy Palacio (1960–2008) A celebrated musician and UNESCO Artist for Peace who became an international icon for popularising Garifuna music and culture through his award-winning album *Wátina*.

Jaguar Paw (active 7th–8th centuries) A powerful Maya ruler whose elaborate tomb at the site of Cahal Pech provided significant archaeological insight into the wealth and power of Classic Period Maya kings.

PLACES

Caracol (flourished c. 250–900 CE) The largest known Maya archaeological site in Belize, once a major political and military centre that rivaled the power of Tikal in present-day Guatemala.

Great Blue Hole A giant marine sinkhole located at the centre of Lighthouse Reef, made famous by Jacques Cousteau. It is a UNESCO World Heritage site and a premier destination for scuba divers.

Belize Barrier Reef Reserve System (UNESCO site 1996) The second-largest coral reef system in the world, a UNESCO World Heritage site comprising seven protected marine areas renowned for their biodiversity.

Caye Caulker A small, laid-back island off the coast known for its motto 'Go Slow.' It is a major hub for tourism, fishing and enjoying the relaxed Caribbean lifestyle.

Xunantunich (active c. 200–900 CE) A Classic Period Maya ceremonial centre in western Belize, famous for its large pyramid 'El Castillo,' which offers panoramic views of the surrounding jungle and nearby Guatemala.

Belmopan (established 1970) The purpose-built capital city of Belize, created after Hurricane Hattie severely damaged the former capital, Belize City, in 1961.

Mennonite Communities (established 1958) Settlements such as Spanish Lookout and Blue Creek, where traditional Mennonite groups live, contributing significantly to Belize's agricultural production and dairy industry.

TIMELINE OF EVENTS

c. 1500 BCE: First Indigenous Settlements: The Maya civilisation developed in present-day Belize, establishing cities, agriculture, trade networks and advanced knowledge long before European contact.

c. 250–900 CE: Classic Maya Period: Major Maya city-states such as Caracol and Lamanai flourished, reaching cultural, scientific and architectural heights.

900–1500: Maya Decline and Continuity: Many southern Maya cities declined, but Maya communities continued to inhabit and adapt across the region.

1502: Columbus Reaches Nearby Waters: Christopher Columbus sailed along the Caribbean coast, marking early European awareness of the region.

1638: First British Settlements: English settlers, known as Baymen, established logging camps focused on harvesting logwood.

1763: Treaty of Paris: Spain recognised British settlement rights in Belize, though sovereignty remained disputed.

1798: Battle of St George's Caye: British settlers and enslaved Africans repelled a Spanish force, securing British control.

1862: British Honduras Declared Colony: Belize was formally designated the Crown Colony of British Honduras.

1931: Belize City Hurricane: A devastating hurricane caused widespread destruction and loss of life, reshaping development priorities.

1948: Currency Devaluation Protests: Economic hardship sparked nationalist movements demanding political reform and self-rule.

1954: Universal Adult Suffrage: Voting rights were extended to most adults, advancing democratic participation.

1964: Self-Government Achieved: Belize gained internal self-government, with Britain retaining control over defence and foreign affairs.

1973: Name Changed to Belize: British Honduras officially became Belize, reflecting growing national identity.

1981: Independence: Belize became an independent nation within the Commonwealth, ending British colonial rule.

1998: Hurricane Mitch Impact: Severe flooding and damage affected agriculture, infrastructure and livelihoods.

2001: Hurricane Iris: A powerful storm caused major destruction, particularly in southern Belize.

2010: Belize Barrier Reef Protection: Conservation efforts intensified to protect the reef, a UNESCO World Heritage Site.

2016: ICJ Referendum Process Begins: Belize advanced steps towards resolving its territorial dispute with Guatemala.

2019: ICJ Referendum Approved: Voters agreed to take the Guatemala dispute to the International Court of Justice.

2020: COVID-19 Pandemic Impact: The pandemic disrupted tourism, health services and economic stability nationwide.

THE REPUBLIC OF GUATEMALA

The Republic of Guatemala, commonly known as Guatemala, occupies a pivotal and strategically significant portion of Central America, bordered by Mexico to the north and west, Belize and the Caribbean Sea to the northeast, Honduras to the east, El Salvador to the southeast and the Pacific Ocean to the south. Formerly the heartland of the Maya civilisation and a core province of the Spanish Empire, Guatemala is the most populous nation in Central America. With an estimated population of approximately 17.6 million people, Guatemala is a demographic and cultural centre of the region. The capital is Guatemala City, which is also the largest urban centre and commercial hub. The Quetzal serves as the national currency. Shaped by ancient Maya civilisations, Spanish colonial rule and a turbulent post-independence history, Guatemala is a distinctive fusion of Indigenous, European and more recent influences. Its complex social fabric, significant natural environment and strategic location contribute to its enduring regional importance.

Geography

Guatemala's geography is remarkably diverse and dramatic. The southern coastal regions consist of fertile lowlands, while the central highlands are dominated by volcanic mountains and highland valleys, home to many of the country's population and its highest point, Tajumulco Volcano. To the north stretch the vast, forested lowlands of the Petén department, which forms part of the Maya Forest. The country boasts numerous lakes, most notably Lake Atitlán, set in a volcanic caldera and Lake Izabal, which drains into the Caribbean. Guatemala's climate is tropical, with variation according to altitude and it is highly vulnerable to volcanic activity, earthquakes, hurricanes and flooding. The country's ecosystems host exceptional biological richness, placing it among the world's biodiversity hotspots, though deforestation, soil erosion and climate change pose severe ongoing threats.

History

Guatemala's history begins with the flourishing of advanced Maya civilisations, which built monumental city-states such as Tikal, El Mirador and Quiriguá, leaving behind a legacy of architecture, astronomy and writing. From the 16th century, the region was comprehensively conquered by Spain, becoming the Captaincy-General of Guatemala, a principal centre of colonial administration. It achieved independence in 1821, first as part of the Mexican Empire and then of the Federal Republic of Central America, before becoming a fully independent republic in 1847. The subsequent history was marked by political instability, authoritarian rule and a protracted 36-year civil war (1960–1996) that left a deep social trauma. The peace accords of 1996 aimed to address issues of human rights, indigenous rights and democratisation, shaping the country's contemporary political landscape.

Government and Politics

Guatemala is a presidential representative democratic republic. Executive power is exercised by an elected President and Vice President, while legislative authority rests with a unicameral Congress of the Republic. The country is divided into 22 departments for administrative purposes. Politics are dominated by a multi-party system, though parties are often volatile and weak, with corruption and impunity forming major challenges to governance. Key domestic political issues include poverty, security, judicial reform, indigenous rights and environmental protection. In foreign affairs, Guatemala maintains active ties within Central America, is a member of the Central American Integration System (SICA) and has a long-standing territorial claim to Belize, which shapes a significant part of its diplomatic engagements.

Economy

Guatemala has the largest economy in Central America but faces profound inequality. It is a mixed economy reliant on a narrow range of sectors. Agriculture remains a cornerstone, with key exports including coffee, sugar, bananas, cardamom and vegetables. Textiles and apparel manufacturing, tourism and remittances from a large diaspora also contribute substantially to national income. Economic growth is hampered by informal employment, inadequate infrastructure and vulnerability to global commodity prices and climate events. Structural challenges include extreme wealth disparity, limited tax revenue and underinvestment in public services. Long-term economic resilience depends on broadening the tax base, improving education and fostering inclusive development.

Demographics and Society

Guatemala is a deeply diverse society with a significant indigenous population. Its people include a plurality of Ladinos (of mixed European and Indigenous ancestry) and over 20 Maya ethnic groups, along with smaller communities of Garifuna, Xinca and others. While Spanish is the official language, 22 Mayan languages are recognised nationally and widely spoken. The population is relatively young and rapidly growing, with a significant portion living in rural areas, often in conditions of poverty. Guatemalan society is marked by stark social stratification along ethnic and economic lines, while facing profound challenges related to malnutrition, limited access to services and the legacy of civil conflict.

Culture

Guatemalan culture is a complex network of enduring Maya tradition and strong Spanish colonial influence. Textiles, weaving and traditional dress are vibrant expressions of indigenous identity and community. Music, from the marimba to contemporary forms and religious festivals blending Catholic and Maya beliefs, are central to cultural life. Holy Week (Semana Santa) processions in Antigua Guatemala are world-renowned. Cuisine is based on maize, beans, rice and chillies, with dishes like tamales, pepián and kak'ik reflecting this heritage. Storytelling, oral history and communal practices play a vital role in preserving a multifaceted heritage deeply connected to the land and history.

Education and Healthcare

Education in Guatemala follows a structure inherited from the Spanish system, with primary, secondary and tertiary levels. While primary education is compulsory, access, completion rates and quality are poor, particularly for girls and indigenous children in rural areas. The country has several public and private universities. Healthcare is delivered through a fragmented mix of public and private services, with severe disparities in access. Challenges are extensive, including high rates of maternal and child mortality, malnutrition, infectious diseases and a critical shortage of medical personnel and facilities in underserved regions.

Infrastructure

Guatemala's infrastructure reflects deep-seated inequalities. The road network is reasonably developed in major cities and between departmental capitals, but is poor or non-existent in many rural and remote areas. Ports on the Caribbean and Pacific coasts are vital to trade. Air travel is centred on La Aurora International Airport in the capital. Telecommunications have improved in urban areas, though digital access remains limited in the countryside. Energy generation relies on a mix of hydropower, imported fuels and biomass. Strengthening infrastructure to withstand seismic and climatic events is a persistent concern.

Tourism

Tourism is a vital and growing sector of Guatemala's economy. The country is celebrated for its profound cultural attractions, including the magnificent archaeological site of Tikal, the well-preserved Spanish colonial city of Antigua Guatemala (both UNESCO World Heritage Sites) and vibrant indigenous markets such as Chichicastenango. Natural attractions like Lake Atitlán, Semuc Champey and numerous volcanoes complement cultural tourism. Eco-tourism and adventure tourism are expanding, though the sector's potential is constrained by infrastructure limitations and security perceptions in some areas.

Current Issues and Future Outlook

Guatemala faces a formidable array of contemporary challenges, including widespread poverty, corruption, violent crime, food insecurity, climate vulnerability and environmental degradation. Political instability and weak institutions hinder progress. However, Guatemala also possesses significant strengths: a resilient and rich cultural heritage, a strategic geographic position, economic potential and an active civil society. Its future prospects rest on strengthening the rule of law, tackling inequality, investing in human capital, managing natural resources sustainably and fostering genuine social inclusion for all its peoples.

Overview

The Republic of Guatemala is a nation of profound contrasts and resilient spirit. Rooted in one of the world's great ancient civilisations and shaped by a complex colonial and post-colonial history, it grapples with a difficult legacy while forging a modern identity. While confronting deep-seated social, economic and political challenges, Guatemala's cultural wealth, historical significance and natural environment provide a foundational patrimony. Its ongoing journey seeks to achieve lasting peace, equitable development and democratic consolidation, honouring its pluralistic heritage to secure a more just and sustainable future for all Guatemalans.

DID YOU KNOW...?

Beneath Guatemala's highlands lie hundreds of ancient reservoirs and canals built by the Maya, revealing a sophisticated water management system few know existed. Beyond monumental cities like Tikal, smaller settlements show evidence of terraces, cisterns and channels that regulated water for agriculture and ritual purposes. Some reservoirs align with the stars, hinting at cosmological significance. These hydraulic systems supported dense populations and demonstrate that the Maya were master engineers, controlling floods and droughts. Today, remnants of these ancient waterworks survive beneath the forest canopy, a testament to the ingenuity of Guatemala's early civilisations, hidden from the casual visitor.

KEY FACTS AND FIGURES

Geography & Environment

• Total area: 108,889 km².

• Coastline: ≈400 km (Pacific Ocean and Caribbean Sea).

• Climate: Tropical, with cooler conditions in the highlands.

• Highest point: Volcán Tajumulco (4,220 m).

• Major features: Volcanic highlands, Pacific coastal plain, Petén lowlands, Lake Atitlán.

• Wildlife: Jaguars, howler monkeys, quetzals, tapirs, crocodiles.

• 3 UNESCO World Heritage sites.

Population & Society

• Population: ≈18 million (2024 estimate).

• Density: ≈165 persons/km².

• Urbanisation: ≈55%.

• Ethnicity:

o Indigenous Maya peoples: ≈43%

o Mestizo/Ladino: ≈56%

o Other: ≈1%

• Languages: Spanish (official), 20+ Mayan languages, Garífuna, Xinca.

• Religion: Christian (Roman Catholic and Protestant): ≈90%.

• Literacy: ≈81%.

• Life expectancy: ≈75 years.

Economy

• GDP (nominal): ≈£80 billion.

• GDP per capita (PPP): ≈£10,000.

• Key industries:

o Agriculture (coffee, sugar, bananas)

o Manufacturing and textiles

o Mining

o Tourism

• Major exports: Coffee, sugar, bananas, textiles, cardamom.

• Currency: Guatemalan quetzal (GTQ; £1 ≈ 10 GTQ).

Government

- Presidential republic.
- System: Constitutional democratic republic.
- Head of State: President of Guatemala.
- Head of Government: President of Guatemala.
- Legislature: Congress of the Republic (160 members).

Infrastructure

- Transport: National road network; limited rail services; air and sea transport.
- Major airports: La Aurora International Airport (Guatemala City).
- Energy mix: Hydropower, fossil fuels, growing renewable energy use.
- Digital connectivity: Well developed in urban areas; limited in rural regions.

Major Urban Centres

- Guatemala City: ≈3 million (metro) – Capital and economic centre.
- Mixco: ≈500,000 – Major urban and industrial city.
- Villa Nueva: ≈600,000 – Key commercial and residential hub.
- Quetzaltenango: ≈250,000 – Regional economic and cultural centre.

GUATEMALA CITY – GUATEMALA'S CAPITAL AND ECONOMIC HUB

The National Flag

The national flag of Guatemala features a sky-blue field with a central white vertical stripe and a national emblem at its heart. The blue symbolises the nation's position between the Pacific and Atlantic oceans, as well as justice and loyalty, while the white represents purity and peace. The emblem depicts the resplendent quetzal, a symbol of liberty, perched above a parchment scroll bearing the date of Central American independence, framed by crossed rifles and sabres and crowned with laurel branches. These elements denote the nation's sovereignty, its historical struggle for freedom and the victory of peace. The flag as a whole represents Guatemala's natural heritage, its hard-won independence and its enduring ideals.

KEY PEOPLE AND PLACES

PEOPLE

Miguel García Granados (1809–1878) Widely regarded as one of Guatemala's founding political leaders, García Granados served as president and played a key role in liberal reforms, education and the modernisation of the nation, shaping Guatemala's political and social landscape in the 19th century.

Justo Rufino Barrios (1835–1885) A military leader and reformist president, Barrios implemented major liberal reforms including education, infrastructure and agricultural modernisation. He sought national unification and played a decisive role in shaping Guatemala's political structure, economy modernisation during the late 19th century.

Rigoberta Menchú (b. 1959) A Nobel Peace Prize laureate, indigenous rights activist and author, Menchú has advocated for the rights of the Maya people, social justice and human rights. Her work has brought international attention to Guatemala's history of civil conflict and cultural heritage.

Juan José Arévalo (1904–1990) President from 1945 to 1951, Arévalo introduced progressive social reforms, education initiatives and democratic policies. His leadership marked a period of political opening and civic engagement that profoundly influenced Guatemala's mid-20th-century development.

Efraín Ríos Montt (1926–2018) A controversial military leader and de facto president, Ríos Montt played a major role in Guatemala's civil conflict. His tenure is noted for authoritarian rule, human rights abuses and military campaigns, leaving a complex legacy in national memory.

PLACES

Guatemala City (founded 1776) The capital and largest city of Guatemala, located in the central highlands. Guatemala City serves as the political, economic and cultural hub, featuring government institutions, universities, historic sites, commercial centres and cultural events that shape national life.

Antigua Guatemala (founded 1543) A UNESCO World Heritage city, Antigua is famous for its well-preserved colonial architecture, cobblestone streets and cultural festivals. It served as the former capital and remains a major centre for tourism, education and historical research.

Tikal (flourished c. 200–900 CE) One of the most important Maya archaeological sites in Guatemala, Tikal was a major political and ceremonial centre during the Classic Period. It provides invaluable insight into Maya architecture, culture, religion and ancient urban planning.

Lake Atitlán A volcanic lake surrounded by mountains and indigenous villages in the western highlands. Lake Atitlán is renowned for its natural beauty, cultural heritage, eco-tourism and recreational opportunities, attracting visitors for hiking, photography and cultural immersion.

Quetzaltenango (founded 1524) Also known as Xela, it is Guatemala's second-largest city. Quetzaltenango is a cultural and economic centre in the western highlands, famous for its colonial architecture, educational institutions, markets and surrounding indigenous communities preserving traditional crafts and customs.

Pacaya Volcano An active volcano near Guatemala City, Pacaya is a prominent natural landmark. It offers hiking, scientific study and eco-tourism opportunities while highlighting the geological activity and volcanic heritage that characterise much of Guatemala's landscape.

TIMELINE OF EVENTS

c. 2000 BCE: Early Maya Civilisation: Early Maya communities developed in present-day Guatemala, establishing agriculture, settlements and complex social structures.

250–900 CE: Classic Maya Period: Powerful Maya city-states such as Tikal flourished, achieving major advances in science, architecture and governance.

900–1200: Postclassic Maya Period: Maya civilisation reorganised into regional centres, maintaining culture, trade and political influence.

1524: Spanish Conquest Begins: Spanish forces led by Pedro de Alvarado defeated major Maya kingdoms, beginning colonial rule.

1542: Captaincy General of Guatemala Established: Spain organised Central America under colonial administration centred in Guatemala City.

1821: Independence from Spain: Guatemala declared independence from Spanish rule as part of a broader Central American movement.

1823: United Provinces of Central America: Guatemala joined a short-lived federation seeking regional unity and stability.

1839: Federation Collapses: The United Provinces dissolved and Guatemala emerged as an independent republic.

1871: Liberal Reforms Implemented: Political reforms modernised the state but often disadvantaged Indigenous populations.

1944: October Revolution: A popular uprising ended dictatorship, ushering in democratic reforms and social change.

1954: CIA-Backed Coup: A US-supported coup overthrew the elected government, destabilising politics and institutions.

1960: Civil War Begins: Armed conflict erupted between government forces and insurgent groups, lasting decades.

1996: Peace Accords Signed: The government and rebels signed accords, formally ending the civil war.

1999: Truth Commission Report: Findings documented widespread human rights abuses, particularly against Indigenous communities.

2006: Indigenous Rights Movements Grow: Indigenous organisations increased activism for political, cultural and land rights.

2015: Anti-Corruption Protests: Mass demonstrations led to the resignation of the president amid corruption scandals.

2017: Migration Crisis Intensifies: Economic hardship and violence drove increased migration from Guatemala.

2019: Political Reforms Debated: Ongoing debates focused on governance, justice and electoral transparency.

2020: COVID-19 Pandemic Impact: The pandemic strained health services, deepened poverty and disrupted daily life.

THE REPUBLIC OF HONDURAS

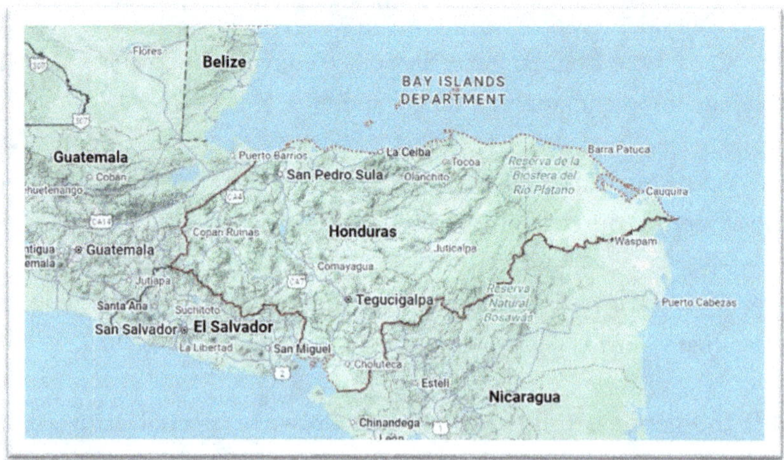

The Republic of Honduras occupies a pivotal yet geographically constrained position in Central America, bordered by Guatemala to the west, El Salvador to the southwest, Nicaragua to the south and east, the Pacific Ocean to the south via the Gulf of Fonseca and the Caribbean Sea to the north. The nation's very name, 'Honduras,' translates from Spanish as 'depths,' a reference to the deep coastal waters encountered by early explorers. With an estimated population of approximately 10.6 million, it is one of the most populous countries in Central America. Its political and administrative capital is Tegucigalpa, while the primary industrial and commercial hub is San Pedro Sula. The national currency is the Lempira. Shaped by powerful pre-Columbian civilisations, centuries of Spanish colonial rule and a modern history marked by political upheaval and natural disasters, Honduras is a nation of profound social and economic contrasts, working to harness its strategic location and natural resources.

Geography

Honduras is a nation defined by its rugged topography. Its interior is dominated by a complex highland plateau, intersected by mountain ranges which create deep, fertile valleys. The northern Caribbean coast features extensive lowlands, including the Mosquito Coast and is fringed by the Bay Islands. The southern Pacific coast is a narrower, hot lowland. The country possesses significant river systems, most notably the Ulúa and Aguán and is home to the largest wilderness area in Central America, the Mosquitia region, which contains the Río Plátano Biosphere Reserve. The climate is predominantly tropical, with seasonal variation marked by a pronounced rainy season. Honduras is highly vulnerable to extreme weather events, particularly hurricanes from the Caribbean, which pose recurrent and severe threats to infrastructure and livelihoods.

History

Ancient Honduras was a significant centre of Maya civilisation, with the city-state of Copán being a major political and artistic centre until its decline around the 9th century. Columbus claimed the territory for Spain in 1502, initiating a colonial period centred on mining and agriculture. Independence from Spain was achieved in 1821, followed by a brief union with the Mexican Empire and then the Federal Republic of Central America, before Honduras emerged as a sovereign republic in 1838. The 20th century was characterised by immense political instability, dominated by military rule, interventions by American fruit companies—giving rise to the term 'banana republic'—and a brief war with El Salvador in 1969. A return to civilian democratic rule began in the 1980s, but the country has continued to grapple with deep-seated institutional weakness, corruption and the aftermath of a 2009 political crisis.

Government and Politics

Honduras is a presidential representative democratic republic. Executive power is vested in a single-term President who serves as both head of state and head of government. Legislative power rests with a unicameral National Congress. The country is divided into 18 departments for administrative purposes. The political landscape is dominated by two traditional parties, the Liberal Party and the National Party, though newer parties have emerged following a constitutional crisis that permitted presidential re-election. Key political challenges include systemic corruption, the pervasive influence of organised crime, profound social inequality and chronic governmental inefficiency. In foreign affairs, Honduras maintains strong ties with the United States, is a member of the Central American Integration System and participates in regional security initiatives.

Economy

Honduras has a lower-middle-income economy that remains heavily dependent on a few vulnerable sectors. It is historically an agricultural exporter, with coffee, bananas, palm oil and shrimp forming traditional pillars. Manufacturing, primarily in maquiladora export-processing zones and remittances from a vast diaspora—which constitute a critical source of national income—are other key economic drivers. Growth has been persistently hampered by widespread informality, a lack of infrastructure, low educational attainment and one of the highest rates of economic inequality in Latin America. Structural challenges also include a significant public debt, vulnerability to commodity price shocks and the devastating economic impact of frequent natural disasters. Long-term prospects hinge on improving governance, investing in human capital and fostering broader economic diversification.

Demographics and Society

Honduran society is predominantly Mestizo, a mix of European and Indigenous ancestry. There are significant indigenous minority groups, including the Lenca, Miskito, Garifuna and Maya Ch'orti', alongside communities of Afro-Hondurans and people of European descent. Spanish is the official and dominant language, though various indigenous languages and English-based creoles are spoken in specific regions. The population is remarkably young, with a high proportion under 25 and is increasingly urbanised, though rural poverty remains endemic. Honduran society is characterised by close-knit family structures and a strong sense of community, but it faces severe challenges including widespread poverty, gang-related violence and one of the world's highest homicide rates, which has driven significant emigration.

Culture

Honduran culture is a rich fusion of Indigenous, Spanish, African and Caribbean influences. This is vividly expressed in music, where the national instrument is the marimba and styles like punta (of Garifuna origin) are widely popular. Traditional folk dances and colourful festivals, such as the Feria de San Isidro in La Ceiba, are central to community life. Honduran cuisine is based on staples of corn, beans, rice and plantains, with dishes like 'baleadas' (folded tortillas), 'sopa de caracol' (conch soup) and 'plátanos fritos'. Oral storytelling and a deep connection to the land and Catholic religious traditions remain vital. The archaeological site of Copán stands as a profound source of national pride and cultural identity.

Education and Healthcare

The Honduran education system, structured into primary, secondary and tertiary levels, is plagued by chronic underfunding and access issues. While primary education is nominally compulsory, dropout rates are high, particularly in rural areas and educational quality is poor. The National Autonomous University of Honduras is the primary public university. The healthcare system is fragmented, with public services often lacking basic resources, equipment and personnel. Challenges are acute, including high infant and maternal mortality rates, outbreaks of dengue and Zika, malnutrition and a concentration of medical services in urban centres, leaving vast segments of the population with inadequate care.

Infrastructure

Honduran infrastructure is generally underdeveloped and a major constraint on economic growth. The road network is limited and often in poor condition, especially in rural and remote regions, where connectivity can be severed in the rainy season. Key ports exist at Puerto Cortés on the Caribbean and San Lorenzo on the Pacific. The primary international gateway is Toncontín Airport in Tegucigalpa. Telecommunications coverage has expanded in urban areas, but reliable internet access remains a luxury in much of the country. Energy generation relies on a mix of thermal plants and hydropower, but the grid suffers from inefficiency and unreliability. Rebuilding and hardening infrastructure against climatic disasters is a perpetual and costly challenge.

Tourism

Tourism holds significant potential but remains an underdeveloped sector compared to regional neighbours. Honduras's primary draw is the magnificent Maya ruins of Copán, renowned for its intricate stone stelae and hieroglyphic staircase. The Bay Islands, particularly Roatán, are a world-class destination for scuba diving and snorkelling on the Mesoamerican Barrier Reef. Other attractions include the colonial town of Gracias, the cloud forests of Celaque National Park and the wildlife of the Mosquitia region. The industry's growth is hampered by perceptions of insecurity, inadequate tourist infrastructure outside key hubs and underinvestment in promotion.

Current Issues and Future Outlook

Honduras confronts a daunting array of contemporary crises: pervasive violence and gang dominance, entrenched corruption at the highest levels, extreme poverty, food insecurity and being on the front line of the climate crisis. These interrelated challenges fuel one of the largest outward migrations in the Western Hemisphere. However, the nation possesses inherent strengths: a strategic geographic position, a young and resilient population, untapped natural resources and a vibrant civil society. Its future prospects depend almost entirely on its ability to strengthen democratic institutions, combat impunity, create meaningful economic opportunities for its youth and build sustainable resilience against environmental shocks.

Overview

The Republic of Honduras is a nation of stark contradictions and enduring spirit. It is a land of immense natural beauty and archaeological wealth, yet also of profound human hardship and instability. Rooted in an ancient past and shaped by a difficult modern history, it stands at a critical juncture. While facing some of the most severe developmental challenges in the hemisphere, Honduras's cultural vitality, demographic energy and geographic assets provide a foundation, however fragile, upon which to build. Its path forward requires nothing less than a fundamental transformation toward greater equity, security and opportunity for all its citizens.

DID YOU KNOW...?

Most visitors to Honduras know Copán for its sculpted stelae, but few realise the city once hosted an elaborate astronomical observatory. Carved into the plazas and temple staircases are alignments that mark solstices and lunar cycles, allowing the Maya to predict eclipses. Beyond the ceremonial centre, hidden platforms suggest ritual observations were conducted over decades, linking elite authority to celestial knowledge. Copán's surrounding valley also preserves networks of agricultural terraces, roads and caves containing red ochre used in sacred rites. Together, these features reveal that Honduras was not just a ceremonial hub, but a centre of cosmic observation and ritual science.

KEY FACTS AND FIGURES

Geography & Environment

• Total area: 112,492 km².

• Coastline: ≈820 km (Caribbean Sea and Pacific Ocean via Gulf of Fonseca).

• Climate: Tropical, with cooler conditions in mountainous interior regions.

• Highest point: Cerro Las Minas (2,870 m).

• Major features: Central highlands, Caribbean lowlands, Gulf of Fonseca, extensive river systems.

• Wildlife: Jaguars, ocelots, sloths, scarlet macaws, crocodiles.

• 2 UNESCO World Heritage sites.

Population & Society

• Population: ≈10.7 million (2024 estimate).

• Density: ≈95 persons/km².

• Urbanisation: ≈57%.

• Ethnicity:

o Mestizo: ≈90%

o Indigenous peoples: ≈7%

o Afro-Honduran (Garífuna and others): ≈2%

o Other: ≈1%

• Languages: Spanish (official); Garífuna and indigenous languages.

• Religion: Christian (Roman Catholic and Protestant): ≈90%.

• Literacy: ≈89%.

• Life expectancy: ≈75 years.

Economy

• GDP (nominal): ≈£25 billion.

• GDP per capita (PPP): ≈£6,000.

• Key industries:

o Agriculture (bananas, coffee, palm oil)

o Manufacturing and maquila textiles

o Mining

o Tourism

• Major exports: Coffee, bananas, palm oil, textiles, shrimp.

• Currency: Honduran lempira (HNL; £1 ≈ 31 HNL).

Government

• Presidential republic.

• System: Constitutional democratic republic.

• Head of State: President of Honduras.

• Head of Government: President of Honduras.

• Legislature: National Congress (128 members).

Infrastructure

• Transport: National road network; limited rail; air and sea transport.

• Major airports: Ramón Villeda Morales International Airport, Toncontín International Airport.

• Energy mix: Hydropower, fossil fuels and growing solar and wind capacity.

• Digital connectivity: Moderate in urban areas; limited in rural regions.

Major Urban Centres

• Tegucigalpa: ≈1.5 million (metro) – Capital and political centre.

• San Pedro Sula: ≈1 million – Industrial and commercial hub.

• Choloma: ≈300,000 – Manufacturing and logistics centre.

• La Ceiba: ≈200,000 – Port city and tourism gateway.

TEGUCIGALPA – HONDURAS'S CAPITAL AND POLITICAL CENTRE

The National Flag

The national flag of Honduras features a turquoise blue field with three equal horizontal stripes and five blue stars arranged in a quincunx pattern at the centre. The two outer blue stripes symbolise the Pacific Ocean and the Caribbean Sea, which border the nation, while the central white stripe represents the land of Honduras itself and its aspiration for peace. The five blue stars denote the five nations of the former Federal Republic of Central America and express the hope for its eventual renewed union. The flag as a whole represents Honduras's geography, its historical federation and its ongoing commitment to regional unity and peace.

KEY PEOPLE AND PLACES

PEOPLE

Francisco Morazán (1792–1842) Widely regarded as a visionary leader in Central America, Morazán served as president of the Federal Republic of Central America and advocated for liberal reforms, national unity and education. He remains a symbol of democracy and progressive ideals in Honduras.

José Trinidad Cabañas (1805–1871) A distinguished military leader and statesman, Cabañas promoted national defence, liberal reforms and economic development in Honduras. He played a key role in stabilising the country during turbulent periods and strengthening its political and administrative institutions.

Porfirio Lobo Sosa (b. 1947) President of Honduras from 2010 to 2014, Lobo Sosa focused on political reconciliation, economic recovery and international relations following a period of political crisis, promoting social programmes, governance reform and regional cooperation.

Berta Cáceres (1971–2016) An indigenous leader and environmental activist, Cáceres fought for the rights of the Lenca people, protection of natural resources and environmental justice. Her advocacy brought global attention to Honduras' social and ecological challenges and inspired human rights movements.

Carlos Roberto Flores (b. 1950) President from 1998 to 2002, Flores oversaw economic reforms, disaster recovery following Hurricane Mitch and international diplomacy. His administration focused on modernisation, infrastructure and strengthening Honduras' political and social institutions during a period of recovery and reform.

PLACES

Tegucigalpa (founded 1578) The capital and largest city of Honduras, located in the central highlands. Tegucigalpa serves as the political, economic and cultural centre, featuring government buildings, universities, museums, markets and a vibrant urban environment combining modern development with colonial heritage.

San Pedro Sula (founded 1536) The second-largest city, located in the northwest. San Pedro Sula is an industrial and commercial hub, known for manufacturing, trade and economic activity, while also serving as a centre for cultural events, education and urban development in Honduras.

Copán (flourished c. 5th–9th centuries CE) A major Maya archaeological site in western Honduras, Copán is famous for its intricate stelae, hieroglyphic inscriptions and ceremonial architecture. It provides invaluable insight into Maya civilisation, culture and social organisation during the Classic Period.

La Ceiba A coastal city on the northern Atlantic coast, La Ceiba is known for tourism, cultural festivals and natural attractions. It serves as a gateway to national parks, islands and eco-tourism destinations, highlighting Honduras' Caribbean heritage and biodiversity.

Lake Yojoa The largest natural lake in Honduras, located in the western highlands. Lake Yojoa is celebrated for its scenic beauty, fishing, birdwatching and eco-tourism opportunities, serving as an important site for recreation, conservation and biodiversity in the country.

Pico Bonito National Park A protected area featuring cloud forests, tropical wildlife, rivers and hiking trails. Pico Bonito is a key site for eco-tourism, environmental preservation and outdoor recreation, highlighting Honduras' diverse ecosystems and natural heritage.

TIMELINE OF EVENTS

c. 2000 BCE: Early Indigenous Settlements: Early Indigenous societies, including ancestors of the Maya and other groups, settled across present-day Honduras, developing agriculture, trade networks and organised communities adapted to environments.

250–900 CE: Classic Maya Period: Maya civilisation flourished in western Honduras, particularly at Copán, which became a major political, cultural and scientific centre within the Maya world.

900–1500: Postclassic Period: Following the decline of major Maya centres, Indigenous groups adapted to regional changes, maintaining local governance systems, trade networks and cultural traditions.

1524: Spanish Conquest Begins: Spanish forces arrived in Honduras, subduing Indigenous societies and establishing colonial rule, leading to major demographic decline and social disruption.

1821: Independence from Spain: Honduras declared independence from Spanish colonial rule as part of the wider Central American independence movement reshaping regional political futures.

1823: United Provinces of Central America: Honduras joined the United Provinces of Central America, a short-lived federation intended to promote regional unity and political stability.

1838: Independent Republic Declared: After the federation collapsed, Honduras formally became an independent republic, beginning challenges of self-governance and nation-building.

1876: Liberal Reforms Introduced: Liberal governments implemented reforms aimed at modernisation, expanding exports and infrastructure while increasing foreign economic influence.

1890s: Banana Industry Expansion: United States banana companies gained dominance over the Honduran economy, heavily influencing politics, land ownership and labour conditions.

1954: Major Labour Strike: A large-scale strike by banana workers led to improved labour rights and marked a turning point in organised labour activism.

1963: Military Coup: A military coup overthrew the democratic government, initiating a prolonged period of military dominance over political life.

1969: Football War: A brief but intense armed conflict with El Salvador disrupted society, strained regional relations and displaced many civilians.

1982: Return to Civilian Rule: A new constitution restored civilian government, reintroducing democratic institutions and limiting the formal role of military forces.

1998: Hurricane Mitch: One of the deadliest hurricanes in Central American history devastated Honduras, causing massive loss of life and long-term economic damage.

2009: Political Crisis: A military-backed coup removed the sitting president, triggering widespread unrest and international condemnation of democratic breakdown.

2017: Contested Elections: Disputed presidential election results sparked protests, political instability and concerns over democratic transparency and governance.

2020: COVID-19 Pandemic Impact: The pandemic severely strained healthcare systems, damaged the economy and intensified poverty and inequality nationwide.

THE REPUBLIC OF EL SALVADOR

The Republic of El Salvador occupies the Pacific coast of Central America, bordered by Guatemala to the west, Honduras to the north and east and the Pacific Ocean to the south. It is the only country in Central America without a Caribbean coastline and with a total area of just 21,041 square kilometres, it is the region's smallest and most densely populated nation. The country's very name, 'El Salvador,' translates as 'The Saviour,' and its indigenous Pipil name, 'Cuscatlán', means 'Land of the Jewel'. With a population estimated at approximately 6.4 million people, it is heavily urbanised, with its capital and largest city being San Salvador. The official currency is the United States Dollar, which replaced the Salvadoran colón in 2001. Shaped by powerful pre-Columbian cultures, a Spanish colonial past and a devastating 12-year civil war in the late 20th century, El Salvador is a nation marked by both profound resilience and deep social challenges, striving for stability and security in the modern era.

Geography

El Salvador's geography is defined by its dramatic and volatile volcanic origins. Known as the 'Land of Volcanoes,' it features more than twenty volcanoes, with two major volcanic ranges running east to west. These ranges create three distinct regions: the southern coastal plain, the fertile central valleys and plateaus and the mountainous northern highlands. The central plateau, though covering only about 25% of the land, holds the majority of the population and major cities. Located atop the confluence of three tectonic plates, it is one of the most seismically active areas on Earth, prone to frequent and often destructive earthquakes and volcanic eruptions. The longest and most important river is the Río Lempa, which is partially navigable. The climate is tropical with a distinct dry season ('verano') from November to April and a wet season ('invierno') from May to October.

History

Ancient El Salvador was inhabited by a succession of cultures, including the Olmecs and Maya, before the Pipil people established the dominant kingdom of Cuscatlán. Spanish conquistadors led by Pedro de Alvarado arrived in 1524, facing fierce resistance from the Pipils before establishing control by 1528. Independence from Spain was achieved in 1821 and after a brief union with the Mexican Empire and the Federal Republic of Central America, El Salvador became a fully sovereign republic in 1841. The late 19th and 20th centuries were defined by rule by a landed coffee oligarchy (the so-called 'Fourteen Families') and a series of military-dominated governments, which culminated in severe socioeconomic inequality and political repression. This led to the brutal Salvadoran Civil War (1979-1992), which pitted the U.S.-backed government against the leftist Farabundo Martí National Liberation Front (FMLN). The war claimed approximately 75,000 lives before peace accords were signed in 1992, converting the FMLN into a legal political party and establishing a fragile democracy.

Government and Politics

El Salvador is a unitary presidential constitutional republic. The president, who serves as both head of state and head of government, is elected by popular vote for a single five-year term, although a controversial 2021 court ruling allowed for consecutive re-election, facilitating President Nayib Bukele's second term beginning in 2024. Legislative power rests with a unicameral Legislative Assembly. Politics was long dominated by two traditional parties—the conservative Nationalist Republican Alliance (ARENA) and the leftist FMLN—until the dramatic rise of President Bukele and his Nuevas Ideas party, which now holds a supermajority in the assembly. Under Bukele, the country has experienced significant democratic backsliding, including the consolidation of executive power and the dismissal of constitutional court justices. In foreign affairs, El Salvador is a member of the United Nations, the Organisation of American States (OAS) and the Central American Integration System (SICA).

Economy

El Salvador has a lower-middle-income economy that has struggled with low growth, historically averaging around 2-2.5% annually. It was once heavily dependent on agricultural exports, particularly coffee, though this sector has diminished in relative importance. The modern economy is now driven by services (including finance and retail), manufacturing (primarily textiles and apparel from maquiladora factories) and, most critically, remittances from a vast diaspora living abroad, which constitute over 20% of GDP and are a vital economic lifeline. The country made global headlines in 2021 by adopting Bitcoin as legal tender alongside the US Dollar, a controversial policy experiment intended to promote financial inclusion and attract investment. Key challenges include widespread informal employment, low productivity, a high fiscal deficit and a reliance on imported food and energy.

Demographics and Society

Salvadoran society is ethnically and culturally homogeneous, with the population being overwhelmingly Mestizo—a mix of indigenous and European ancestry. The once-significant indigenous population, primarily of Nahua-Pipil descent, was largely decimated and assimilated following the Spanish conquest, though recent efforts aim to recognise indigenous identity. The primary language is Spanish and the dominant religion is

Roman Catholicism, with a rapidly growing Protestant evangelical population. Society is youthful, with a high proportion of the population under 30 years old. A defining characteristic is the massive Salvadoran diaspora, with an estimated 2 to 3 million people (nearly a third of the native population) living abroad, primarily in the United States, whose remittances are indispensable to the national economy and social stability.

Culture

Salvadoran culture is a vibrant and deeply rooted fusion of indigenous Pipil and Spanish traditions. It is perhaps most famously expressed through its cuisine, centred on the staple food of corn, with the national dish being the 'pupusa'—a thick, hand-made corn tortilla stuffed with cheese, beans, pork, or other fillings and served with curtido (pickled cabbage slaw). Music is integral, with genres like folkloric 'cumbia' and 'salsa' being popular. Vibrant religious festivals honouring local patron saints are central to community life in towns and villages across the country. Religious art and crafts are significant and the preservation of pre-Columbian traditions, particularly in pottery and weaving, remains important in some communities.

Education and Healthcare

The education system in El Salvador follows a structure of primary, secondary and higher education. Primary education is compulsory and attendance is relatively high, but the system is challenged by issues of quality, overcrowding and high dropout rates, particularly in secondary grades, which contributes to gang recruitment. Public university education is provided by the University of El Salvador. The healthcare system is a mix of public and private providers. The public system, managed by the Ministry of Health, offers basic services but is often strained by limited resources, leading to long wait times and shortages of medicines and equipment. Chronic diseases, maternal health and violence-related injuries are significant public health concerns.

Infrastructure

El Salvador's infrastructure is among the more developed in Central America but faces strain from natural disasters, lack of maintenance and urban congestion. The Pan-American Highway is a vital artery running through the country. The main international airport is Monseñor Óscar Arnulfo Romero y Galdámez International Airport, located near San Salvador. The primary seaports are Acajutla on the Pacific coast and La Unión in the east. Telecommunications infrastructure is relatively advanced, with high mobile phone penetration and growing internet access, though rural-urban divides persist. The energy grid relies on a mix of geothermal (harnessed from its volcanoes), hydroelectric and imported fossil fuels, with efforts underway to expand renewable sources.

Tourism

Tourism in El Salvador is a growing sector with significant potential, centred on its dramatic Pacific surf beaches, archaeological sites and colonial heritage. Popular destinations include the Ruta de las Flores, a scenic route of colourful towns, coffee farms and waterfalls; the archaeological site of Joya de Cerén, a pre-Columbian farming village remarkably preserved under volcanic ash (often called the 'Pompeii of the Americas'); and the Mayan ruins of Tazumal and San Andrés. Surfing hotspots like El Tunco and El Sunzal attract international visitors. The industry's growth has been historically hampered by the country's reputation for insecurity, though the recent security crackdown has led to a surge in domestic tourism and renewed international interest.

Current Issues and Future Outlook

El Salvador faces a pivotal and uncertain future shaped by its dramatic recent policy shifts. The defining issue is the unprecedented security crackdown under President Nayib Bukele's state of exception, which has drastically reduced homicide rates and is immensely popular domestically but has drawn intense international criticism for alleged human rights abuses, mass arbitrary detentions and the erosion of democratic institutions. The economy faces pressure from high public debt, the uncertain experiment with Bitcoin and a need to create formal jobs. Long-term challenges include profound socioeconomic inequality, vulnerability to climate change and natural disasters and the need to reintegrate a generation affected by gang violence. The nation's trajectory will depend on whether it can build sustainable economic growth and true democratic stability upon its newfound, but contentious, security.

Overview

The Republic of El Salvador is a nation of intense contrasts, emerging from a turbulent past and navigating a highly unconventional present. It is a land of remarkable volcanic beauty and resilient cultural traditions, yet also of deep-seated social wounds and profound political transformation. Having endured a bitter civil war and decades of gang violence, it has embarked on a radical and controversial path under President Bukele, prioritising security and challenging democratic norms. Its future hinges on whether this new model can deliver lasting peace, economic opportunity and a functional social contract for all Salvadorans, or if it will trade one set of profound challenges for another.

DID YOU KNOW...?

El Salvador conceals evidence of pre-Columbian metallurgical skill that few know existed. Long before European arrival, the Pipil and related groups worked native copper and gold, creating small bells, ornaments and ritual objects. Excavations at sites such as Cihuatán show traces of smelting furnaces, crucibles and moulds, demonstrating local mastery of heat and alloying techniques. These artefacts were often deposited in tombs or ceremonial centres, connecting craft with spirituality. Beyond metallurgy, El Salvador's volcanic soils also supported intensive terraced farming, allowing dense populations to thrive in a geologically active landscape. This forgotten technological heritage highlights the ingenuity of ancient Salvadoran societies.

KEY FACTS AND FIGURES

Geography & Environment

• Total area: 21,041 km^2 (smallest country in Central America).
• Coastline: ≈307 km (Pacific Ocean).
• Climate: Tropical, with a distinct wet and dry season.
• Highest point: Cerro El Pital (2,730 m).
• Major features: Volcanic mountain chain, Pacific coastal plain, Lake Ilopango, Lake Coatepeque.
• Wildlife: Howler monkeys, deer, armadillos, sea turtles, tropical bird species.
• 1 UNESCO World Heritage site.

Population & Society

• Population: ≈6.4 million (2024 estimate).
• Density: ≈300 persons/km^2 (one of the highest in the Americas).
• Urbanisation: ≈73%.
• Ethnicity:
o Mestizo: ≈86%
o White: ≈12%
o Indigenous: ≈1%
o Other: ≈1%
• Languages: Spanish (official); Nahuatl spoken by small communities.
• Religion: Christian (Roman Catholic and Protestant): ≈90%.
• Literacy: ≈90%.
• Life expectancy: ≈74 years.

Economy

• GDP (nominal): ≈£30 billion.
• GDP per capita (PPP): ≈£9,000.
• Key industries:
o Manufacturing and textiles
o Agriculture (coffee, sugar, maize)
o Services and commerce
o Tourism

• Major exports: Textiles, electrical components, coffee, sugar.
• Currency: US dollar (USD) and Bitcoin (legal tender).

Government

• Presidential republic.
• System: Constitutional democratic republic.
• Head of State: President of El Salvador.
• Head of Government: President of El Salvador.
• Legislature: Legislative Assembly (84 members).

Infrastructure

• Transport: National road network; no active passenger rail; air and sea transport.
• Major airports: El Salvador International Airport (San Óscar Arnulfo Romero).
• Energy mix: Hydropower, geothermal, fossil fuels, growing solar capacity.
• Digital connectivity: Well developed in urban areas; moderate in rural regions.

Major Urban Centres

• San Salvador: ≈1.8 million (metro) – Capital and economic centre.
• Santa Ana: ≈260,000 – Regional commercial hub.
• San Miguel: ≈250,000 – Eastern regional centre.
• Soyapango: ≈300,000 – Industrial and manufacturing city.

SAN SALVADOR – EL SALVADOR'S CAPITAL AND ECONOMIC CENTRE

The National Flag

The national flag of El Salvador features a horizontal triband of cobalt blue, white and cobalt blue, with the national coat of arms centred on the white band. The blue symbolises the sky and the two great oceans, while the white represents peace. The coat of arms depicts a triangle encircling five volcanoes above a sea, framed by flags and laurel wreaths and bearing the national motto. This represents the nation's ideals of liberty, its federation with Central America and its hard-won independence. The flag as a whole embodies El Salvador's history, sovereignty and enduring pursuit of unity and peace.

KEY PEOPLE AND PLACES

PEOPLE

José Matías Delgado (1767–1832) Widely regarded as a founding father of El Salvador, Delgado was a priest and revolutionary leader who played a key role in the country's independence from Spanish colonial rule. He promoted civic engagement, education and national identity during the early 19th century.

Manuel José Arce (1787–1847) A military leader and politician, Arce served as the first President of the Federal Republic of Central America, including El Salvador. He contributed to early political organisation, governance and the establishment of republican institutions during the formative period of Salvadoran history.

Farabundo Martí (1893–1932) A revolutionary activist and intellectual, Martí became a symbol of resistance for the working class and peasant movements. He advocated social justice, equality and workers' rights and his legacy continues to influence Salvadoran political thought and activism.

Óscar Romero (1917–1980) Archbishop of San Salvador, Romero was a prominent human rights advocate who spoke out against social injustice, poverty and political repression during El Salvador's civil conflict. His assassination made him a symbol of moral courage and national conscience.

Agustín Farabundo Martí National Liberation Front Leaders (1980s) Key political and revolutionary figures who contributed to the Salvadoran civil war and peace process, advocating for social reform, justice and democracy. Their efforts shaped modern El Salvador's political landscape and commitment to equality.

PLACES

San Salvador (founded c. 1525) The capital and largest city of El Salvador, San Salvador serves as the political, economic and cultural hub of the country. It features government institutions, historic architecture, bustling markets, universities and vibrant cultural and commercial activity.

Santa Ana (founded 1569) The second-largest city in El Salvador, located in the western region. Santa Ana is known for its historic architecture, cultural festivals, coffee plantations and its role as an important economic and commercial centre in the country.

Suchitoto A historic colonial town celebrated for its cobblestone streets, cultural heritage and art scene. Suchitoto attracts tourists, artists and historians, providing insight into El Salvador's colonial past, traditional crafts and the preservation of national culture and identity.

Izalco Volcano Located in western El Salvador, Izalco is one of the country's most iconic volcanoes, often called the 'Lighthouse of the Pacific.' It is significant for its geological activity, eco-tourism and cultural importance in Salvadoran history and local folklore.

Lake Coatepeque A large volcanic crater lake in western El Salvador, renowned for its natural beauty, recreational opportunities and ecological significance. Lake Coatepeque attracts tourists for boating, swimming and nature appreciation, making it an important feature of the country's landscape.

Joya de Cerén A UNESCO World Heritage site and pre-Columbian Maya village preserved by volcanic ash. Known as the 'Pompeii of the Americas,' it provides invaluable archaeological insight into daily life, agriculture and social structures of early Salvadoran societies.

TIMELINE OF EVENTS

c. 2000 BCE: Early Indigenous Settlements: Early Indigenous groups, including the Lenca and later the Pipil peoples, settled present-day El Salvador, developing agriculture, trade networks and organised communities.

900–1200 CE: Pipil Dominance: The Pipil civilisation became dominant, establishing city-states, controlling trade routes and shaping cultural and political life across the region.

1524: Spanish Conquest Begins: Spanish forces led by Pedro de Alvarado conquered Indigenous societies, initiating colonial rule and significant population decline.

1540: Incorporation into Spanish Empire: El Salvador was incorporated into the Captaincy General of Guatemala, becoming part of Spain's Central American administration.

1821: Independence from Spain: El Salvador declared independence from Spanish rule as part of Central America's broader independence movement.

1823: United Provinces of Central America: El Salvador joined the regional federation seeking political unity and economic cooperation.

1841: Independent Republic Declared: Following the federation's collapse, El Salvador became a fully independent republic.

1881: Liberal Land Reforms: Government reforms privatised communal lands, expanding coffee production while displacing many rural Indigenous communities.

1932: Peasant Uprising and Repression: A rural uprising was brutally suppressed, resulting in tens of thousands of deaths and lasting political trauma.

1969: Football War: A brief war with Honduras disrupted society, caused displacement and strained regional relations.

1979: Military Coup and Reform Attempts: A coup led to attempted reforms but increasing political violence and instability.

1980–1992: Civil War: A prolonged civil war between government forces and guerrilla groups caused widespread human rights abuses.

1992: Peace Accords Signed: The Chapultepec Peace Accords formally ended the civil war, initiating democratic reforms and reconciliation.

2001: Adoption of the US Dollar: El Salvador adopted the US dollar as legal tender, reshaping economic policy and monetary stability.

2015: Gang Violence Crisis: Escalating gang violence significantly affected public security, migration and daily life.

2019: Election of Nayib Bukele: The election of a non-traditional candidate signalled major political change and public discontent with established parties.

2020: COVID-19 Pandemic Impact: The pandemic strained healthcare systems, disrupted the economy and deepened social inequality nationwide.

THE REPUBLIC OF NICARAGUA

The Republic of Nicaragua occupies a strategic and geographically dominant position in Central America, bordered by Honduras to the north, Costa Rica to the south, the Pacific Ocean to the west and the Caribbean Sea to the east. It is the largest country in the Central American isthmus by land area. The country's very name, derived from the indigenous chief Nicarao, is believed to be linked to its defining abundance of major bodies of water, most notably Lake Nicaragua, the largest lake in Central America. With an estimated population of approximately 6.9 million people, its capital and largest political and cultural centre is Managua. The national currency is the Córdoba. Shaped by a pre-Columbian heritage, a Spanish colonial past, a violent 20th-century revolution and a contemporary period of consolidated political control, Nicaragua is a nation of profound social and political divisions, possessing significant untapped economic potential and natural wealth.

Geography

Nicaragua is often described as the 'Land of Lakes and Volcanoes,' a fitting name for its dramatic physical geography. The country is bisected by a central mountain range, creating distinct Pacific and Caribbean regions. The Pacific lowlands are dotted with a chain of active volcanoes and contain Lake Managua and the vast Lake Nicaragua. The Caribbean lowlands form part of the larger Mosquito Coast, a vast, sparsely populated region of tropical rainforests, wetlands and river deltas. Lake Nicaragua is notable for housing the world's only freshwater sharks and numerous volcanic islands. The climate is tropical, with the Pacific side experiencing a pronounced dry season, while the Caribbean coast is consistently hot, humid and receives immense rainfall, making it one of the wettest regions in the hemisphere. The country is vulnerable to hurricanes, volcanic eruptions and earthquakes.

History

Ancient Nicaragua was a cultural crossroads inhabited by various indigenous groups, including the Maya-influenced Chorotegas in the Pacific and the Miskito, Sumo and Rama peoples on the Caribbean coast. The Spanish colonised the Pacific region beginning in the 1520s, establishing Granada and León as rival colonial centres, but exerted little control over the Caribbean coast, which fell under British influence. Independence from Spain was achieved in 1821, followed by a brief union with the Mexican Empire and the Federal Republic of Central America before Nicaragua became a fully independent republic in 1838. The 19th and early 20th centuries were marked by intense political infighting, Conservative-Liberal civil wars and repeated military interventions by the United States. The long, oppressive dictatorship of the Somoza family (1936–1979) was overthrown by the Sandinista National Liberation Front (FSLN) in the 1979 Revolution. The subsequent 1980s saw a devastating U.S.-backed Contra war against the Sandinista government. The FSLN lost elections in 1990 but returned to power under Daniel Ortega in 2007, beginning a period of increasing authoritarian rule.

Government and Politics

Nicaragua is nominally a presidential representative democratic republic, but in practice, it has evolved into a highly centralised, authoritarian state under the control of the FSLN and President Daniel Ortega, who has governed continuously since 2007 with his wife, Rosario Murillo, as Vice President. All branches of government, the judiciary, the electoral council and the security forces are under the effective control of the ruling party. Opposition parties have been systematically outlawed, their leaders imprisoned or exiled and independent media shuttered. The last general elections in 2021 were widely condemned by the international community as a sham. Key political dynamics revolve around the consolidation of a family dynasty, the suppression of all dissent following massive 2018 protests and deepening international isolation. In foreign affairs, Nicaragua maintains close ideological and economic ties with allies such as Russia, China, Cuba and Venezuela, while relations with the United States and many Western democracies are severely strained.

Economy

Nicaragua has a lower-middle-income economy, one of the poorest in the Western Hemisphere. It is heavily dependent on agriculture, with key exports including coffee, beef, gold, sugar and peanuts. Textile manufacturing (in free trade zones), tourism (which has declined sharply due to political unrest) and remittances from a large diaspora are other critical economic pillars. Growth has been historically volatile, vulnerable to commodity price swings, natural disasters and, increasingly, political crises and international sanctions. The Ortega government maintains close control over large sectors of the economy. Structural challenges are profound and include widespread poverty, extreme income inequality, a large informal sector and a lack of economic diversification. The confiscation of private property and the exodus of entrepreneurs and professionals have further weakened the private sector.

Demographics and Society

Nicaraguan society is predominantly Mestizo, a mix of European and Indigenous ancestry. The Pacific region is the most heavily populated and

Mestizo, while the Caribbean Coast (comprising two autonomous regions) is home to distinct indigenous and Afro-descendant communities, including the Miskito, Sumo, Rama, Garifuna and Creole peoples. Spanish is the official language, but English-based creoles and indigenous languages are spoken on the Caribbean Coast. The population is relatively young. Society has been deeply polarised since the 2018 anti-government protests and subsequent crackdown, which led to hundreds of deaths, thousands of injuries and a mass exodus of citizens seeking asylum abroad. Family and community ties remain strong, but trust in public institutions is extremely low.

Culture

Nicaraguan culture is a rich fusion of indigenous, Spanish and African influences, with notable regional variation. Literature holds a place of national pride, with poet Rubén Darío (1867–1916) celebrated as the father of the Spanish-American literary movement known as 'Modernismo'. Music and dance are vibrant, featuring the marimba, folkloric dances like the 'Palo de Mayo' (of Afro-Caribbean origin) and popular genres such as 'son nica' and salsa. Traditional cuisine is based on corn and beans, with dishes like 'gallo pinto' (red beans and rice), 'nacatamales' (steamed corn dough) and 'vigorón' (yuca, pork rinds and cabbage salad). Festivals, particularly the elaborate celebrations honouring patron saints in cities like León and Granada, are central to cultural and religious life.

Education and Healthcare

The education system in Nicaragua, structured into primary, secondary and higher education, has suffered from chronic underfunding and, in recent years, from intense political indoctrination and the closure of independent universities. While literacy rates were once a source of national pride following the 1980 literacy crusade, educational quality has declined sharply. The National Autonomous University of Nicaragua in León is a historic institution. The healthcare system is public, with services nominally free but severely hampered by a lack of resources, equipment and medicines. The system is highly politicised and during the 2018 crisis and the COVID-19 pandemic, there were widespread reports of denial of care to perceived government opponents. Preventable diseases and maternal mortality remain significant concerns.

Infrastructure

Nicaraguan infrastructure is generally underdeveloped and has deteriorated due to a lack of maintenance and investment. The road network is limited; while major highways connect principal cities in the Pacific region, roads in the Caribbean and northern interior are often unpaved and impassable in the rainy season. The main seaports are Corinto on the Pacific and El Bluff on the Caribbean. The primary international airport is Augusto C. Sandino International Airport in Managua. A highly controversial and ultimately abandoned project to build a trans-oceanic canal with Chinese backing exemplified both the grand ambitions and profound governance problems of the current administration. Telecommunications are controlled by companies with close ties to the ruling family and internet access is monitored and subject to censorship and shutdowns during periods of unrest.

Tourism

Tourism was once a promising growth sector for Nicaragua, leveraging its dramatic natural landscapes, colonial cities and Pacific beaches. Key attractions included the well-preserved Spanish colonial architecture of Granada and León, the volcanic islands of Lake Nicaragua (Ometepe and the Isletas) and the Pacific surf beaches of San Juan del Sur. However, the industry has been devastated by the political crisis that began in 2018. Government violence against protesters, the imprisonment of opponents, the silencing of independent media and associated international travel advisories have led to a catastrophic drop in international visitors, with many hotels, tour operators and related businesses closing permanently.

Current Issues and Future Outlook

Nicaragua faces a profound and multifaceted crisis under what is widely regarded as a dictatorial regime. The most pressing issues are the complete erosion of democratic institutions and civil liberties, the systematic persecution of all opposition (including the Catholic Church and civil society), a severe economic downturn exacerbated by sanctions and a continuing mass exodus of its citizens. The country is increasingly isolated internationally, subject to targeted sanctions from the United States, the European Union and other bodies. Long-term challenges include rebuilding a shattered social fabric, addressing extreme poverty and managing the impacts of climate change. The future outlook is exceptionally bleak in the short to medium term, with the potential for further internal repression and international confrontation. Any positive transformation would require a fundamental political change and a long, difficult process of national reconciliation.

Overview

The Republic of Nicaragua is a nation of immense natural beauty and tragic political circumstances. It is a land endowed with spectacular lakes, volcanoes and biodiversity, yet cursed by a history of foreign intervention, revolution and, now, entrenched familial authoritarianism. From the hope of the 1979 Sandinista Revolution, it has descended into one of the most consolidated dictatorships in the Americas. While its people have shown remarkable resilience, the current path leads toward deeper poverty, isolation and conflict. The nation's true potential—rooted in its resources, its culture and the spirit of its people—remains locked away, awaiting a future where democracy, rule of law and social justice might once again become possible.

DID YOU KNOW...?

While Nicaragua is famous for Lake Nicaragua, few realise the lake hides archaeological treasures. Under its waters lie ancient Zapatera Island cemeteries, containing stone statues, ceramics and effigies deliberately placed in burial grounds. These objects suggest highly organised religious practices and ancestor veneration. The Zapatera statues, carved from volcanic stone, depict humans, animals and hybrid beings, reflecting complex symbolic thought. Some were positioned to face cardinal directions, hinting at astronomical or cosmological significance. Combined with evidence of pre-Columbian settlements on nearby islands, these submerged and hidden sites reveal that Nicaragua's history is not only on land but also beneath its waters, guarding secrets of ritual and artistry.

KEY FACTS AND FIGURES

Geography & Environment

• Total area: 130,373 km² (largest country in Central America).

• Coastline: ≈910 km (Caribbean Sea and Pacific Ocean).

• Climate: Tropical, with wetter Caribbean lowlands and drier Pacific regions.

• Highest point: Mogotón Peak (2,107 m).

• Major features: Lake Nicaragua, Lake Managua, volcanic chain, extensive rainforests.

• Wildlife: Jaguars, pumas, howler monkeys, sloths, sea turtles.

• 2 UNESCO World Heritage sites.

Population & Society

• Population: ≈6.9 million (2024 estimate).

• Density: ≈53 persons/km².

• Urbanisation: ≈59%.

• Ethnicity:

o Mestizo: ≈69%

o White: ≈17%

o Afro-descendant and Indigenous: ≈14%

• Languages: Spanish (official); English and indigenous languages on the Caribbean coast.

• Religion: Christian (Roman Catholic and Protestant): ≈85–90%.

• Literacy: ≈83%.

• Life expectancy: ≈75 years.

Economy

• GDP (nominal): ≈£15 billion.

• GDP per capita (PPP): ≈£6,000.

• Key industries:

o Agriculture (coffee, beef, sugar, peanuts)

o Manufacturing and textiles

o Mining (gold)

o Tourism

• Major exports: Coffee, beef, gold, sugar, textiles.
• Currency: Nicaraguan córdoba (NIO; £1 ≈ 46 NIO).

Government
• Presidential republic.
• System: Constitutional republic (highly centralised).
• Head of State: President of Nicaragua.
• Head of Government: President of Nicaragua.
• Legislature: National Assembly (92 members).

Infrastructure
• Transport: National road network; limited rail; air and sea transport.
• Major airports: Augusto C. Sandino International Airport (Managua).
• Energy mix: Hydropower, geothermal, wind, biomass and fossil fuels.
• Digital connectivity: Moderate in urban areas; limited in rural regions.

Major Urban Centres
• Managua: ≈1.6 million (metro) – Capital and economic centre.
• León: ≈210,000 – Cultural and university centre.
• Masaya: ≈180,000 – Industrial and artisan hub.
• Chinandega: ≈170,000 – Agricultural and commercial centre.

MANAGUA – NICARAGUA'S CAPITAL AND ECONOMIC CENTRE

The National Flag

The national flag of Nicaragua features a horizontal triband of cobalt blue, white and cobalt blue, with the national coat of arms centred on the white band. The blue symbolises justice, loyalty and the nation's position between the Pacific Ocean and the Caribbean Sea, while the white represents purity, integrity and peace. The coat of arms depicts a triangle encircling five volcanoes, a rainbow and a Phrygian cap, framed by the text 'REPÚBLICA DE NICARAGUA - AMÉRICA CENTRAL'. This represents the nation's liberty, its natural beauty and its historical membership in the Central American federation. The flag as a whole embodies Nicaragua's sovereignty, its ideals of peace and its enduring unity within the region.

KEY PEOPLE AND PLACES

PEOPLE

José Santos Zelaya (1853–1919) Widely regarded as one of Nicaragua's most influential leaders, Zelaya served as President from 1893 to 1909. He promoted national modernisation, infrastructure development, education reform and attempted to assert Nicaraguan sovereignty, leaving a lasting impact on the country's political landscape.

Augusto César Sandino (1895–1934) A revolutionary leader who led resistance against U.S. military occupation in the 1920s and 1930s, Sandino became a national hero and symbol of sovereignty, anti-imperialism and social justice, inspiring generations of Nicaraguans and Latin American activists.

Anastasio Somoza García (1896–1956) A military officer and politician, Somoza served as President and established the Somoza dynasty, which dominated Nicaragua's politics for decades. His rule shaped the country's mid-20th-century political structure, economic development and authoritarian governance.

Violeta Chamorro (b. 1929) The first female President of Nicaragua, serving from 1990 to 1997. Chamorro oversaw the country's transition to democracy following the Sandinista era, promoting national reconciliation, political stability and economic reconstruction while advocating for social reform.

Ernesto Cardenal (1925–2020) A renowned poet, priest and political figure, Cardenal contributed to Nicaragua's cultural and intellectual life, blending literature with activism. He played a key role in the Sandinista government and promoted social justice, education and liberation theology throughout Latin America.

PLACES

Managua (founded 1812) The capital and largest city of Nicaragua, located on the southwestern shore of Lake Managua. Managua serves as the political, economic and cultural centre, featuring government institutions, historic sites, markets, universities and vibrant commercial and cultural activities.

Granada (founded 1524) One of Nicaragua's oldest cities, Granada is known for its colonial architecture, churches and historic plazas. It serves as a cultural and tourist hub, showcasing the country's Spanish colonial heritage, arts and traditions, while contributing to regional commerce.

León (founded 1524) A historic city in western Nicaragua, León is renowned for its colonial architecture, universities and cultural institutions. It has been a centre of education, political activism and literature, playing an important role in Nicaragua's history and intellectual development.

Ometepe Island An island formed by two volcanoes in Lake Nicaragua, Ometepe is celebrated for its biodiversity, archaeological sites, natural beauty and eco-tourism opportunities. It represents the country's volcanic landscape and is a major destination for hiking, nature exploration and cultural heritage.

Masaya Volcano An active volcano and national park near Masaya city, featuring lava craters, hiking trails and visitor facilities. Masaya Volcano is significant for its geological features, tourism, cultural legends and contributions to Nicaragua's natural heritage and scientific research.

Corn Islands A pair of islands in the Caribbean Sea, known for their beaches, coral reefs and fishing communities. The Corn Islands attract tourists seeking sun, sea and marine activities while highlighting the cultural and ecological diversity of Nicaragua's Caribbean coast.

TIMELINE OF EVENTS

c. 2000 BCE: Early Indigenous Settlements: Early Indigenous groups, including ancestors of the Nicarao and other Mesoamerican peoples, settled in present-day Nicaragua, developing agriculture, fishing, trade networks and organised communities.

250–900 CE: Classic Period Societies: Indigenous cultures in western Nicaragua, influenced by Mesoamerican civilisations, built settlements, ceremonial centres and trade networks connecting the region.

1522: Spanish Conquest Begins: Spanish forces arrived, led by Gil González Dávila, subduing Indigenous communities and establishing colonial control over Nicaragua.

1531: Colony of Nicaragua Established: Nicaragua was formally incorporated into the Spanish Empire, governed from León and connected to the wider Captaincy General of Guatemala.

1821: Independence from Spain: Nicaragua declared independence from Spain alongside other Central American provinces, joining a regional movement reshaping governance.

1823: United Provinces of Central America: Nicaragua joined the short-lived federation aimed at regional political unity and economic cooperation.

1838: Independent Republic Declared: Following the federation's collapse, Nicaragua emerged as an independent republic, beginning its own national governance and development.

1855: William Walker Expedition: American filibuster William Walker briefly seized power, causing political instability and resistance that shaped national identity.

1893: Liberal Reforms Implemented: Liberal governments modernisation policies, expanded agriculture and strengthened authority.

1912–1933: US Military Interventions: US forces intervened, affecting politics, stabilising governments and protecting economic interests.

1936: Anastasio Somoza García Takes Power: Somoza became president, beginning a long period of family dictatorship and authoritarian rule in Nicaragua.

1972: Managua Earthquake: A devastating earthquake destroyed much of the capital, causing massive casualties and challenging the Somoza regime.

1979: Sandinista Revolution: The Sandinista National Liberation Front overthrew the Somoza dictatorship, establishing a revolutionary government and initiating social reforms.

1980s: Contra War: A US-backed insurgency, the Contras, fought against the Sandinista government with violence and economic disruption.

1990: Democratic Elections Restored: Violeta Chamorro was elected president, ending Sandinista rule and beginning a period of democratic transition.

2006: Daniel Ortega Elected President: Ortega returned to power, marking a consolidation of Sandinista influence in Nicaraguan politics.

2018: Nationwide Protests: Mass protests against social security reforms were met with violent government suppression, creating political crisis and international concern.

2020: COVID-19 Pandemic Impact: The pandemic affected healthcare, economic activity and daily life, exacerbating existing social and political challenges.

THE REPUBLIC OF COSTA RICA

The Republic of Costa Rica occupies a central position in Central America, bordered by Nicaragua to the north, Panama to the southeast, the Pacific Ocean to the west and the Caribbean Sea to the east. It is a nation celebrated globally for its remarkable commitment to environmental conservation and stable democracy. The country's name, 'Costa Rica,' translates from Spanish as 'Rich Coast.' With an estimated population of approximately 5.2 million people, its capital and largest urban centre is San José. The national currency is the Costa Rican colón. Shaped by a unique colonial history that fostered an egalitarian society and a pivotal 20th-century decision to abolish its military, Costa Rica has forged a distinctive national identity centred on peace, education and sustainability. It is widely regarded as one of the most stable, prosperous and environmentally conscious nations in Latin America.

Geography

Costa Rica's geography is exceptionally diverse and dramatic for its size, encompassing a stunning variety of ecosystems within a compact area. The country is bisected by a series of rugged mountain ranges, primarily the Cordillera Volcánica and the Cordillera de Talamanca, which form the spine of the nation and separate the Pacific and Caribbean slopes. This volcanic activity has created fertile valleys, including the Central Valley where most of the population resides. Costa Rica boasts over 1,200 kilometers of coastline, featuring everything from sandy beaches on the Caribbean to rocky cliffs on the Pacific. The climate is tropical, with a dry season (December to April) and a rainy season (May to November), though microclimates vary greatly with elevation. The country's most significant geographic feature is its extraordinary biodiversity, protected by a system of national parks and reserves that cover over a quarter of its land area.

History

Human habitation in Costa Rica dates back thousands of years. In the pre-Columbian era, the region was a cultural crossroads, influenced by both Mesoamerican and South American indigenous groups. Christopher Columbus arrived on the Caribbean coast in 1502. Spanish colonisation was formalised in the 1560s, but the colony remained poor and isolated due to a lack of precious metals and a small indigenous labor force, which inadvertently led to the development of a society of small landowners. Costa Rica peacefully gained independence from Spain in 1821, subsequently joining first the Mexican Empire and then the Federal Republic of Central America before becoming a fully sovereign republic in 1838.

The late 19th century saw the rise of coffee and banana exports, which shaped the economy and attracted foreign investment. The defining moment of modern Costa Rican history was the brief but impactful civil war of 1948, which resulted in the abolition of the national army by the victorious junta under José Figueres Ferrer. This bold move, enshrined in the 1949 constitution, allowed for massive reinvestment into health, education and environmental protection, setting the country on its unique path of demilitarised democracy.

Government and Politics

Costa Rica is a unitary presidential constitutional republic, consistently rated as one of the most stable and full democracies in Latin America. Executive power is held by a President who is both head of state and head of government, elected for a single four-year term. Legislative power is vested in a unicameral Legislative Assembly. The political system is multi-party, though historically dominated by the social-democratic National Liberation Party and the conservative Social Christian Unity Party; in recent decades, newer parties have gained prominence. Key political issues typically revolve around economic management, infrastructure development, environmental policy and combating corruption. In foreign affairs, Costa Rica is renowned for its active and principled diplomacy, emphasising human rights, disarmament and environmental treaties. It is a founding member of the United Nations University for Peace.

Economy

Costa Rica has an advanced, upper-middle-income economy that is the most stable and diversified in Central America. It has successfully transitioned from a dependence on agricultural exports (notably coffee, bananas and pineapples) to an economy driven by technology, advanced manufacturing and services. It is a major hub for high-tech manufacturing (including microprocessors and medical devices) and a global leader in ecotourism. Other vital sectors include business process outsourcing and medical tourism. The economy faces challenges including a large fiscal deficit, high public debt, significant income inequality and infrastructure gaps. However, its long-term prospects are bolstered by a highly educated workforce, political stability and a strong brand associated with sustainability and innovation.

Demographics and Society

Costa Rican society is predominantly homogeneous, with the vast majority of the population being of European (mainly Spanish) or mixed European and indigenous ancestry. There are small but significant minority groups, including people of African descent (primarily on the Caribbean coast), indigenous peoples from eight recognised groups and communities of Chinese and Nicaraguan origin. The official language is Spanish. A defining characteristic of Costa Rican society is its large and stable middle class, a product of decades of investment in public education and healthcare. The population is increasingly urban and aging. Society places a high cultural value on peace, education and environmental stewardship, encapsulated in the national ethos of 'Pura Vida' (Pure Life), which signifies a philosophy of optimism, simplicity and well-being.

Culture

Costa Rican culture is a vibrant blend of Spanish, indigenous and Afro-Caribbean influences, with a distinctly laid-back and family-oriented character. The phrase 'Pura Vida' permeates everyday life as a greeting, a farewell and an expression of contentment. Music and dance are important, with genres like *música folklórica* (folk music), salsa and the calypso and soca of the Caribbean coast being popular. Traditional *oxcart painting*, recognised by UNESCO, is a famous craft. Cuisine is based on staples of rice, beans, corn and plantains, with the national dish being *gallo pinto* (rice and beans mixed with spices), typically eaten for breakfast. Community festivals, religious processions and local town fiestas are central to social life.

Education and Healthcare

Costa Rica boasts one of the most effective social investment models in the developing world. Education is free and compulsory through secondary school and the country enjoys one of the highest literacy rates in the Americas. The public university system, led by the University of Costa Rica, is highly respected. Healthcare is provided through a universal, single-payer system run by the Costa Rican Social Security Fund, which offers comprehensive coverage to all citizens and legal residents. This system has produced outstanding public health outcomes, including one of the highest life expectancies in the Western Hemisphere and low infant mortality rates. Access to both education and healthcare is a cornerstone of national pride and social stability.

Infrastructure

Costa Rica's infrastructure is generally good by regional standards but faces strain from underinvestment and rapid urbanization. The road network is extensive, though many secondary roads require maintenance and traffic congestion is a major issue in the Greater Metropolitan Area of San José. The country has several international airports, with Juan Santamaría International Airport near San José being the primary gateway. Ports on both the Caribbean (Limón) and Pacific (Puntarenas) coasts handle trade. A significant achievement is that nearly 100% of the country's electricity is generated from renewable sources, primarily hydropower, geothermal, wind and solar. Telecommunications are modern, with widespread mobile and internet access.

Tourism

Tourism is a cornerstone of the Costa Rican economy and its international identity. The country pioneered the concept of ecotourism, attracting visitors with its 'green' brand and unparalleled access to nature. Key attractions include its system of magnificent national parks (such as Manuel Antonio, Tortuguero and Corcovado), active volcanoes (Arenal and Poás), pristine beaches on both coasts and vast tropical rainforests teeming with wildlife. Adventure tourism (zip-lining, white-water rafting, surfing) and wellness tourism are also major draws. The industry is largely oriented toward sustainability, with many lodges and tour operators holding eco-certifications, though balancing tourist numbers with conservation remains an ongoing challenge.

Current Issues and Future Outlook

Costa Rica faces a set of challenges distinct from its regional neighbours, centred on sustaining its successful model. The most pressing issues are a persistent fiscal deficit and high public debt, which constrain investment in much-needed infrastructure upgrades, particularly in roads, water management and public transportation. Other concerns include rising living costs, pockets of poverty and the need to manage tourism growth sustainably to avoid environmental degradation. However, the country possesses immense strengths: deep democratic institutions, a commitment to human development, a globally respected environmental legacy and a diversified, innovation-friendly economy. Its future prospects are among the brightest in the region, dependent on its ability to enact necessary fiscal reforms while preserving the social and environmental pillars of its national success.

Overview

The Republic of Costa Rica stands as a remarkable and inspiring anomaly, not just in Central America but in the wider world. It is a nation that deliberately chose a different path—investing in its people and its natural heritage instead of a military—and has reaped the rewards in stability, prosperity and global admiration. While it must navigate modern economic pressures, its foundation of peace, education and environmental stewardship remains unshaken. Costa Rica demonstrates that a small country can achieve outsized influence through principled policy and a profound respect for both human dignity and the natural world, offering a compelling model of sustainable development for the 21st century.

DID YOU KNOW...?

Costa Rica's Diquís region is home to the mysterious stone spheres, thousands of perfectly rounded boulders scattered across the southern plains. Few know their true origin or purpose: some weigh several tonnes, yet ancient peoples moved them into precise alignments with hills, rivers and settlements. Archaeologists speculate they marked ceremonial sites, territorial boundaries, or celestial events, but no written record explains them. Made from gabbro and basalt, some spheres show remarkable precision, reflecting advanced stone-working skill. Beyond their aesthetic impact, these spheres hint at a complex social and spiritual culture in pre-Columbian Costa Rica that remains partially hidden beneath forest and farmland.

KEY FACTS AND FIGURES

Geography & Environment

• Total area: 51,100 km².

• Coastline: ≈1,290 km (Pacific Ocean and Caribbean Sea).

• Climate: Tropical, with distinct wet and dry seasons; cooler temperatures in highlands.

• Highest point: Cerro Chirripó (3,820 m).

• Major features: Central mountain ranges, tropical rainforests, Pacific and Caribbean coastal plains, rich biodiversity.

• Wildlife: Sloths, jaguars, howler monkeys, toucans, sea turtles.

• 4 UNESCO World Heritage sites.

Population & Society

• Population: ≈5.2 million (2024 estimate).

• Density: ≈102 persons/km².

• Urbanisation: ≈80%.

• Ethnicity:

o Mestizo/White: ≈83%

o Mulatto: ≈7%

o Indigenous: ≈2%

o Afro-descendant and other: ≈8%

• Languages: Spanish (official); English and indigenous languages spoken regionally.

• Religion: Christian (predominantly Roman Catholic): ≈70–75%.

• Literacy: ≈98%.

• Life expectancy: ≈80 years (among the highest in the Americas).

Economy

• GDP (nominal): ≈£60 billion.

• GDP per capita (PPP): ≈£18,000.

• Key industries:

o Ecotourism

o High-tech manufacturing and medical devices

o Agriculture (coffee, bananas, pineapples)

o Services and finance
• Major exports: Medical devices, bananas, pineapples, coffee, electronics.
• Currency: Costa Rican colón (CRC; £1 ≈ 670 CRC).

Government
• Presidential republic.
• System: Constitutional democratic republic.
• Head of State: President of Costa Rica.
• Head of Government: President of Costa Rica.
• Legislature: Legislative Assembly (57 members).

Infrastructure
• Transport: National road network; no intercity rail; air and sea transport.
• Major airports: Juan Santamaría International Airport, Daniel Oduber Quirós International Airport.
• Energy mix: Predominantly renewable (hydropower, geothermal, wind, solar).
• Digital connectivity: Well developed in urban areas; improving in rural regions.

Major Urban Centres
• San José: ≈1.7 million (metro) – Capital and economic centre.
• Alajuela: ≈300,000 – Industrial and commercial hub.
• Cartago: ≈170,000 – Historic and regional administrative centre.
• Heredia: ≈150,000 – Education and technology centre.

SAN JOSÉ – COSTA RICO'S CAPITAL AND ECONOMIC CENTRE

The National Flag

The national flag of Costa Rica features a horizontal triband of blue, white and red, with the white band being twice the width and containing a simplified national coat of arms towards the hoist on the state flag. The blue symbolises the sky, idealism and perseverance, the white represents peace, wisdom and happiness and the red denotes the warmth, generosity and blood spilt for freedom by the Costa Rican people. The coat of arms depicts three volcanoes between two oceans, under a sky of seven stars, representing the nation's provinces and a rising sun, all framed by golden beads. This signifies Costa Rica's natural beauty, its peaceful democracy and its sovereign unity. The flag as a whole embodies the nation's history, its commitment to peace and its vibrant, independent spirit.

KEY PEOPLE AND PLACES

PEOPLE

Juan Rafael Mora Porras (1814–1860) Widely regarded as one of Costa Rica's most influential leaders, Mora Porras served as president from 1849 to 1859. He is celebrated for defending national sovereignty during the Filibuster War, promoting economic development and strengthening democratic institutions.

José Figueres Ferrer (1906–1990) Known as 'Don Pepe,' Figueres served multiple terms as president and abolished Costa Rica's military in 1948. He introduced social reforms, expanded education and promoted democracy, leaving a lasting impact on the country's political stability and progressive governance.

Óscar Arias Sánchez (b. 1941) President and Nobel Peace Prize laureate, Arias played a key role in promoting peace and democratic governance in Central America. His initiatives strengthened Costa Rica's international profile, economic development and commitment to human rights and regional diplomacy.

Claudia Poll (b. 1972) Costa Rica's most decorated Olympic athlete, Poll won multiple medals in swimming, bringing international recognition to the country. She inspired national pride, promoted sports development and encouraged youth participation in athletics throughout Costa Rica.

Laura Chinchilla (b. 1959) The first female President of Costa Rica, serving from 2010 to 2014. Chinchilla focused on social programs, security, environmental protection and economic development, becoming a symbol of female leadership and progressive governance in the country.

PLACES

San José (founded 1737) The capital and largest city of Costa Rica, located in the Central Valley. San José serves as the political, economic and cultural hub, featuring government buildings, universities, museums, historic theatres and vibrant commercial and cultural activities.

Cartago (founded 1563) The former capital and an important historic city, Cartago is known for its colonial architecture, basilicas and role in early Costa Rican history. It remains a centre for culture, religion and tourism while preserving national heritage.

Arenal Volcano One of Costa Rica's most famous volcanoes, located near La Fortuna. Arenal is a major tourist destination, known for hiking, hot springs and its dramatic eruptions. It highlights the country's volcanic activity, natural beauty and eco-tourism opportunities.

Monteverde Cloud Forest A renowned ecological reserve in the central highlands, famous for its biodiversity, hiking trails and conservation efforts. Monteverde Cloud Forest attracts scientists, tourists and nature enthusiasts, showcasing Costa Rica's commitment to environmental protection and sustainable tourism.

Tamarindo A coastal town on the Pacific coast, Tamarindo is celebrated for surfing, beaches and tourism development. It attracts visitors from around the world and contributes significantly to Costa Rica's tourism industry while highlighting local culture and natural beauty.

Guanacaste Province Located in northwestern Costa Rica, Guanacaste is known for its dry tropical forests, beaches, national parks and cattle ranching. The province is a hub for tourism, eco-adventures and cultural festivals, showcasing the diversity and heritage of Costa Rica's landscapes and communities.

TIMELINE OF EVENTS

c. 3000 BCE: Early Indigenous Settlements: Indigenous peoples, including ancestors of the Chorotega, Huetar and Bribri, settled in present-day Costa Rica, developing agriculture, trade networks and organised communities.

1502: Columbus Arrives on the Coast: Christopher Columbus explored the Caribbean coast during his fourth voyage, marking the first European contact with the region.

1561: Spanish Colonisation Begins: Spanish settlers established permanent settlements, introducing colonial administration, Catholicism and European agriculture.

1570s: Indigenous Resistance and Adaptation: Indigenous communities resisted Spanish encroachment while adapting to new social, economic and environmental conditions.

1821: Independence from Spain: Costa Rica declared independence alongside other Central American provinces, joining the wider independence movement.

1823: United Provinces of Central America: Costa Rica joined the short-lived Central American federation aiming for political unity and regional stability.

1838: Independent Republic Declared: Costa Rica became a fully independent republic after the federation collapsed, establishing its own governance systems.

1856–1857: Filibuster Wars: Costa Rica successfully repelled American filibuster William Walker, strengthening national identity and regional influence.

1870s: Coffee Economy Expansion: Coffee production expanded, driving economic growth, social change and integration into global markets.

1948: Civil War and New Constitution: A brief civil war led to democratic reforms, abolition of the army and adoption of a new constitution.

1950s: Social and Economic Development: Costa Rica invested in education, healthcare and infrastructure, laying foundations for modern development.

1980s: Environmental Protection Initiatives: The government promoted conservation, establishing national parks and protected areas to preserve biodiversity.

1990s: Democratic Consolidation: Costa Rica strengthened democratic institutions, human rights protections and electoral transparency.

2007: Renewable Energy Expansion: The country invested in renewable energy, becoming a global leader in sustainable power generation.

2010: Hosting International Conferences: Costa Rica hosted global summits on climate change and environmental policy, highlighting its diplomatic influence.

2018: Political Stability Maintained: Elections proceeded peacefully, reflecting a strong democratic culture and social cohesion.

2020: COVID-19 Pandemic Impact: The pandemic disrupted tourism, public health systems and the economy, testing Costa Rica's social and institutional resilience.

THE REPUBLIC OF PANAMA

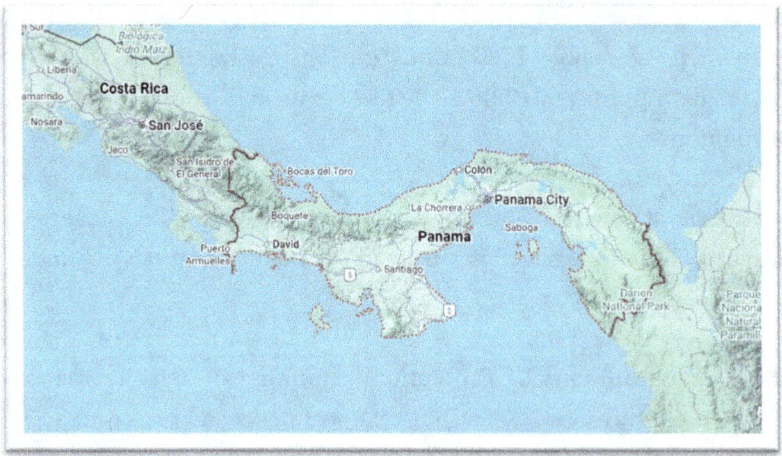

The Republic of Panama occupies the strategic southernmost portion of Central America, bordered by Costa Rica to the west, Colombia to the southeast, the Caribbean Sea to the north and the Pacific Ocean to the south. It is the transcontinental isthmus that connects North and South America. The country's name likely derives from a pre-colonial indigenous word meaning 'abundance of fish'. With an estimated population of approximately 4.3 million people, its capital and largest metropolitan centre is Panama City. The official currency is the Panamanian balboa, which is pegged to and circulates interchangeably with the United States Dollar. Forged by its unique role as a global crossroads, Panama is a nation defined by its maritime canal, a highly service-based economy and a complex blend of cultures from across the world.

Geography

Panama's geography is dominated by its function as a land bridge. A central spine of mountains, including the Cordillera Central, runs the length of the isthmus, creating a distinct divide between the Caribbean and Pacific coasts. The most significant physical feature is the man-made Panama Canal, which cuts through the continental divide, utilising a series of locks and the vast artificial Gatun Lake. The Caribbean coast is characterised by rainforests and fewer natural harbours, while the Pacific coast is more indented with gulfs and has a more pronounced dry season. The Darién Gap, a dense and largely roadless tropical forest in the east, forms a natural break in the Pan-American Highway. Panama's tropical climate is characterised by high humidity and temperatures, with a rainy season from May to December.

History

Panama's history is fundamentally shaped by its geography as the narrowest crossing between two great oceans. Before European arrival, it was home to a number of indigenous groups. Spanish explorer Rodrigo de Bastidas first claimed the isthmus for Spain in 1501 and it quickly became a crucial part of the Spanish Empire's trade route, transporting silver from Peru to Spain via the Camino Real. After gaining independence from Spain in 1821, Panama joined the Republic of Gran Colombia. Following a US-backed separatist movement, it seceded from Colombia in 1903, a move directly orchestrated to facilitate the building of an American-controlled canal. The construction of the Panama Canal by the United States (1904-1914) was an epochal engineering feat that permanently altered global trade and defined modern Panama. The country operated under a series of authoritarian and military governments for much of the 20th century. A landmark moment was the signing of the Torrijos–Carter Treaties in 1977, which set in motion the transfer of the Canal from US to Panamanian control, a process completed on 31 December 1999 under the leadership of General Manuel Noriega, whose regime was later removed by a US invasion in 1989.

Government and Politics

Panama is a unitary presidential constitutional republic. Executive power is vested in a President who is both head of state and head of government, elected for a single five-year term. Legislative power rests with a unicameral National Assembly. The political system is multi-party, though politics have historically been dominated by a few traditional families and parties, including the Democratic Revolutionary Party (PRD) and Panameñista Party. Corruption remains a significant and pervasive challenge, influencing politics and business at high levels. Key political issues include economic inequality, transparency and the management of the canal and associated revenues. In foreign affairs, Panama maintains a neutral and business-oriented stance, is a major centre for global banking and trade and maintains close, if complex, relations with the United States.

Economy

Panama possesses one of the fastest-growing and most robust economies in Latin America, classified as an upper-middle-income economy. Its economic model is uniquely centred on services. The Panama Canal is the economic cornerstone, generating substantial toll revenues and supporting massive related industries in logistics, shipping and port operations. The Colón Free Trade Zone, the second-largest free port in the world, is another critical pillar. Panama is also a major international banking and financial centre. Other significant sectors include tourism, particularly centred on the canal, modern Panama City and coastal resorts, as well as a small but productive agricultural sector. Despite impressive macroeconomic growth, the country grapples with high levels of income inequality and economic prosperity are not evenly distributed.

Demographics and Society

Panamanian society is a rich and complex mosaic of ethnicities and cultures, a direct result of its history as a global crossroads. The population is predominantly mestizo (mixed European and indigenous ancestry). There are also significant Afro-Caribbean communities (descendants of Antillean workers who built the canal), distinct indigenous groups (such as the Guna, Emberá and Ngäbe-Buglé) and sizable communities of European, Chinese and Middle Eastern descent. Spanish is the official language, but English is widely spoken in business circles and many indigenous languages are in use. Society is marked by stark contrasts between the modern, cosmopolitan capital and rural provinces where development lags. Family and religious faith are central social institutions.

Culture

Panamanian culture is a vibrant fusion of African, Spanish, indigenous and North American influences. This is most famously expressed in its music and dance, particularly through *música típica* and the *tamborito* (the national dance), as well as the Afro-Caribbean rhythms of *salsa* and *reggaeton*. The pollera, an elaborate and colourful hand-stitched dress, is the national symbol of traditional costume. Panamanian cuisine reflects its diversity, featuring staples like rice, beans and plantains, with signature dishes including *sancocho* (a chicken stew), *ropa vieja* (shredded beef) and fresh seafood. Carnival celebrations, especially in Las Tablas, are extravagant, nationally important events.

Education and Healthcare

Panama's education system comprises primary, secondary and tertiary levels. While primary education is compulsory, the system faces challenges with quality and access, particularly in rural and indigenous communities, leading to disparities in outcomes. The University of Panama is the leading public university. Healthcare is provided through a dual system of public and private services. The public system, managed by the Ministry of Health and the Social Security Fund, offers coverage but can be strained, leading to long wait times. Private healthcare is of a high standard but accessible primarily to the wealthy and those with insurance. Public health challenges include managing chronic diseases and ensuring equitable access to services.

Infrastructure

Panama's infrastructure is among the most advanced in Central America, heavily centred on supporting its role as a global logistics hub. The centrepiece is, of course, the Panama Canal, which underwent a major expansion completed in 2016. The country boasts the region's most developed port and maritime facilities. Tocumen International Airport near Panama City is a major aviation hub for the Americas. The road network is relatively good, with the Pan-American Highway traversing the country, though roads in remote areas can be poor. Panama City has a modern skyline, a metro system and extensive banking and telecommunications infrastructure.

Tourism

Tourism in Panama is a growing sector that capitalises on the country's unique mix of modern wonders and natural beauty. The undisputed top attraction is the Panama Canal and its visitor centres at Miraflores and Agua Clara. Beyond the canal, tourists are drawn to the modern architecture and historic Casco Viejo district of Panama City, the pristine beaches and islands of the Bocas del Toro and San Blas archipelagos (the latter governed by the Guna people) and highland towns like Boquete. Ecotourism, particularly birdwatching and rainforest exploration, is also significant. The industry benefits from the country's stability, developed services and use of the US dollar.

Current Issues and Future Outlook

Panama faces a critical juncture defined by both economic success and profound social challenges. The most pressing issues are tackling deep-seated corruption, which has eroded public trust and addressing one of the highest levels of income inequality in the world. Environmental challenges, including deforestation and vulnerability to climate change, also pose risks. Recent years have seen significant social protests focused on the cost of living and government transparency. However, the country's strategic assets—the canal, its dollarised economy, its geographic position and its well-developed service sector—provide a formidable foundation. The future outlook hinges on the nation's ability to translate its macroeconomic wealth into more inclusive and sustainable development for all its citizens.

Overview

The Republic of Panama is a nation of profound contrasts and global significance. It is a place where immense engineering prowess meets ancient indigenous cultures, where gleaming financial skyscrapers overlook historic colonial plazas. Defined by its canal, it has leveraged its geography to build a prosperous, outward-looking economy. Yet, this success has not been universally shared and the country grapples with the social and political tensions that such inequality breeds. As the steward of one of the world's most vital commercial arteries, Panama carries a unique global responsibility. Its continued success will depend on its ability to bridge not just oceans, but also the divides within its own society.

DID YOU KNOW...?

Most recognise Panama for its canal, yet the country conceals the lesser-known Coclé culture, which produced extraordinarily intricate polychrome ceramics and goldwork between 500–1500 CE. Beyond tombs in Sitio Conte and El Caño, some burials include multiple skeletons arranged with elaborate grave goods, suggesting complex social hierarchies and ritual practices. Gold pendants, figurines and musical instruments demonstrate both artistic sophistication and symbolic communication. Less explored are the agricultural terraces and causeways linking these communities, revealing that Coclé peoples organised landscapes for farming, trade and ceremonial life. Panama's underground and rural archaeology preserve a forgotten world of craftsmanship and ritual, overshadowed by later colonial and modern developments.

KEY FACTS AND FIGURES

Geography & Environment

• Total area: 75,417 km².

• Coastline: ≈2,490 km (Pacific Ocean and Caribbean Sea).

• Climate: Tropical, with a pronounced wet and dry season.

• Highest point: Volcán Barú (3,475 m).

• Major features: Panama Canal, Central Cordillera, Darién rainforest, extensive coastlines and islands.

• Wildlife: Jaguars, sloths, tapirs, harpy eagles, sea turtles.

• 5 UNESCO World Heritage sites.

Population & Society

• Population: ≈4.4 million (2024 estimate).

• Density: ≈58 persons/km².

• Urbanisation: ≈68%.

• Ethnicity:

o Mestizo: ≈65%

o Afro-Panamanian: ≈15%

o White: ≈10%

o Indigenous peoples: ≈10%

• Languages: Spanish (official); English widely spoken; indigenous languages.

• Religion: Christian (predominantly Roman Catholic): ≈85%.

• Literacy: ≈95%.

• Life expectancy: ≈78 years.

Economy

• GDP (nominal): ≈£60 billion.

• GDP per capita (PPP): ≈£30,000.

• Key industries:

o Canal operations and logistics

o Banking and financial services

o Trade and shipping

o Tourism

• Major exports: Copper, bananas, seafood, refined petroleum products.
• Currency: Panamanian balboa (PAB) and US dollar (USD).

Government
• Presidential republic.
• System: Constitutional democratic republic.
• Head of State: President of Panama.
• Head of Government: President of Panama.
• Legislature: National Assembly (71 members).

Infrastructure
• Transport: Well-developed road network; Panama Canal; major ports; air transport hub.
• Major airports: Tocumen International Airport (Panama City).
• Energy mix: Hydropower, fossil fuels and growing wind and solar capacity.
• Digital connectivity: Well developed, particularly in urban and commercial areas.

Major Urban Centres
• Panama City: ≈1.9 million (metro) – Capital, financial and logistics hub.
• San Miguelito: ≈400,000 – Major urban residential centre.
• Colón: ≈250,000 – Key Caribbean port city.
• David: ≈200,000 – Regional commercial centre in western Panama.

PANAMA CITY – PANAMA'S CAPITAL, FINANCIAL AND LOGISTICS HUB.

The National Flag

The national flag of Costa Rica features five horizontal stripes of blue, white, red, white and blue, with the central red stripe being twice the width of the others. The blue symbolises the expansive sky and the opportunities it presents, while the white represents peace. The prominent red band signifies both the warmth of the people and the blood shed for the nation's liberty. In its state version, the flag bears the national coat of arms on the red stripe, depicting a landscape of three volcanoes between two oceans under a rising sun and seven stars, representing the country's natural beauty, its seven provinces and its sovereignty. Collectively, the design embodies Costa Rica's enduring peace, democratic ideals and independent spirit.

KEY PEOPLE AND PLACES

PEOPLE

Manuel Amador Guerrero (1833–1909) Widely regarded as the first President of Panama, serving from 1904 to 1908, Amador Guerrero played a central role in Panama's independence from Colombia and the establishment of the republic, laying the foundation for its political institutions and national identity.

Omar Torrijos Herrera (1929–1981) A military leader and statesman, Torrijos is celebrated for negotiating the Torrijos-Carter Treaties, which eventually transferred control of the Panama Canal to Panama. He implemented social and infrastructure reforms, strengthened national sovereignty and remains a revered figure in Panamanian history.

Mireya Moscoso (b. 1946) The first female President of Panama, serving from 1999 to 2004. She promoted social development, education, women's empowerment and economic growth while representing Panama in international diplomacy and advancing national policies during her tenure.

Rubén Blades (b. 1948) A world-renowned musician, actor and activist, Blades brought international attention to Panamanian culture through salsa music, songwriting and advocacy. His work celebrates Latin American identity, promotes social justice and has made him a global cultural ambassador for Panama.

Belisario Porras (1856–1942) A prominent political leader and journalist, Porras served multiple terms as President of Panama. He was instrumental in nation-building, developing infrastructure, modernising public institutions and promoting education, economic growth and political stability in the early 20th century.

PLACES

Panama City (founded 1519) The capital and largest city of Panama, located on the Pacific coast. Panama City serves as the political, economic and cultural hub, featuring modern skyscrapers, historic Casco Viejo district, government buildings, cultural institutions and the gateway to the Panama Canal.

Colon A port city on the Caribbean coast, Colon is strategically important for commerce, shipping and trade through the Panama Canal. It is also known for its free-trade zone, historic architecture and proximity to natural and cultural attractions along the Caribbean coast.

Panama Canal (completed 1914) A world-famous engineering marvel connecting the Atlantic and Pacific Oceans. The Panama Canal is vital for global maritime trade, economic development and national sovereignty, symbolising Panama's strategic importance, engineering achievement and international influence.

San Blas Islands An archipelago along Panama's Caribbean coast, home to the Guna Yala indigenous community. The islands are known for their pristine beaches, cultural heritage, eco-tourism and the preservation of traditional Guna customs, language and governance systems.

Bocas del Toro A province and archipelago on Panama's Caribbean coast, celebrated for its natural beauty, biodiversity and tourism opportunities. Bocas del Toro attracts eco-tourists, divers and travellers seeking beaches, rainforests and cultural experiences in Panama's tropical landscapes.

Boquete A mountain town in Chiriquí province, famous for its coffee plantations, cool climate and eco-tourism. Boquete is a centre for hiking, birdwatching and agricultural innovation, showcasing Panama's natural diversity, rural culture and sustainable tourism initiatives.

TIMELINE OF EVENTS

c. 2000 BCE: Early Indigenous Settlements: Indigenous peoples, including the Coclé, Ngäbe and other groups, settled in present-day Panama, developing agriculture, trade networks and organised communities across diverse environments.

1501: Spanish Exploration Begins: Rodrigo de Bastidas explored the Panamanian coast, marking the first European contact with the isthmus and initiating Spanish interest in the region.

1519: Founding of Panama City: Spanish settlers established Panama City, creating a key colonial port and administrative centre for trans-Pacific and trans-Atlantic trade.

1520s: Spanish Colonial Rule Established: Panama became part of the Spanish Empire, serving as a transit route for gold, silver and other goods between the Americas and Europe.

1821: Independence from Spain: Panama declared independence from Spain, joining the newly independent Republic of Gran Colombia under Simón Bolívar.

1831: Gran Colombia Dissolves: Panama became part of the Republic of Colombia after the dissolution of Gran Colombia, maintaining its strategic importance.

1903: Independence and US Involvement: With support from the United States, Panama separated from Colombia and established the Republic of Panama, allowing construction of the Panama Canal.

1914: Panama Canal Opens: The Panama Canal officially opened, transforming global trade routes and establishing Panama as a strategic international hub.

1968: Military Coup: A military coup brought General Omar Torrijos to power, initiating a period of authoritarian rule with major infrastructure and social reforms.

1977: Torrijos-Carter Treaties Signed: Treaties with the United States set the path for full Panamanian control over the canal by 1999.

1989: US Invasion: The United States invaded Panama to remove Manuel Noriega from power, restoring democratic governance.

1999: Panama Canal Transferred: Full control of the Panama Canal was handed over to Panama, boosting national sovereignty and economic opportunity.

2000s: Economic Growth and Infrastructure: Panama invested in infrastructure, banking, tourism and international trade, becoming one of Central America's fastest-growing economies.

2014: Expansion of Panama Canal Completed: Expansion of the canal allowed larger ships to transit, increasing global trade significance and economic benefits.

2019: International Diplomatic Initiatives: Panama hosted key international conferences and strengthened its role as a regional diplomatic and trade hub.

2020: COVID-19 Pandemic Impact: The pandemic disrupted commerce, public health systems and daily life, challenging Panama's economy and social services.

THE CARIBBEAN

The Caribbean is a region defined by its intricate geography and profound historical transformations, encompassing island nations, coastal territories and numerous Indigenous and diasporic communities. Its archipelagos, coral reefs, volcanic peaks and turquoise seas have sustained diverse societies intimately connected to the maritime environment and to evolving Atlantic networks. Historically, the region was shaped by powerful pre-Columbian civilisations such as the Taíno and Kalinago, the catastrophic forces of European colonisation and plantation slavery and the protracted rise of modern independent states, playing a pivotal role in global movements of commodities, labour and ideas through the triangular trade and imperial rivalry. Following centuries of colonial exploitation and relentless struggle for emancipation and sovereignty, the modern era has seen these societies forge distinct political identities while engaging in regional co-operation through frameworks such as CARICOM, all while grappling with the complex legacies of the plantation economy, migration and climate vulnerability. The petroglyphs of the Caguana Ceremonial Park, the Haitian Declaration of Independence, the literary works of Derek Walcott and the engineering of the Panama Canal underscore the Caribbean's enduring influence on global culture, political thought and transnational connectivity. This chapter examines the region's foundational heritage, its ongoing quest for reparatory justice and sustainable development and its significant role in shaping the modern world's social and economic fabric.

THE COMMONWEALTH OF BAHAMAS

The Bahamas occupies an expansive archipelago in the Atlantic Ocean, bordered by the crystal-clear waters of the Florida Straits and the Caribbean Sea. With an estimated population of around 400,000 people, the capital city is Nassau, while centres such as Freeport exert major cultural, economic and political influence. English is the official national language, with a distinctive Bahamian dialect spoken across the islands. The Bahamian Dollar serves as the national currency. Shaped by millennia of Lucayan civilisation, British colonisation and the legacy of the transatlantic slave trade, the nation blends deep historical roots with deliberate modern development. Its maritime resources, commitment to regional cooperation and relatively high quality of life contribute significantly to its international stature and domestic prosperity. This combination of historical depth and contemporary stability defines the identity of The Bahamas.

Geography

Spanning a scattered and varied seascape, The Bahamas features extraordinary geographical diversity. It includes thousands of low-lying limestone islands and cays, surrounded by expansive shallow banks and deep oceanic trenches. The landscape is characterised by karst topography, with caves, blue holes and sandy beaches. Coastal regions offer sheltered estuaries and mangrove forests, while the interiors feature pine forests and coppice. Major waterways include the Tongue of the Ocean, the Northeast Providence Channel and countless tidal creeks. The climate is tropical maritime, with a wet season and risk of hurricanes. Natural hazards such as tropical storms, hurricanes, saltwater intrusion and coastal erosion significantly shape regional life. The country hosts remarkable marine biodiversity, though ecosystems face pressure from tourism, development and climate change. Conservation efforts and sustainable marine management remain central to preserving the nation's diverse natural heritage.

History

The history of The Bahamas begins thousands of years before European contact with the Lucayan people, a branch of the Taíno. European exploration and settlement began in the late 15th century, leading to Spanish depopulation and later British colonisation. The islands became a haven for pirates and privateers before establishing as a formal British colony. Following the American War of Independence, the 18th and 19th centuries saw an influx of Loyalists and enslaved Africans, establishing a plantation economy. The Bahamas' abolition of slavery, its role in blockade-running during the American Civil War and Prohibition and its emergence from colonial status to full sovereignty shaped its modern identity. The latter half of the 20th century was marked by the movement for majority rule, independence in 1973 and the development of a tourism-based economy. Modern The Bahamas continues to navigate its complex past while reaffirming its role as a stable and diverse society.

Government and Politics

The Bahamas is a unitary parliamentary democracy and a constitutional monarchy, with the British monarch as the ceremonial head of state represented by the Governor-General. Government authority is central, with local administration on the Family Islands. The system comprises three branches: executive, legislative and judicial. Executive power is vested in the Prime Minister and the Cabinet, drawn from the elected House of Assembly. Legislative power rests with the bicameral Parliament, consisting of the elected House of Assembly and the appointed Senate. The Supreme Court of The Bahamas heads the judiciary. Regular elections, a robust constitution and an independent judiciary underpin political stability. Political life is characterised by two dominant national parties, the Free National Movement and the Progressive Liberal Party. Domestically, debates centre on crime, economic diversification, climate policy and healthcare, while internationally The Bahamas maintains a strong commitment to regional cooperation (CARICOM), financial governance and environmental advocacy.

Economy

The Bahamas possesses one of the most stable and prosperous economies in the Caribbean, characterised as a service-based, high-income system with a significant tourism base. Key sectors include tourism, international financial services, maritime registry and light manufacturing. The nation is a regional leader in offshore banking and wealth management. Fisheries and agriculture remain present, though limited by terrain. Despite its economic strength, challenges include income inequality, vulnerability to external shocks, high costs for imports and energy and managing the transition to greater economic resilience. The Bahamian Dollar is pegged to the US Dollar and the economy is deeply integrated with that of the United States. Continued investment in tourism product, sustainable development, financial sector regulation and digital infrastructure is viewed as essential for sustaining long-term prosperity.

Demographics and Society

With a population of approximately 400,000, The Bahamas is one of the most densely populated archipelagic nations. The population is highly urbanised, concentrated on the islands of New Providence and Grand Bahama. Bahamian society is fundamentally shaped by a history of slavery and migration, resulting in a majority Afro-Bahamian demographic with European, Asian and mixed-race minorities. English is the universal language, with Bahamian Creole widely spoken. High living standards relative to the region coexist with challenges, including the cost of living, violent crime and addressing historical inequities. The concepts of community, resilience and social cohesion remain central to the national ethos.

Culture

Bahamian culture has achieved distinct regional recognition, shaped by its island setting, history and African diaspora roots. Indigenous Lucayan, African, British and American influences form essential cultural foundations. Junkanoo, music (goombay, rake 'n' scrape), storytelling and visual arts enjoy prominence. Sport plays a major role in national life, particularly sailing, athletics, basketball and cricket. Cultural expression frequently explores themes of identity, the sea, freedom and celebration. While deeply influenced by global trends and its northern neighbour, Bahamian culture continues to evolve with a focus on local heritage and artistic support, reflecting ongoing debates about preservation, modernity and national purpose.

Education and Healthcare

The Bahamas maintains a well-regarded education system, encompassing public and private institutions at primary, secondary and tertiary levels. It is home to the University of The Bahamas and several technical colleges, attracting regional students. Education is primarily managed at the national level. Healthcare operates through a mix of public and private systems, with a National Insurance scheme. While access to medical care is available, challenges include wait times for certain specialties, managing non-communicable diseases and serving remote Family Islands. Policy debates focus on sustaining healthcare quality, improving technical education and addressing public health issues in a dispersed island nation.

Infrastructure

Infrastructure across The Bahamas reflects both unique geographic challenges and significant investment. Internal air and sea networks are critical for connectivity between islands, with the Family Islands reliant on ferries and domestic flights. Major ports in Nassau and Freeport and international airports facilitate global trade and tourism. Digital infrastructure is generally robust in urban centres, though disparities in broadband access persist in the more remote cays. Energy systems are largely dependent on imported fossil fuels, with growing interest in solar and renewable capacity. Infrastructure priorities include climate-resilient design, water supply security and upgrading utilities. Balancing connectivity, sustainability and resilience remains a national priority.

Tourism

Tourism is the dominant contributor to the Bahamian economy, offering exceptional diversity of attractions. Natural landmarks include the Exuma Cays Land and Sea Park, Thunderball Grotto, Dean's Blue Hole and the pristine beaches of Harbour Island and Eleuthera. Iconic resorts and cruise ports in Nassau and Freeport provide world-renowned hospitality, gaming and culinary experiences. Outdoor activities like diving, fishing, sailing and boating attract millions of visitors annually. Historic sites from the Loyalist and colonial eras, along with Junkanoo shacks, offer insight into the nation's complex past. Sustainable tourism initiatives increasingly aim to protect fragile marine ecosystems and support local economies.

Current Issues and Future Outlook

The Bahamas faces significant challenges alongside considerable strengths. Climate change and sea-level rise, crime and public safety, economic diversification and building greater resilience to external shocks remain central national concerns. Internationally, navigating its relationship with the United States and asserting leadership in regional climate advocacy require careful diplomatic engagement. At the same time, the country benefits from political stability, a resilient tourism brand, a strategic location and a respected financial sector. The future outlook depends on fostering youth opportunity, managing environmental vulnerabilities, investing in a digital transition and upholding social cohesion. How effectively these issues are managed will shape The Bahamas' regional role and domestic stability in the decades ahead.

Overview

The Bahamas is a nation defined by its archipelago, maritime culture and commitment to democratic governance. Rooted in Lucayan heritage and shaped by a distinct colonial past, the African diaspora and a tradition of enterprise, it has emerged as a respected regional actor. Its island geography presents both immense tourism appeal and profound environmental vulnerability. Moving forward, the nation seeks to reconcile its aspirational values with persistent social and economic challenges while sustaining its quality of life and democratic institutions. Continued innovation, inclusion and principled leadership remain key to ensuring a resilient and prosperous future for The Bahamas.

DID YOU KNOW...?

The Bahamas is home to one of the world's deepest known blue holes, Dean's Blue Hole on Long Island. Plunging approximately 202 metres (663 feet), it is a dramatic vertical cave system in a sheltered bay. It has become a world-renowned site for free-diving competitions and scientific research, offering insights into geological history, unique marine life and low-oxygen environments. This monumental natural wonder stands as a stark symbol of the archipelago's unique karst landscape, oceanic mystery and the enduring human fascination with exploration.

KEY FACTS AND FIGURES

Geography & Environment

• Total area: 13,880 km² (archipelago of over 700 islands and cays).
• Coastline: ≈3,500 km.
• Climate: Tropical marine climate, moderated by trade winds.
• Highest point: Mount Alvernia, Cat Island (63 m).
• Major features: Great Bahama Bank andros Barrier Reef, Exuma Cays, extensive coral reefs.
• Wildlife: Flamingos, iguanas, dolphins, sea turtles, reef fish.
• 0 UNESCO World Heritage sites.

Population & Society

• Population: ≈410,000 (2024 estimate).
• Density: ≈30 persons/km².
• Urbanisation: ≈83%.
• Ethnicity:
o Afro-Bahamian: ≈90%
o White: ≈5%
o Mixed and other: ≈5%
• Languages: English (official); Bahamian Creole widely spoken.
• Religion: Christian (predominantly Protestant): ≈95%.
• Literacy: ≈96%.
• Life expectancy: ≈75 years.

Economy

• GDP (nominal): ≈£11 billion.
• GDP per capita (PPP): ≈£30,000.
• Key industries:
o Tourism and hospitality
o Financial and offshore services
o Real estate
o Maritime services
• Major exports: Seafood, salt, rum, chemicals.
• Currency: Bahamian dollar (BSD; pegged 1:1 to the US dollar).

Government

- Constitutional monarchy (Commonwealth realm).
- System: Parliamentary democracy.
- Head of State: King Charles III.
- Head of Government: Prime Minister of The Bahamas.
- Parliament: Bicameral Parliament (House of Assembly and Senate).

Infrastructure

- Transport: Inter-island travel by air and sea; limited road networks on major islands.
- Major airports: Lynden Pindling International Airport (Nassau).
- Energy mix: Predominantly fossil fuels; growing interest in solar energy.
- Digital connectivity: Well developed in urban and tourist areas; limited on remote islands.

Major Urban Centres

- Nassau: ≈280,000 (metro) – Capital and economic centre.
- Freeport: ≈50,000 – Industrial and port city on Grand Bahama.
- West End: ≈15,000 – Regional settlement and transport hub.
- Marsh Harbour: ≈10,000 – Commercial centre of the Abaco Islands.

NASSAU - BAHAMAS'S CAPITAL AND ECONOMIC CENTRE

The National Flag

The national flag of The Bahamas features an equilateral black triangle at the hoist set against three horizontal stripes of aquamarine, gold and aquamarine. The gold stripe symbolises the sun and the nation's sandy shores, while the aquamarine represents the surrounding Caribbean Sea. The black triangle denotes the strength and vigour of the Bahamian people, with its forward-pointing direction embodying their collective enterprise and determination to cultivate the land's abundant resources. This flag, designed by Hervis Bain and first raised on 10 July 1973, marks the country's independence from the United Kingdom. Together, these elements reflect the Bahamian people's unity, their connection to a distinctive natural environment and their forward-looking spirit.

KEY PEOPLE AND PLACES

PEOPLE

Sir Lynden Pindling (1930–2000) Widely regarded as the 'Father of the Nation,' Pindling served as the first Prime Minister of The Bahamas after independence in 1973. He championed majority rule, political reform, economic development and social progress, shaping the modern Bahamian state and national identity.

Perry Christie (b. 1943) A prominent political leader and former Prime Minister, Christie implemented economic policies, social programmes and infrastructure projects, while promoting regional cooperation, governance reform and strengthening democratic institutions throughout The Bahamas during his periods in office.

Sir Cecil Wallace-Whitfield (1900–1977) An influential politician and social advocate, Wallace-Whitfield promoted workers' rights, education and civic engagement. He played a crucial role in advancing political representation and social reform, contributing significantly to The Bahamas' mid-20th-century social and political development.

Sidney Poitier (1927–2022) Born in Miami to Bahamian parents, Poitier is celebrated globally as an Academy Award-winning actor and civil rights pioneer. His career brought international attention to Bahamian heritage and culture, highlighting the country's contributions to arts and global identity.

Shaunae Miller-Uibo (b. 1994) An Olympic gold medallist in sprinting, Miller-Uibo represents The Bahamas on the international stage. Her athletic achievements have inspired national pride, encouraged youth participation in sports and raised global awareness of Bahamian talent and excellence.

PLACES

Nassau (founded 1695) The capital and largest city of The Bahamas, located on New Providence Island. Nassau serves as the political, economic and cultural hub, featuring government institutions, historic colonial architecture, museums, marketplaces and a major port central to tourism and commerce.

Freeport (founded 1955) Located on Grand Bahama Island, Freeport is a centre for commerce, shipping and tourism. It hosts a free-trade zone, industrial facilities and cultural sites, playing a key role in the economic development and international trade of The Bahamas.

Exuma Cays A chain of over 365 islands and cays known for turquoise waters, white sand beaches and marine biodiversity. The Exuma Cays attract tourists, divers and sailors, highlighting The Bahamas' natural beauty, eco-tourism opportunities and luxury travel offerings.

Harbour Island Renowned for its pink sand beaches and historic settlements, Harbour Island combines natural beauty with local culture. It attracts tourists seeking leisure, history and traditional Bahamian experiences, supporting the island's economy and preserving its unique heritage.

Andros Island The largest island in The Bahamas andros is famous for its blue holes, barrier reef and ecological diversity. It supports eco-tourism, scientific research and conservation efforts while preserving traditional lifestyles, agriculture and marine ecosystems.

Abaco Islands A northern chain of islands and cays known for sailing, boating and natural scenery. The Abaco Islands contribute to the country's tourism economy, showcase ecological diversity and preserve local culture, fishing communities and recreational activities across the archipelago.

TIMELINE OF EVENTS

c. 1500 BCE: First Indigenous Settlements: Lucayan Taíno peoples settled the islands of the Bahamas, developing fishing, farming and trade networks, with organised communities long before European contact.

1492: Columbus Arrives in the Bahamas: Christopher Columbus made his first landfall in the Americas on an island in the Bahamas, marking the beginning of European awareness of the region.

1520s: Decline of the Lucayan Population: Disease, enslavement and Spanish raids led to the rapid decline of the Lucayan Taíno population across the islands.

1648: English Settlement at Eleuthera: English Puritans, known as the Eleutheran Adventurers, established the first lasting European settlement, promoting Protestantism and self-governance.

1670: Bahamas Becomes a British Crown Colony: The islands were formally incorporated into the British Empire, establishing colonial administration and maritime control.

1718: Piracy Suppressed: The Royal Navy eradicated piracy in the Bahamas, securing trade routes and strengthening colonial governance.

1783: Loyalist Migration: After the American Revolutionary War, Loyalists settled in the Bahamas, bringing enslaved Africans and establishing plantations.

1834: Abolition of Slavery: The British Empire abolished slavery, transforming social, economic and political structures across the islands.

1862: Nassau Becomes the Colonial Capital: Nassau developed as the administrative, commercial and cultural centre of the Bahamas under British rule.

1950s: Push for Self-Government: Political movements advocating greater autonomy and social reform began gaining momentum in the Bahamas.

1964: Internal Self-Government Achieved: The Bahamas gained control over domestic affairs, establishing a ministerial government while Britain retained foreign affairs and defence.

1973: Independence from Britain: The Bahamas became an independent Commonwealth nation, joining the Commonwealth of Nations while retaining the British monarch as head of state.

1980s: Tourism and Financial Sector Growth: Economic development focused on tourism, offshore banking and international trade, increasing prosperity and global connections.

1990s: Environmental Conservation Efforts: Policies were implemented to protect marine life, coral reefs and natural habitats while promoting sustainable tourism.

2010: International Recognition for Tourism: The Bahamas gained global recognition for luxury tourism, cultural festivals and ecological initiatives.

2019: Climate Change Focus: Rising sea levels and hurricanes highlighted the Bahamas' vulnerability, prompting national and international climate advocacy.

2020: COVID-19 Pandemic Impact: The pandemic severely affected tourism, public health and the economy, demonstrating the islands' reliance on global travel and trade.

THE REPUBLIC OF CUBA

Cuba occupies the largest island in the Caribbean Sea, positioned at the entrance to the Gulf of Mexico and bordered by the Straits of Florida and the Windward Passage. With an estimated population of over 11 million people, the capital city is Havana, while regional centres such as Santiago de Cuba and Camagüey exert major cultural and historical influence. Spanish is the official national language. The Cuban Peso serves as the national currency. Shaped by millennia of Indigenous civilisations, Spanish colonisation, the African diaspora, revolution and a protracted geopolitical standoff, the nation blends deep historical roots with a distinctive political path. Its strategic location, cultural richness and social policies contribute significantly to its regional stature and national character. This combination of historical depth and revolutionary ideology defines the identity of Cuba.

Geography

Spanning a long and narrow island with over 4,000 surrounding cays and keys, Cuba features varied geographical diversity. It includes vast lowland plains, rugged mountain systems such as the Sierra Maestra—home to the highest point, Pico Turquino (1,974 m)—and the unique limestone landscapes of the Sierra de los Órganos. The country's extensive coastline, over 5,700 km long, is dotted with white-sand beaches, coral reefs and vital mangrove ecosystems like the Zapata Swamp. Major waterways are limited, with the Cauto River being the longest. The climate is tropical, moderated by trade winds, with a distinct wet season from May to October and a risk of hurricanes. Natural hazards, particularly tropical cyclones, significantly shape regional life. The country hosts remarkable biodiversity, including many endemic species, though ecosystems face pressure from climate change, which brings increased temperatures, sea-level rise and shifting rainfall patterns. Conservation efforts in marine protected areas remain central to preserving the nation's natural heritage.

History

The history of Cuba begins thousands of years before European contact with the cultures of the Guanahatabey, Ciboney and Taíno peoples. European exploration began in 1492 with Christopher Columbus, leading to Spanish conquest and settlement in the early 16th century. The colonial economy, built on sugar plantations and sustained by the transatlantic slave trade, defined centuries of Spanish rule, interrupted only by a brief British occupation of Havana in 1762. A series of wars for independence in the late 19th century culminated in U.S. intervention in the Spanish-American War and the end of Spanish rule in 1898. Following a period of U.S. military administration, Cuba gained formal independence in 1902, though it remained under strong American influence. The 20th century was marked by political instability and dictatorship until the 1959 Cuban Revolution, led by Fidel Castro, established a socialist state aligned with the Soviet Union. The subsequent Cold War era was defined by the U.S. embargo, the 1961 Bay of Pigs invasion and the 1962 Cuban Missile Crisis. The collapse of the Soviet Union plunged Cuba into a severe economic crisis known as the Special Period in the 1990s. Modern Cuba continues to navigate economic challenges and a complex relationship with the United States while maintaining its socialist system.

Government and Politics

Cuba is a single-party Marxist–Leninist socialist republic, with the Communist Party of Cuba constitutionally designated as the 'leading force of society and of the state'. Government authority is centralised, with the country divided into provinces and municipalities. The political system comprises three branches: executive, legislative and judicial. Executive power is vested in the President, who is head of state and the Council of Ministers. Legislative power rests with the unicameral National Assembly of People's Power. The judiciary is headed by the People's Supreme Court. Elections are held for the National Assembly and municipal assemblies, with suffrage universal for citizens aged 16 and older; voting is legally mandatory. Political life is characterised by the absence of legal opposition parties and mass organisations like the Committees for the Defense of the Revolution play a significant role in social control. Domestically, debates centre on economic management, while internationally Cuba maintains a policy of opposing U.S. influence and engaging with global allies.

Economy

Cuba possesses a centrally planned, state-controlled economy. Key sectors include professional services, tourism and the export of medical services, nickel, tobacco and sugar. The nation has developed significant biotechnological and pharmaceutical industries. Agriculture remains important, though the country imports a substantial portion of its food. Persistent economic challenges include low productivity, infrastructure decay, scarcity of consumer goods and the long-standing U.S. trade embargo. The economy operates with a dual currency system, though recent reforms have sought to unify it. The Cuban Peso (CUP) is the primary national currency. The economy has been deeply affected by the loss of Soviet subsidies and relies on strategic partnerships for fuel and investment. Continued reform, foreign investment and increased agricultural output are viewed as essential for improving economic conditions.

Demographics and Society

With a population of approximately 11 million, Cuba is the most populous island nation in the Caribbean. The population is moderately urbanised, concentrated in cities like Havana, Santiago de Cuba and Camagüey. Cuban society is fundamentally shaped by a history of colonisation, slavery and revolution, resulting in a multiracial population of primarily European, African and mixed descent. Spanish is the universal language. Relatively high social development indicators, such as literacy and life expectancy, coexist with significant challenges, including low wages, limited political freedoms and difficulties in obtaining basic necessities. The concepts of social equality, national sovereignty and resilience remain central to the national ethos.

Culture

Cuban culture has achieved profound global recognition, shaped by its diverse population, island setting and revolutionary history. Indigenous remnants, Spanish colonial heritage and deep African influences form essential cultural foundations, particularly in music, dance and religion. Literature, visual arts, cinema and dance from Cuba enjoy international acclaim. Music, such as son, rumba and salsa, is ubiquitous and influential. Sport plays a major role in national life, particularly baseball, which is the dominant sport. Cultural expression frequently explores themes of identity, love, hardship and social justice. While deeply influenced by its own history and global trends, Cuban culture continues to evolve with state support and within the framework of its political system, reflecting ongoing debates about cultural identity and autonomy.

Education and Healthcare

Cuba maintains a state-operated and fully subsidised education system, encompassing all levels from primary to university. It has one of the highest literacy rates in the world and is home to extensive medical training facilities, attracting international students, particularly in medicine. Education is managed at the national level, with a strong emphasis on ideology and technical training. Healthcare operates through a universal, free public system with an extensive network of community-based clinics and hospitals. The system is credited with achieving health indicators comparable to developed nations, including low infant mortality. Challenges include shortages of medical supplies, outdated equipment and the strain of providing international medical missions. Policy debates focus on maintaining quality amidst economic constraints.

Infrastructure

Infrastructure across Cuba reflects both historical investment and protracted economic challenges. An extensive central railway and road network connects major towns, though maintenance and vehicle availability are persistent issues. Major ports in Havana, Santiago de Cuba and Cienfuegos facilitate trade. Digital infrastructure has limited bandwidth, with state-controlled internet access, though mobile data availability has increased. Energy systems rely heavily on imported fossil fuels, with frequent outages, prompting investments in renewable sources like solar power. Infrastructure priorities include upgrading the electrical grid, improving public transportation and increasing housing stock. Balancing development needs with limited resources remains a national challenge.

Tourism

Tourism is a vital contributor to the Cuban economy, offering a distinct blend of attractions. Natural landmarks include the Viñales Valley, the beaches of Varadero and the coral reefs of Jardines de la Reina archipelago. Iconic cities such as Havana, Trinidad and Santiago de Cuba provide renowned cultural, historical and architectural experiences. Activities like music, classic car tours and hiking attract visitors. Historic sites from the colonial, sugar plantation and revolutionary eras offer insight into the nation's complex past. Tourism development increasingly aims to attract foreign investment while managing social impacts.

Current Issues and Future Outlook

Cuba faces profound challenges alongside distinctive strengths. Navigating a severe and protracted economic crisis, managing the effects of the U.S. embargo and addressing pressing issues like housing shortages, low wages and outward migration remain central national concerns. Internationally, balancing relationships with traditional allies and seeking new economic partnerships require careful diplomatic engagement. At the same time, the country benefits from a highly educated workforce, a strong sense of national identity and proven social resilience. The future outlook depends on the pace and success of domestic economic reforms, the evolution of U.S.-Cuba relations and managing the generational transition in political leadership. How effectively these issues are managed will shape Cuba's social stability and role in the region in the decades ahead.

Overview

Cuba is a nation defined by its revolutionary ideology, cultural potency and enduring defiance. Rooted in a tumultuous colonial past and decisively shaped by the Cold War, it has emerged as a unique and influential socialist state in the Americas. Its island geography presents both strategic importance and vulnerability. Moving forward, the nation seeks to preserve its socialist system and social gains while overcoming deep economic hardships and engaging with a changing world. Continued adaptation, amid sustained external pressure and internal debate, remains key to determining the future of Cuba.

DID YOU KNOW...?

Cuba is home to one of the world's most extensive and well-preserved systems of colonial fortifications. The Castillo de los Tres Reyes Magos del Morro in Havana, completed in 1630, was built to defend the Spanish treasure fleet from pirates and rival empires. Its strategic location at the entrance to Havana Bay allowed it to control all maritime traffic. Following the British capture of Havana in 1762 via a landward attack, an even larger fortress, La Cabaña, was constructed alongside it. These monumental structures, now UNESCO World Heritage sites, stand as stark symbols of colonial power, imperial rivalry and the immense wealth that once flowed through the Spanish Main.

KEY FACTS AND FIGURES

Geography & Environment

• Total area: 109,884 km² (largest island in the Caribbean).

• Coastline: ≈5,746 km.

• Climate: Tropical, with a wet and dry season; hurricane-prone.

• Highest point: Pico Turquino (1,974 m).

• Major features: Sierra Maestra mountains, fertile plains, extensive coral reefs and wetlands.

• Wildlife: Cuban crocodile, hutia, flamingos, manatees, diverse bird species.

• 9 UNESCO World Heritage sites.

Population & Society

• Population: ≈11.1 million (2024 estimate).

• Density: ≈101 persons/km².

• Urbanisation: ≈78%.

• Ethnicity:

o White: ≈64%

o Mixed (Mulatto/Mestizo): ≈27%

o Black: ≈9%

• Languages: Spanish (official).

• Religion: Christian and folk religions (Roman Catholic, Protestant, Santería): ≈60–65%; significant non-religious population.

• Literacy: ≈99%.

• Life expectancy: ≈78 years.

Economy

• GDP (nominal): ≈£90 billion.

• GDP per capita (PPP): ≈£9,000.

• Key industries:

o State services and public administration

o Tourism

o Biotechnology and pharmaceuticals

o Agriculture (sugar, tobacco)

• Major exports: Medical products, nickel, tobacco, sugar.
• Currency: Cuban peso (CUP).

Government
• Socialist republic.
• System: One-party socialist state.
• Head of State: President of Cuba.
• Head of Government: Prime Minister of Cuba.
• Legislature: National Assembly of People's Power (470 members).

Infrastructure
• Transport: National road and rail networks; air and sea transport.
• Major airports: José Martí International Airport (Havana).
• Energy mix: Predominantly fossil fuels; growing solar and biomass use.
• Digital connectivity: Improving in urban areas; limited speed and access compared to regional peers.

Major Urban Centres
• Havana: ≈2.1 million – Capital, political and cultural centre.
• Santiago de Cuba: ≈500,000 – Major eastern city and port.
• Camagüey: ≈300,000 – Agricultural and regional centre.
• Holguín: ≈350,000 – Industrial and tourism hub.

HAVANA – CUBA'S CAPITAL, POLITICAL AND CULTURAL CENTRE

The National Flag

The national flag of the Republic of Cuba features five alternating horizontal stripes of blue and white, with a red equilateral triangle at the hoist bearing a single white star. The three blue stripes symbolise the three old administrative departments of the island, while the two white stripes represent the purity of the independence cause. The red triangle denotes the blood shed for freedom and the white star signifies independence itself. The flag as a whole embodies Cuba's struggle for liberty, its unity as a nation and its sovereign future.

KEY PEOPLE AND PLACES

PEOPLE

José Martí (1853–1895) Widely regarded as the 'Apostle of Cuban Independence,' he was a poet, journalist and revolutionary leader who dedicated his life to freeing Cuba from Spanish colonial rule, inspiring generations of Cubans and Latin Americans with his vision of justice and liberty.

Fidel Castro (1926–2016) A revolutionary and political leader who served as Prime Minister and later President of Cuba from 1959 to 2008, he led the Cuban Revolution, establishing a socialist state and profoundly shaping Cuba's domestic policies and international relations.

Che Guevara (1928–1967) An Argentine-born revolutionary, he became a key figure in the Cuban Revolution, assisting in overthrowing the Batista regime, implementing reforms and later promoting socialist and anti-imperialist movements throughout Latin America, leaving a lasting legacy.

Raúl Castro (b. 1931) Brother of Fidel Castro, he served as Cuba's President from 2008 to 2018, overseeing gradual economic reforms, maintaining socialist governance, continuing revolutionary policies and representing Cuba in international diplomacy and regional cooperation initiatives.

Camilo Cienfuegos (1932–1959) A charismatic revolutionary leader during the Cuban Revolution, remembered for his bravery, popularity and role in the successful overthrow of the Batista government, becoming a symbol of courage, loyalty and revolutionary spirit in Cuba.

Nicolás Guillén (1902–1989) Cuba's national poet, known for his Afro-Cuban poetry and literary contributions, celebrating Cuban identity, culture and social justice, while highlighting the lives of ordinary people and advocating for equality and cultural pride in the nation.

PLACES

Havana (founded 1519) The capital and largest city of Cuba, located on the northern coast, serving as the nation's cultural, political and economic centre, renowned for its colonial architecture, historic old town, music, art and vibrant urban life.

Trinidad (founded 1514) A UNESCO World Heritage site, this colonial town is famous for its cobbled streets, pastel-coloured buildings and preservation of 18th- and 19th-century architecture, offering a rich cultural experience and insight into Cuba's colonial past.

Santiago de Cuba (founded 1515) The country's second-largest city, a historic centre of Afro-Cuban culture and music and a key location in Cuba's revolutionary history, known for its festivals, architecture and vibrant local traditions.

Viñales Valley A scenic limestone valley in western Cuba, renowned for its tobacco plantations, mogotes (karst hills) and agricultural heritage, recognised as a UNESCO World Heritage site, attracting tourists, researchers and nature enthusiasts from around the world.

Varadero One of the Caribbean's most famous beach destinations, known for its white sands, clear waters, luxury resorts, recreational activities and international tourism appeal, contributing significantly to Cuba's economy and global reputation as a tropical paradise.

Baracoa (founded 1512) Cuba's oldest Spanish settlement, located on the eastern coast, notable for its rich cultural traditions, tropical landscapes, historic architecture and unique heritage, representing the early colonial history and enduring local identity of the region.

TIMELINE OF EVENTS

c. 5000–2000 BCE: Early Indigenous Settlements: Taíno and Ciboney peoples settled Cuba, developing agriculture, fishing, trade networks and organised communities before European contact.

1492: Columbus Arrives in Cuba: Christopher Columbus reached Cuba, marking European contact, mapping the island and beginning future colonisation.

1511: Spanish Conquest Begins: Spanish forces led by Diego Velázquez conquered Indigenous communities, establishing colonial rule, European governance, religion and agriculture systems.

1514: Havana Founded: Havana became a central port of trade, administration, military defence and Spanish control in the Caribbean.

1762–1763: British Occupation: Britain briefly occupied Havana during the Seven Years' War, returning it to Spain under the Treaty of Paris.

1868–1878: Ten Years' War: Cuba's first independence war against Spain involved widespread fighting, destruction and foundations for later revolutionary movements.

1895–1898: Cuban War of Independence: José Martí and other leaders renewed independence struggles, challenging Spanish rule and inspiring revolutionary activity.

1898: Spanish-American War: US intervention defeated Spain, ending Spanish colonial control, increasing American political, economic and military influence in Cuba.

1902: Republic of Cuba Established: Cuba became an independent republic, though the Platt Amendment gave the United States substantial political and military influence.

1933: Revolution and Machado's Fall: Popular uprisings overthrew President Machado, triggering political instability, reforms and social and governmental transformations.

1953–1959: Cuban Revolution: Fidel Castro's forces overthrew Batista, establishing socialism and transforming Cuba's society, politics, economy and international relations.

1961: Bay of Pigs Invasion: United States-backed exiles attempted to overthrow Castro, but the invasion failed, strengthening Cuba's revolutionary government internationally.

1962: Cuban Missile Crisis: Soviet missiles in Cuba made Cold War confrontations, nearly causing global nuclear conflict with the US.

1970s–1980s: Socialist Consolidation: Cuba aligned with the Soviet Union, focusing on social programmes, healthcare, education, infrastructure and international diplomatic influence.

1991–1994: Special Period: Soviet collapse caused severe economic hardship, prompting rationing, reforms and adaptation to reduced trade, resources and production.

2008: Raul Castro Presidency: Leadership passed to Raul Castro, introducing gradual economic and political reforms while maintaining Cuba's socialist governance identity.

2015: US-Cuba Diplomatic Thaw: Diplomatic relations partially restored with the United States, easing restrictions, promoting trade, tourism and global engagement.

2020: COVID-19 Pandemic Impact: The pandemic disrupted healthcare systems, tourism, the economy and daily life, testing Cuba's resilience and public health capacity.

JAMAICA

Jamaica is a mountainous tropical island located in the Caribbean Sea, situated approximately 145 kilometres south of Cuba. With an estimated population of around 2.8 million people, the capital city is Kingston, while major centres such as Montego Bay, Ocho Rios and Spanish Town are significant economic and tourism hubs. English is the official national language, with the English-based creole, Jamaican Patois, widely spoken across the island. The Jamaican Dollar serves as the national currency. Shaped by millennia of Indigenous Taino civilisation, Spanish and later British colonisation, the plantation economy and the African diaspora, the nation blends deep historical roots with vibrant cultural development. Its renowned music, athletic prowess, tourism appeal and diaspora influence contribute significantly to its international stature. This combination of resilience, creativity and cultural strength defines the identity of Jamaica.

Geography

Spanning a compact but topographically dramatic landscape, Jamaica features remarkable geographical diversity for its size. The island is dominated by a central spine of mountains, most notably the Blue Mountains in the east, which contain the highest point, Blue Mountain Peak, at 2,256 metres. The interior features a unique karst landscape, with the Cockpit Country in the west showcasing dramatic conical hills and sinkholes. The coastline stretches for 1,022 kilometres, offering a contrast between the calm seas and white-sand beaches of the north and the rugged cliffs and black sand beaches of the south. Major rivers include the Black River, the longest, which courses through the Great Morass wetlands in the southwest. The climate is tropical, with a wet season from May to October, moderated by trade winds. The country is highly biodiverse, with many endemic species like the swallow-tail hummingbird, but faces natural hazards from hurricanes. Environmental issues include deforestation and coastal water pollution.

History

The history of Jamaica begins with the Taino people, who arrived from South America centuries before European contact, calling the island Xaymaca, 'land of wood and water'. European contact began with Christopher Columbus in 1494, leading to Spanish settlement and the decimation of the Taino population. The British captured the island in 1655, establishing a brutal plantation economy based on sugar and sustained by the transatlantic slave trade. Jamaica became one of the largest slave markets in the Western Hemisphere. Slavery was abolished in 1838 and the 20th century saw the rise of a movement for self-government. Jamaica gained full independence from the United Kingdom in 1962. The post-independence era has been shaped by a two-party democratic system, economic challenges and the powerful global influence of its culture, particularly reggae music. Modern Jamaica continues to navigate issues of economic development, social equity and its role in the Caribbean community.

Government and Politics

Jamaica is a unitary parliamentary democracy and a constitutional monarchy, with the British monarch as the ceremonial head of state represented by a Governor-General. Government authority is central, with local administration through 14 parishes. The political system comprises three branches: executive, legislative and judicial. Executive power is vested in the Prime Minister and the Cabinet, drawn from the elected House of Representatives. Legislative power rests with the bicameral Parliament, consisting of the elected House of Representatives and the appointed Senate. The judiciary, headed by the Court of Appeal, is independent and based on English common law. Political life is characterised by two dominant national parties, the Jamaica Labour Party (JLP) and the People's National Party (PNP). Domestically, debates centre on economic management, crime and public services, while internationally Jamaica maintains active membership in the Commonwealth, CARICOM and the United Nations.

Economy

Jamaica possesses a mixed but service-dominated economy, with tourism, remittances and bauxite/alumina as traditional pillars. The services sector accounts for over 70% of GDP. Key industries beyond tourism include agriculture (sugarcane, bananas, coffee), mining (bauxite, alumina, gypsum) and light manufacturing. Despite its strengths, the economy has been characterised by low growth over decades, high public debt and vulnerability to external shocks like hurricanes. The Jamaican Dollar is the national currency, managed by the Bank of Jamaica. The economy is deeply integrated with those of the United States and Canada, both key trading partners and sources of tourist arrivals and remittances. Continued efforts at fiscal reform, attracting foreign investment and promoting sectors like information technology are viewed as essential for improving long-term economic resilience.

Demographics and Society

With a population of approximately 2.8 million, Jamaica is the third most populous anglophone country in the Americas. The population is predominantly of African descent, a legacy of the transatlantic slave trade, with smaller minorities of mixed, East Indian, Chinese and European descent. The national motto, 'Out of Many, One People,' reflects this multi-ethnic heritage. Society is highly urbanised, with about one-third of all Jamaicans living in the capital, Kingston. English is the official language, but Jamaican Patois is the lingua franca of daily life. Religious life is diverse, with Christianity predominating and the Rastafari movement holding significant cultural influence. Social challenges include managing crime, poverty and economic inequality, but the society is also known for its strong family structures, religious conviction and community spirit.

Culture

Jamaican culture has achieved profound global recognition, shaped by its history, African roots and spirit of resilience and innovation. It is most famously expressed through music, with genres like ska, rocksteady and especially reggae and dancehall enjoying worldwide popularity. The global icon Bob Marley remains its most famous ambassador. Cuisine is another cultural pillar, featuring dishes like jerk chicken, ackee and saltfish (the national dish) and curry goat. The Rastafari movement, with its distinct philosophy, use of language and symbolism (such as the colours red, gold and green), is an internationally recognised aspect of Jamaican identity. Jamaican Patois is a rich vehicle for oral traditions, poetry and song. Sport is central to national life, with athletics (sprinters in particular) and cricket commanding massive followings and international success.

Education and Healthcare

Jamaica maintains an education system based on the British model, encompassing primary, secondary and tertiary levels. Literacy rates are relatively high. The University of the West Indies, Mona campus, is a major regional institution. Healthcare operates through a public system offering universal access, supplemented by private providers. The system provides basic care but can be strained by resource limitations. Key public health challenges include managing non-communicable diseases like diabetes and hypertension. Policy discussions often focus on improving the quality and reach of education and healthcare services across all parishes.

Infrastructure

Infrastructure across Jamaica reflects the challenges and opportunities of its island geography. A main highway network circles the island and connects key north-south routes, though rural roads can be less developed. The country's last major passenger railway service was suspended in the 1990s, though limited lines serve the bauxite industry. Major ports in Kingston and Montego Bay and international airports in these cities, facilitate tourism and trade. Energy systems have traditionally relied on imported fossil fuels, driving efforts to diversify with liquefied natural gas (LNG) and renewable sources. Broadband internet access is good in urban areas but variable in rural regions. Infrastructure priorities include improving water supply reliability and building resilience against natural disasters.

Tourism

Tourism is the primary engine of the Jamaican economy and an essential part of its global identity. Natural attractions include the renowned white-sand beaches of Negril and Montego Bay, the dramatic Dunn's River Falls near Ocho Rios and the misty heights of the Blue Mountains. Iconic cities such as Kingston and the colonial capital of Spanish Town provide cultural and historical experiences, from reggae museums to historic Georgian architecture. Activities like river rafting on the Martha Brae, visiting Great Houses (plantations) and experiencing vibrant nightlife attract millions of visitors annually. Sustainable tourism and community-based tourism initiatives are increasingly important, aiming to better distribute economic benefits.

Current Issues and Future Outlook

Jamaica faces a clear set of challenges alongside its world-renowned strengths. Tackling high levels of violent crime, reducing public debt, fostering stronger and more equitable economic growth and building climate resilience against hurricanes and coastal erosion remain central national concerns. Internationally, navigating global economic volatility and maintaining strong diaspora links are key. At the same time, the country benefits from immense cultural soft power, a stable democratic system and a strategic location. The future outlook depends on successful implementation of economic reforms, investments in human capital and infrastructure and leveraging its unique cultural assets. How effectively these issues are managed will shape Jamaica's prosperity and social stability in the decades ahead.

Overview

Jamaica is a nation defined by its cultural might, athletic brilliance and complex post-colonial journey. Rooted in a painful history of plantation slavery and shaped by a triumphant struggle for independence and identity, it has emerged as a disproportionate global influencer. Its island geography presents both a tourism paradise and developmental challenges. Moving forward, the nation seeks to harness its creative energy and spirit to overcome socio-economic hurdles while sustaining its democratic institutions and unique place in the world. Continued focus on inclusive growth, security and innovation remains key to ensuring a resilient and prosperous future for Jamaica.

DID YOU KNOW...?

Jamaica is the birthplace of one of the world's fastest land animals, the Jamaican national animal, the Doctor Bird or Swallow-tail Hummingbird. This spectacular endemic species, noted for its long, forked tail and iridescent feathers, is found nowhere else on Earth. It is celebrated in Jamaican folklore and culture, believed to be a reincarnated spirit of the Taino people and seen as a symbol of good luck. Its image is prominent on the national coat of arms and it is fiercely protected. This small, dazzling bird stands as a vibrant symbol of the island's unique biodiversity, rich heritage and enduring spirit.

KEY FACTS AND FIGURES

Geography & Environment

• Total area: 10,991 km².

• Coastline: ≈1,022 km.

• Climate: Tropical, with a wet and dry season; hurricane-prone.

• Highest point: Blue Mountain Peak (2,256 m).

• Major features: Mountains, fertile plains, limestone plateaus, coral reefs.

• Wildlife: Jamaican iguana, crocodiles, hummingbirds (including the national bird, the Doctor Bird).

• 1 UNESCO World Heritage site.

Population & Society

• Population: ≈2.9 million (2024 estimate).

• Density: ≈265 persons/km².

• Urbanisation: ≈56%.

• Ethnicity:

o Black: ≈92%

o Mixed: ≈6%

o Other: ≈2%

• Languages: English (official); Jamaican Patois widely spoken.

• Religion: Christian (predominantly Protestant): ≈85–90%.

• Literacy: ≈88%.

• Life expectancy: ≈75 years.

Economy

• GDP (nominal): ≈£13 billion.

• GDP per capita (PPP): ≈£11,000.

• Key industries:

o Tourism

o Mining (bauxite and alumina)

o Agriculture (sugar, bananas, coffee)

o Manufacturing and services

• Major exports: Alumina, bauxite, sugar, coffee, rum.

• Currency: Jamaican dollar (JMD; £1 ≈ 200 JMD).

Government

- Constitutional monarchy (Commonwealth realm).
- System: Parliamentary democracy.
- Head of State: King Charles III.
- Head of Government: Prime Minister of Jamaica.
- Parliament: Bicameral Parliament (House of Representatives and Senate).

Infrastructure

- Transport: Road-based transport network; no rail; air and sea transport.
- Major airports: Norman Manley International Airport, Sangster International Airport.
- Energy mix: Predominantly fossil fuels; growing renewable energy.
- Digital connectivity: Moderate, with better access in urban areas.

Major Urban Centres

- Kingston: ≈670,000 (metro) – Capital and cultural centre.
- Spanish Town: ≈160,000 – Historic former capital.
- Montego Bay: ≈150,000 – Major tourism hub.
- Portmore: ≈180,000 – Large residential and commercial city.

KINGSTON – JAMAICA'S CAPITAL AND CULTURAL CENTRE

The National Flag

The national flag of Jamaica, known as 'The Cross,' consists of a gold (or yellow) saltire (diagonal cross) dividing the flag into four triangles. The top and bottom triangles are green, representing hope and agricultural wealth. The hoist and fly triangles are black, symbolising the strength and creativity of the people. It is one of only two national flags in the world that does not feature the colours red, white or blue (the other being Mauritania's).

KEY PEOPLE AND PLACES

PEOPLE

Marcus Garvey (1887–1940) Widely regarded as a national hero, he was a political leader, publisher and activist who promoted Pan-Africanism, the empowerment of people of African descent worldwide and self-determination, inspiring global movements for racial pride, economic independence and social justice.

Alexander Bustamante (1884–1977) The first Prime Minister of independent Jamaica, serving from 1962 to 1967, he was a labour leader and founder of the Jamaica Labour Party, playing a decisive role in the country's independence, political development and early social reforms.

Norman Manley (1893–1969) A key political figure and founder of the People's National Party, he led constitutional reforms, advocated for self-governance and helped lay the foundations for Jamaica's democratic institutions and eventual independence from British colonial rule.

Bob Marley (1945–1981) An internationally renowned musician and cultural icon, he popularised reggae music globally, became a symbol of Jamaican identity, peace and social justice and used his art to promote awareness of oppression, spirituality and the struggles of ordinary people.

Mary Seacole (1805–1881) Of Jamaican and Scottish heritage, she was a pioneering nurse and humanitarian, celebrated for her work during the Crimean War, inspiring Jamaican contributions to medicine and care and promoting public health and compassionate nursing practices internationally.

Usain Bolt (b. 1986) The world's fastest sprinter, Olympic champion and national hero, he brought international acclaim to Jamaica in athletics, breaking multiple world records, inspiring generations of athletes and raising global awareness of Jamaica's sporting talent and excellence.

PLACES

Kingston (founded 1692) The capital and largest city of Jamaica, located on the southeastern coast, serving as the nation's political, economic and cultural centre, featuring historic sites, music venues, bustling markets and the heart of Jamaican artistic and commercial life.

Montego Bay A major tourist destination on the northwestern coast, famous for its white sand beaches, luxury resorts, cruise ports, recreational facilities and vibrant nightlife, contributing significantly to Jamaica's economy, tourism industry and international recognition.

Negril Famous for its Seven Mile Beach, dramatic cliffs and relaxed atmosphere, Negril is a major destination for eco-tourism, leisure and beach-focused holidays, attracting visitors from around the world seeking natural beauty and Caribbean culture.

Port Antonio A scenic coastal town on the northeastern coast, known for its lush tropical landscapes, Blue Lagoon, waterfalls, historical sites and cultural heritage, attracting tourists, filmmakers and nature enthusiasts seeking adventure and authentic local experiences.

Blue Mountains A mountain range in eastern Jamaica, celebrated for its biodiversity, hiking trails, world-famous Blue Mountain coffee and scenic landscapes, forming an essential part of Jamaica's natural heritage, agriculture, eco-tourism and outdoor recreational activities.

Spanish Town (founded 1534) Jamaica's former capital and historic city, notable for colonial architecture, old churches, civic buildings and its role in the island's early governance under Spanish and later British rule, preserving centuries of political, religious and cultural history.

TIMELINE OF EVENTS

c. 600–1500 CE: Indigenous Settlements: Taíno peoples settled Jamaica, developing agriculture, fishing, trade networks, villages and complex social organisation, thriving long before European contact occurred.

1494: Columbus Arrives in Jamaica: Christopher Columbus landed in Jamaica, marking European contact, mapping the island, initiating colonisation and beginning Spanish influence over the region.

1509–1655: Spanish Rule Established: Spain colonised Jamaica, introducing European governance, Catholic religion, agriculture and enslaving Indigenous populations, profoundly reshaping society, economy and culture on the island.

1655: British Conquest of Jamaica: Britain captured Jamaica from Spain, establishing plantations, using enslaved African labour and creating a long-lasting colonial administration across the island.

1670: Treaty of Madrid: Spain formally ceded Jamaica to Britain, confirming British control, reinforcing the island's strategic importance and ensuring its position in Caribbean trade.

1713–1807: Expansion of Plantation Economy: Sugar and coffee plantations expanded rapidly, driven by enslaved African labour, making Jamaica a central economic and colonial power in the Caribbean.

1834: Abolition of Slavery: Enslaved Africans were emancipated under British law, transforming Jamaica's society, economy, plantation structures and initiating significant social and political changes.

1865: Morant Bay Rebellion: A major uprising highlighted social inequalities and injustice, leading to harsher colonial control but eventual reforms in governance and society.

1944: Universal Adult Suffrage Introduced: Voting rights were extended to most adults, paving the way for democratic participation, political representation and local leadership development.

1962: Independence from Britain: Jamaica became an independent nation within the Commonwealth, establishing its own government while retaining symbolic ties to the British monarchy.

1970s–1980s: Political and Economic Challenges: Jamaica faced economic instability, social unrest, political tension and challenges while pursuing industrialisation, development and modernisation strategies.

1990s: Economic and Social Reform: Structural adjustments, investment in tourism and social programmes improved infrastructure, public services, economic stability and global integration across Jamaica.

2010: Natural Disaster Recovery: Hurricanes and tropical storms caused severe damage, prompting Jamaica to strengthen disaster preparedness, resilience strategies and emergency response systems nationwide.

2020: COVID-19 Pandemic Impact: The pandemic disrupted tourism, trade, public health and daily life, testing Jamaica's healthcare, economy and social resilience extensively.

THE REPUBLIC OF HAITI

Haiti, known in Haitian Creole as Ayiti, is the Caribbean's second-largest island nation, occupying the western third of the island of Hispaniola, east of Cuba and south-east of the Bahamas. It is a sovereign republic. The national. With an estimated population of around 11.5 million people, the capital and largest city is Port-au-Prince, which serves as the political, economic and cultural centre. Haitian Creole (Kreyòl) and French are the official languages. The Haitian gourde is the official currency. Shaped by Indigenous Taíno civilisation, French colonial rule and the legacy of the world's first successful slave revolution, Haiti blends deep African-derived traditions with a complex post-colonial history. Its tropical environment, strategic location and vibrant culture contrast with profound socio-economic challenges. This balance between a proud heritage and contemporary struggle defines the identity of Haiti.

Geography

Haiti spans a rugged tropical landscape dominated by mountain ranges and coastal plains. Approximately two-thirds of the territory is mountainous, with the Massif de la Selle rising to the country's highest point at Pic la Selle. The coastline is indented with bays and coves, while fertile valleys support agriculture. Deforestation is severe, with less than 3% of original forest cover remaining. The climate is predominantly tropical, with warm temperatures year-round and a rainy season from April to October. Natural hazards include earthquakes, hurricanes, flooding and droughts, which frequently devastate infrastructure and agriculture. Haiti hosts unique Caribbean biodiversity, though habitat loss is acute, making environmental restoration a critical concern.

History

The history of Haiti extends back to Indigenous Taíno settlements, followed by Spanish claim in 1492. The western part of the island was ceded to France in the 17th century, becoming the wealthy colony of Saint-Domingue. Enslaved Africans, through the Haitian Revolution (1791–1804), overthrew the system, establishing the world's first black republic and the second independent nation in the Americas. The 19th and 20th centuries were marked by political instability, foreign intervention (including a US occupation from 1915–1934) and authoritarian rule. Modern Haiti continues to navigate the legacy of revolution, international isolation and socio-political turmoil while strengthening national identity and democratic self-determination.

Government and Politics

Haiti operates as a unitary semi-presidential republic, with its own parliament, the National Assembly and government, headed by a Prime Minister. The head of state is the President. Political life is characterised by frequent upheaval, institutional fragility and debates over governance, security, economic development and the role of international aid. Democratic processes are often disrupted by crises, though community resilience and civil society engagement remain central to the political landscape in a densely populated and vibrant society.

Economy

Haiti's economy is the poorest in the Western Hemisphere, characterised by informal activity and significant external aid dependence. Agriculture, particularly coffee and mangoes, remains a key sector alongside textile manufacturing and remittances from the diaspora, which form a critical financial backbone. International donors provide substantial financial support. In recent years, interest has grown in potential tourism and light industry, though these are hampered by instability. Environmental degradation and natural disasters pose severe risks to traditional livelihoods. Challenges include extreme poverty, high unemployment, reliance on imports and balancing reconstruction with long-term development. Sustainable growth remains a central, yet elusive, economic objective.

Demographics and Society

With a population of approximately 11.5 million, Haiti is among the most densely populated nations in the Caribbean. Most residents are of African descent, with a small minority of mixed European and African ancestry. The population is concentrated in urban coastal areas and the central plains. Haitian culture emphasises community, spiritual faith and resilience in the face of adversity. While a small elite enjoys relative wealth, challenges include widespread poverty, limited access to basic services, health crises and rural-urban divides. Language, Vodou culture and youth activism play key roles in shaping modern Haitian society.

Culture

Haitian culture is deeply rooted in African traditions, shaped by centuries of adaptation and resistance. Vodou cosmology, oral storytelling, drumming and vibrant visual arts remain culturally significant. Modern cultural expression includes music (such as kompa and rasin), dance and literature that blend Indigenous heritage with contemporary themes. Festivals and communal gatherings reinforce social bonds and cultural identity. While influenced by French and global culture, Haiti maintains a distinct artistic voice that reflects themes of freedom, struggle and beauty.

Education and Healthcare

Education in Haiti is theoretically provided by both public and private systems, though quality and access are highly uneven. Schooling is provided in French and Haitian Creole, with Creole instruction increasingly promoted. Higher education opportunities are limited, leading many students to study abroad. Healthcare is underfunded and fragmented, aiming for but struggling to provide universal access. Geographic and economic barriers create severe challenges in service delivery. International NGOs play a critical role. Public health priorities include infectious disease, maternal health, malnutrition and improving outcomes in remote and urban slum communities.

Infrastructure

Haiti's infrastructure reflects its challenging topography and chronic underinvestment. Road networks are poorly maintained, with transport often relying on informal means. The port of Port-au-Prince and Toussaint Louverture International Airport are essential for trade and travel. Digital connectivity is limited outside urban centres. Energy production is unreliable, with frequent blackouts affecting homes and businesses. Natural disasters place severe strain on infrastructure resilience, requiring constant reconstruction.

Tourism

Tourism is a potential yet underdeveloped sector in Haiti, attracting visitors seeking historical sites and cultural experiences. Key attractions include the Citadelle Laferrière, a UNESCO World Heritage site, colonial architecture in Jacmel and Caribbean beaches. Activities range from historical tours and hiking to cultural festivals. Port-au-Prince and Cap-Haïtien serve as major hubs. Sustainable tourism is emphasised to support economic development while respecting local communities and heritage.

Current Issues and Future Outlook

Haiti faces profound challenges and uncertain opportunities. Political instability, gang violence and humanitarian crises threaten daily life and development. Environmental degradation and climate vulnerability affect traditional ways of life while complicating reconstruction. Economic self-sufficiency, security and the strengthening of democratic institutions remain central political issues. At the same time, Haiti benefits from an immensely resilient population, a powerful diaspora and a unique cultural legacy. The future will depend on achieving stability, equitable development and the effective use of international partnership.

Overview

Haiti is a nation defined by resilience, cultural richness and historical significance. Rooted in a revolutionary past and shaped by centuries of challenge, it is striving to forge a stable modern identity within the Caribbean. Its dramatic history and geography present immense challenges, demanding just governance and a sustainable vision. As Haiti looks ahead, strengthening institutions, protecting the vulnerable and supporting community resilience will be central to ensuring a peaceful and prosperous future for the country and its people.

DID YOU KNOW…?

Haiti is home to the Citadelle Laferrière, a monumental early 19th-century fortress built atop a mountain in northern Haiti. Constructed following independence, the fortress was part of a defensive system conceived by King Henry Christophe to deter a potential French invasion. The Citadelle consists of massive stone walls and ramparts rising directly from the peak, housing hundreds of cannons and extensive quarters for a garrison of thousands. It included royal apartments, storage vaults and rainwater cisterns, representing a feat of engineering and labour. Changing political fortunes eventually led to its abandonment as a military site. Today, it stands as a UNESCO World Heritage site, serving as a striking reminder of post-revolutionary ambition, Haitian engineering ingenuity and the long-term cultural legacy of national defiance in one of the world's first post-colonial nations.

KEY FACTS AND FIGURES

Geography & Environment

- Total area: 27,750 km².
- Coastline: ≈1,771 km.
- Climate: Tropical, with a wet and dry season; highly hurricane-prone.
- Highest point: Pic la Selle (2,680 m).
- Major features: Mountainous terrain, coastal plains, Massif de la Selle and Massif du Nord ranges.
- Wildlife: Hutias, flamingos, sea turtles, tropical bird species.
- 0 UNESCO World Heritage sites.

Population & Society

- Population: ≈11.8 million (2024 estimate).
- Density: ≈425 persons/km² (among the highest in the Caribbean).
- Urbanisation: ≈58%.
- Ethnicity:
  - o Black: ≈95%
  - o Mixed and other: ≈5%
- Languages: Haitian Creole and French (both official).
- Religion: Christian (predominantly Roman Catholic and Protestant), with Vodou widely practised: ≈95%.
- Literacy: ≈62%.
- Life expectancy: ≈64 years.

Economy

- GDP (nominal): ≈£15 billion.
- GDP per capita (PPP): ≈£3,000.
- Key industries:
  - o Agriculture (coffee, mangoes, cocoa)
  - o Apparel manufacturing
  - o Trade and services
  - o Remittances
- Major exports: Apparel, agricultural products, essential oils.
- Currency: Haitian gourde (HTG; £1 ≈ 165 HTG).

Government

• Republic.

• System: Semi-presidential republic (currently unstable governance).

• Head of State: President of Haiti (office often vacant or transitional).

• Head of Government: Prime Minister of Haiti.

• Legislature: Bicameral Parliament (often non-functional).

Infrastructure

• Transport: Limited road network; no active rail; air and sea transport constrained.

• Major airports: Toussaint Louverture International Airport (Port-au-Prince).

• Energy mix: Predominantly biomass and fossil fuels; very limited electricity access.

• Digital connectivity: Limited; concentrated mainly in urban areas.

Major Urban Centres

• Port-au-Prince: ≈2.6 million (metro) – Capital and main economic centre.

• Cap-Haïtien: ≈300,000 – Northern port city and tourism gateway.

• Les Cayes: ≈200,000 – Southern regional centre.

• Gonaïves: ≈350,000 – Historic city and agricultural hub.

PORT-AU-PRINCE – HAITI'S CAPITAL AND MAIN ECONOMIC CENTRE

The National Flag

The national flag of the Republic of Haiti features a horizontal bicolour of blue and red, with the national coat of arms centred on a white panel on the state flag. The blue symbolises Haiti's Black citizens and its historical alliance with France, while the red represents the nation's people of mixed heritage and its hard-won independence. The coat of arms depicts a palm tree surmounted by a liberty cap, flanked by cannons and flags, with the national motto 'L'Union Fait La Force' ('Union Makes Strength') below. This signifies the nation's victory in revolution, its liberty and its enduring unity. The flag as a whole embodies Haiti's history as the world's first Black republic, its resilience and its sovereign pride.

KEY PEOPLE AND PLACES

PEOPLE

Toussaint Louverture (1743–1803) Widely regarded as the 'Father of Haiti,' he led the Haitian Revolution, uniting enslaved and free people of colour to overthrow French colonial rule, establish Haiti as the first Black republic and inspire global movements for freedom.

Jean-Jacques Dessalines (1758–1806) A key revolutionary general and the first ruler of independent Haiti, He declared the nation's independence in 1804, abolished slavery completely, resisted colonial domination and became a lasting symbol of courage, resilience and Haitian national pride.

Henri Christophe (1767–1820) A revolutionary leader then King, Christophe built the Citadelle Laferrière fortress, strengthening Haiti's political and economic independence and establishing post-revolutionary governance shaping the country's early history and national identity.

Alexander Pétion (1770–1818) President of southern Haiti, Pétion helped stabilise the new republic, promoted education, supported regional liberation movements across Latin America and introduced reforms that defined Haiti's political, social and economic structures during the early post-revolutionary period.

Jean-Bertrand Aristide (b. 1953) A former Catholic priest and political leader, Aristide served multiple presidential terms, advocating social justice, democratic governance and policies for the poor, while navigating political instability, coups and international pressures during his leadership in modern Haiti.

Jacques Roumain (1907–1944) A celebrated Haitian writer, poet and activist, Roumain focused on rural life, social inequality and Haitian identity. His works promoted cultural awareness, social justice and national pride, inspiring generations of Haitians and leaving a lasting literary legacy.

PLACES

Port-au-Prince (founded 1749) The capital and largest city of Haiti, Port-au-Prince sits on the Gulf of Gonâve and serves as the nation's political, cultural and economic hub, featuring historic sites, government institutions, urban communities, education and arts centres.

Cap-Haïtien (founded 1670) A historic northern coastal city, Cap-Haïtien was once the capital of the French colony of Saint-Domingue. It is known for its colonial architecture, cultural heritage and proximity to Citadelle Laferrière, remaining an important economic and historic centre.

Citadelle Laferrière (built 1805–1820) A massive fortress constructed by Henri Christophe atop a mountaintop, Citadelle Laferrière symbolises Haitian independence, resistance against colonial powers and post-revolutionary architectural ingenuity. It is recognised as a UNESCO World Heritage site and a key national landmark.

Jacmel A coastal town celebrated for its colonial architecture, artistic community and vibrant Carnival. Jacmel plays a central role in Haitian culture, visual arts, tourism and heritage preservation, representing the creativity, craftsmanship and enduring identity of the nation.

Labadee A northern coastal area known for pristine beaches, natural beauty and as a cruise ship destination. Labadee offers recreational activities, Caribbean landscapes and cultural experiences while contributing significantly to Haiti's tourism industry and local economy.

Sans-Souci Palace (built 1810–1813) The former royal residence of King Henri Christophe near Cap-Haïtien, now a UNESCO World Heritage site. Sans-Souci Palace symbolises the ambition, resilience and historical legacy of Haiti's early revolutionary leaders and the nation's struggle for independence.

TIMELINE OF EVENTS

c. 500–1492 CE: Indigenous Settlements: Taino and Arawak peoples settled Hispaniola, including present-day Haiti, developing agriculture, fishing, trade networks, villages and complex social and cultural structures.

1492: Columbus Arrives in Hispaniola: Christopher Columbus landed on the island during his first voyage, beginning European contact, colonisation, mapping and eventual Spanish control over Haiti.

1503–1697: Spanish Colonial Rule: Spain established colonial settlements, introduced Catholicism, agriculture and European governance, enslaving Indigenous populations and reshaping society, economy and culture throughout Hispaniola.

1697: Treaty of Ryswick: Spain ceded the western part of Hispaniola to France, officially creating the French colony of Saint-Domingue, today's Haiti.

1700s: Expansion of Plantation Economy: French colonial Saint-Domingue became a major sugar and coffee producer using enslaved African labour, creating immense wealth and harsh social hierarchies.

1791–1804: Haitian Revolution: Enslaved Africans and free people of colour led a successful revolt, overthrowing colonial rule and establishing Haiti as a sovereign nation.

1804: Independence Declared: Haiti became the first Black republic in the world, abolishing slavery and securing independence from France under Jean-Jacques Dessalines.

1804–1825: Early Republic and Challenges: Haiti faced political instability, economic isolation and international embargoes, including reparations demanded by France for independence recognition.

1915–1934: US Occupation: United States occupied Haiti, controlling finances, infrastructure and governance, while prompting social unrest and nationalist movements demanding sovereignty.

1957–1986: Duvalier Dictatorship: François 'Papa Doc' Duvalier and later Jean-Claude 'Baby Doc' ruled Haiti with authoritarianism, corruption, repression and human rights abuses.

1986: Fall of Duvalier Regime: Popular uprisings overthrew Jean-Claude Duvalier, ending decades of dictatorship and opening the country to democratic reform attempts.

1990: Election of Jean-Bertrand Aristide: Haiti elected Aristide, a former priest, marking a historic democratic moment and a shift toward popular political representation.

2004: Political Crisis and Rebel Uprising: President Aristide was removed amid political unrest and armed rebellion, leading to international intervention and governance instability.

2010: Devastating Earthquake: A 7.0 magnitude earthquake struck Haiti, causing widespread death, destruction and humanitarian crises, severely affecting infrastructure and daily life.

2020: COVID-19 Pandemic Impact: The pandemic compounded Haiti's challenges, disrupting public health, economy, education and exacerbating pre-existing social and political instability.

THE DOMINICAN REPUBLIC

The Dominican Republic is a mountainous tropical nation located in the Caribbean, occupying the eastern two-thirds of the island of Hispaniola, which it shares with Haiti to the west. With an estimated population of approximately 11.3 million people, it is the second-largest country in the Caribbean by population. The capital city is Santo Domingo, the oldest continuously inhabited European-founded city in the Americas, while major urban centres such as Santiago de los Caballeros, La Romana and Punta Cana serve as important economic, cultural and tourism hubs. Spanish is the official national language, spoken throughout the country. The Dominican Peso serves as the national currency. Shaped by Indigenous Taíno civilisation, Spanish colonisation, African enslavement and centuries of political transformation, the nation blends deep historical foundations with dynamic cultural development. Its music, baseball legacy, tourism industry and growing diaspora contribute significantly to its international profile. This combination of resilience, diversity and cultural vitality defines the identity of the Dominican Republic.

Geography

Spanning a geographically diverse and topographically complex landscape, the Dominican Republic features some of the most varied terrain in the Caribbean. The country is dominated by several mountain ranges, most notably the Cordillera Central, which contains Pico Duarte, the highest point in the Caribbean at 3,098 metres. Fertile valleys such as the Cibao lie between mountain chains and support extensive agriculture. The coastline stretches for over 1,600 kilometres, offering a wide contrast between white-sand beaches, coral reefs, mangroves and rugged cliffs along both the Atlantic Ocean and the Caribbean Sea. Major rivers include the Yaque del Norte, the longest river in the Caribbean and the Yuna. The climate is tropical, with regional variation influenced by altitude and trade winds and a hurricane season from June to November. The country is highly biodiverse, with many endemic species, but is vulnerable to hurricanes, earthquakes and flooding. Environmental challenges include deforestation, water management and coastal degradation.

History

The history of the Dominican Republic begins with the Taíno people, who inhabited the island of Hispaniola long before European contact and referred to it as Ayiti or Quisqueya. Christopher Columbus arrived in 1492 and Spain established its first permanent settlement in the Americas at Santo Domingo in 1496. Spanish colonisation led to the rapid decline of the Taíno population due to disease, forced labour and violence, followed by the introduction of enslaved Africans. Over centuries, the eastern part of Hispaniola experienced shifting fortunes, periods of neglect and foreign occupation. The Dominican Republic declared independence from Haiti in 1844, following a 22-year period of Haitian rule. The modern nation was shaped by political instability, foreign intervention, including a United States occupation in the early 20th century and the long dictatorship of Rafael Trujillo from 1930 to 1961. Since the late 20th century, the country has transitioned toward democratic governance and economic growth.

Government and Politics

The Dominican Republic is a unitary presidential republic with a democratic system of government. Executive power is vested in the President, who serves as both head of state and head of government. The country is administratively divided into provinces and municipalities. Legislative authority resides in the bicameral National Congress, consisting of the Senate and the Chamber of Deputies, both elected by popular vote. The judiciary is independent and based on civil law traditions, with the Supreme Court serving as the highest judicial authority. Political life is dominated by several major parties, including the Modern Revolutionary Party (PRM), the Dominican Liberation Party (PLD) and the Social Christian Reformist Party (PRSC). Domestically, political debates focus on economic management, corruption, migration and public security. Internationally, the Dominican Republic maintains active membership in the United Nations, the Organisation of American States and CARICOM as an observer.

Economy

The Dominican Republic possesses one of the largest and most diversified economies in the Caribbean. The economy is service-dominated, with tourism, free trade zones, remittances and telecommunications forming key pillars. Manufacturing in export processing zones includes medical devices, textiles and electronics, while agriculture remains important, producing sugarcane, coffee, cocoa and tobacco. Tourism is a major driver of growth, centred on resort areas such as Punta Cana, Puerto Plata and La Romana. Despite strong growth in recent decades, the economy faces challenges including income inequality, informal employment and exposure to external shocks. The Dominican Peso is managed by the Central Bank of the Dominican Republic. The economy is closely integrated with that of the United States, its principal trading partner and source of remittances. Continued efforts to strengthen institutions, infrastructure and human capital are central to sustaining long-term growth.

Demographics and Society

With a population of approximately 11.3 million, the Dominican Republic is one of the most populous countries in the Caribbean. The population reflects a complex mix of European, African and Indigenous ancestry, shaped by centuries of migration and cultural exchange. Urbanisation is high, with a significant proportion of the population living in Santo Domingo and Santiago. Spanish is universally spoken and serves as a central marker of national identity. Roman Catholicism has historically predominated, though Protestant denominations have grown in recent decades. The country hosts a significant population of Haitian migrants and descendants, making migration and citizenship important social and political issues. Social challenges include poverty, inequality and access to public services, but Dominican society is also characterised by strong family networks, community ties and cultural expression.

Culture

Dominican culture is internationally recognised for its vibrancy, rhythm and diversity, shaped by Taíno heritage, Spanish traditions and African influences. Music is central to national life, with merengue and bachata designated as UNESCO Intangible Cultural Heritage forms. Dance, festivals and carnival celebrations play a major role in cultural expression. Cuisine blends African, Spanish and Indigenous elements, featuring dishes such as *la bandera* (rice, beans and meat), *sancocho* and *mangu*. Language, humour and oral tradition are important cultural vehicles. Sport holds significant social importance, with baseball occupying a central place in national identity and producing numerous internationally renowned players. Cultural creativity remains a powerful source of national pride and global influence.

Education and Healthcare

The Dominican Republic operates an education system providing compulsory primary and secondary education, with expanding access to tertiary institutions. Literacy rates have improved steadily, though disparities remain between urban and rural areas. Major universities are concentrated in Santo Domingo and Santiago. Healthcare is delivered through a mixed public and private system, with public hospitals offering basic services and private facilities providing higher levels of specialised care. Access and quality vary by region and income level. Public health priorities include reducing maternal mortality, addressing non-communicable diseases and strengthening healthcare infrastructure. Ongoing reforms aim to improve coverage, efficiency and equity within the education and healthcare systems.

Infrastructure

Infrastructure development in the Dominican Republic reflects its growing economy and strategic regional role. The country has an extensive road network linking major cities, tourism zones and industrial centres, though congestion and maintenance remain challenges. There is no national passenger railway system. Major ports such as Santo Domingo, Caucedo and Haina facilitate trade, while international airports serve multiple regions, supporting tourism and commerce. Energy production relies on a mix of fossil fuels and renewable sources, including hydroelectric, wind and solar power. Telecommunications infrastructure is well developed, with widespread mobile and internet access, particularly in urban areas. Infrastructure priorities include improving public transport, water management and climate resilience.

Tourism

Tourism is a cornerstone of the Dominican Republic's economy and a central element of its international image. The country is renowned for its all-inclusive beach resorts, particularly in Punta Cana, Bávaro and Puerto Plata, as well as cultural and historical attractions in Santo Domingo's Colonial Zone, a UNESCO World Heritage Site. Ecotourism opportunities include national parks, mountain regions and whale watching in Samaná Bay. Golf, cruise tourism and nightlife further enhance the visitor offering. Sustainable tourism initiatives are increasingly emphasised to balance economic growth with environmental protection and community development.

Current Issues and Future Outlook

The Dominican Republic faces a range of challenges alongside its economic and cultural strengths. Key issues include managing migration, reducing inequality, improving public services and addressing environmental pressures. Climate change poses risks through hurricanes, coastal erosion and water stress. At the same time, the country benefits from relative political stability, strong economic momentum and strategic geographic location. The future outlook depends on continued institutional reform, investment in education and infrastructure and sustainable management of natural resources. How effectively these challenges are addressed will shape the country's long-term development and social cohesion.

Overview

The Dominican Republic is a nation defined by its historical significance, cultural dynamism and economic ambition. From its role as the first European colony in the Americas to its modern position as a regional economic leader, it has undergone profound transformation. Its diverse geography supports both agricultural productivity and global tourism, while its culture exerts wide international influence. Looking forward, the country seeks to consolidate democratic governance, promote inclusive growth and strengthen resilience in the face of environmental and social challenges.

DID YOU KNOW...?

The Dominican Republic is home to Pico Duarte, the highest mountain in the Caribbean at 3,098 metres above sea level. Located within the Cordillera Central, the peak is a symbol of national pride and a popular destination for hikers. Named after Juan Pablo Duarte, one of the country's founding fathers, Pico Duarte represents the Dominican Republic's dramatic natural landscape, historical legacy and enduring sense of national identity.

KEY FACTS AND FIGURES

Geography & Environment

• Total area: 48,671 km² (shares the island of Hispaniola with Haiti).

• Coastline: ≈1,288 km (Caribbean Sea and Atlantic Ocean).

• Climate: Tropical; wet and dry seasons; hurricane-prone.

• Highest point: Pico Duarte (3,098 m).

• Major features: Cordillera Central, Cibao Valley, fertile coastal plains, Lake Enriquillo.

• Wildlife: Jaguars, manatees, parrots, iguanas, tropical bird species.

• 3 UNESCO World Heritage sites.

Population & Society

• Population: ≈11.3 million (2024 estimate).

• Density: ≈232 persons/km².

• Urbanisation: ≈83%.

• Ethnicity:

o Mixed (Mestizo/White): ≈73%

o Black: ≈16%

o White: ≈11%

• Languages: Spanish (official).

• Religion: Christian (predominantly Roman Catholic; Protestant minority): ≈90%.

• Literacy: ≈93%.

• Life expectancy: ≈74 years.

Economy

• GDP (nominal): ≈£150 billion.

• GDP per capita (PPP): ≈£13,000.

• Key industries:

o Tourism

o Agriculture (sugar, coffee, cocoa, tobacco)

o Manufacturing (textiles, beverages)

o Mining (nickel, gold)

• Major exports: Gold, sugar, medical instruments, textiles, tobacco.
• Currency: Dominican peso (DOP; £1 ≈ 65 DOP).

Government
• Presidential republic.
• System: Constitutional democratic republic.
• Head of State: President of the Dominican Republic.
• Head of Government: President of the Dominican Republic.
• Legislature: National Congress (Senate and Chamber of Deputies).

Infrastructure
• Transport: National road network; limited rail; air and sea transport.
• Major airports: Las Américas International, Cibao International.
• Energy mix: Fossil fuels, hydropower, wind and solar.
• Digital connectivity: Moderate to well developed in urban and tourist areas; limited in rural regions.

Major Urban Centres
• Santo Domingo: ≈3.3 million (metro) – Capital and economic centre.
• Santiago de los Caballeros: ≈1.2 million – Major commercial hub.
• La Romana: ≈130,000 – Industrial and tourism centre.
• San Pedro de Macorís: ≈200,000 – Port city and sugar industry hub

SANTO DOMINGO - DOMINICAN REPUBLIC'S CAPITAL AND ECONOMIC CENTRE

The National Flag

The national flag of the Dominican Republic features a centred white cross extending to the edges, dividing the field into four rectangles of ultramarine blue and vermilion red. At the centre lies the national coat of arms. The blue symbolises liberty, the white cross represents salvation and the red denotes the blood of heroes. The coat of arms displays a shield with a cross, a Bible and four flags, flanked by olive and palm branches and topped by a blue ribbon bearing the national motto 'Dios, Patria, Libertad' ('God, Fatherland, Liberty'). This represents the nation's Christian faith, its sovereignty and its enduring struggle for independence. The flag as a whole embodies the Dominican Republic's identity, its historical victory and its commitment to core national values.

KEY PEOPLE AND PLACES

PEOPLE

Juan Pablo Duarte (1813–1876) Widely regarded as the 'Father of the Nation,' Duarte was a visionary revolutionary leader who founded the secret society La Trinitaria and had a central role in Dominican's struggle for independence from Haitian rule, inspiring national unity and pride.

Francisco del Rosario Sánchez (1817–1861) A founding father of the Dominican Republic, He was a key figure in the fight for independence and a symbol of patriotism, courage and sacrifice, remembered for his unwavering commitment to liberty and the sovereignty of the nation.

Pedro Santana (1801–1864) A military and political leader, Santana was the first president of the Dominican Republic. He played a big role in the country's early political development, influencing national policy, defence and international relations in the nation's formative years.

Rafael Trujillo (1891–1961) A long-serving military dictator who ruled from 1930 to 1961, Trujillo's regime was marked by authoritarian control, economic development and infrastructure projects, but also widespread human rights abuses, political repression and the consolidation of power through fear and propaganda.

Salvador Estrella Sadhalá (1900–1985) A political and cultural leader recognised for his contributions to literature, education and the promotion of Dominican identity. He worked to strengthen cultural awareness, historical knowledge and national pride among the Dominican people throughout the 20th century.

Duarte, Sánchez y Mella Collectively celebrated as the founding fathers of the Dominican Republic, they led the nation to independence from Haiti in 1844 and the foundation for democratic governance, national identity and patriotic ideals that remain central to Dominican society.

PLACES

Santo Domingo (founded 1498) The capital and largest city of the Dominican Republic, located on the southern coast, Santo Domingo is the oldest continuously inhabited European settlement in the Americas, known for its colonial architecture, historical sites, vibrant culture and UNESCO World Heritage designation.

Punta Cana A major tourist destination on the eastern coast, famous for its white sand beaches, luxury resorts, recreational tourism and water sports. Punta Cana attracts international visitors, providing economic growth and establishing the region as a key hub of Caribbean tourism.

Santiago de los Caballeros (founded 1495) The second-largest city in the country, Santiago is an important economic, cultural and educational centre in the northern region. It is known for its historic architecture, vibrant urban life and significant contributions to industry, commerce and education.

La Romana A coastal city known for tourism, sugar production and as a gateway to Isla Catalina and Casa de Campo resort. La Romana combines economic development with cultural attractions, offering visitors access to history, leisure and luxury experiences along the coast.

Jarabacoa A mountain town in the central highlands, Jarabacoa is celebrated for its temperate climate, scenic rivers, waterfalls and adventure tourism opportunities. It attracts hikers, eco-tourists and nature enthusiasts while promoting sustainable tourism and appreciation of the Dominican Republic's natural landscapes.

Fortaleza Ozama (built 1502–1505) A historic fortress in Santo Domingo, Fortaleza Ozama is one of the oldest military constructions in the Americas. It represents colonial history, defence strategies and the city's strategic importance during the early European settlement and early defence of the territory.

TIMELINE OF EVENTS

c. 500–1492 CE: Indigenous Settlements: Taíno peoples settled Hispaniola, including present-day Dominican Republic, developing agriculture, fishing, trade networks, villages and complex social, cultural and spiritual systems.

1492: Columbus Arrives in Hispaniola: Christopher Columbus landed on Hispaniola, marking European contact, mapping and the beginning of Spanish colonisation in the region.

1493–1500s: Spanish Colonial Rule Established: Spain established settlements, introduced Catholicism, European governance and agriculture, enslaving Indigenous populations and reshaping society, economy and culture.

1503: Santo Domingo Founded: The city of Santo Domingo was established as the first permanent European settlement in the Americas, becoming a major administrative and colonial centre.

1697: Treaty of Ryswick: Spain ceded the western part of Hispaniola to France, confirming French control of Saint-Domingue, separating it from Spanish Hispaniola.

1795: Treaty of Basel: Spain ceded the eastern part of Hispaniola to France, placing the Dominican territory under French colonial administration temporarily.

1808–1821: Resistance and Independence Movements: Dominicans resisted French rule, leading to short-lived independence under leaders like José Núñez de Cáceres.

1822–1844: Haitian Occupation: Haiti occupied the eastern part of Hispaniola, integrating Dominican territory while creating social, political and economic tensions among the population.

1844: Dominican Republic Declared Independence: Dominicans, led by Juan Pablo Duarte and others, declared independence from Haiti, establishing a sovereign republic.

1861–1865: Annexation by Spain and Restoration War: Spain briefly annexed the Dominican Republic, prompting the Restoration War and restoration of independence.

1916–1924: US Occupation: The United States occupied the Dominican Republic, controlling finances, infrastructure and governance while prompting nationalist movements demanding sovereignty.

1930–1961: Trujillo Dictatorship: Rafael Trujillo ruled with authoritarianism, suppression and human rights abuses, transforming the country's politics, economy and society drastically.

1965: Civil War and US Intervention: Political unrest and civil war prompted US military intervention to restore order and stabilise governance structures.

1966–1978: Post-Trujillo Political Reconstruction: Democratic governments emerged, attempting to rebuild institutions, infrastructure and economic stability after decades of dictatorship and unrest.

1990s: Economic and Social Development: The Dominican Republic experienced economic growth, tourism expansion and social reforms, strengthening infrastructure, public services and international relations.

2010: Earthquake in Neighboring Haiti Impacts Country: Humanitarian crises in Haiti affected the Dominican Republic, prompting disaster relief, migration management and regional cooperation.

2020: COVID-19 Pandemic Impact: The pandemic disrupted public health, tourism, economy and social services, challenging the Dominican Republic's resilience and institutional capacity.

THE COMMONWEALTH OF PUERTO RICO

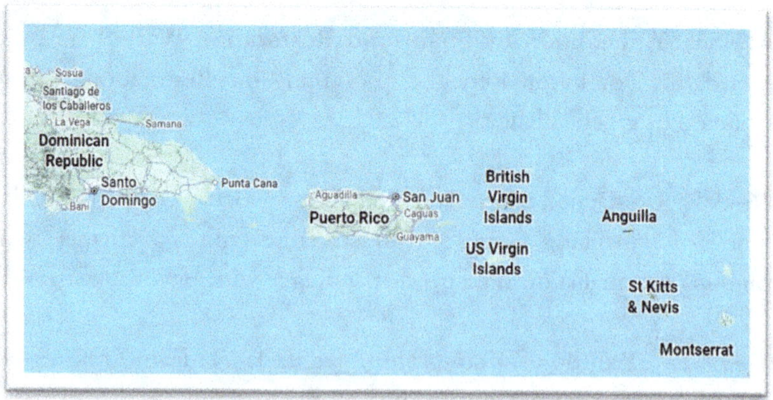

Puerto Rico, known officially as the Commonwealth of Puerto Rico and locally as Borinquén, is a self-governing unincorporated territory of the United States located in the northeastern Caribbean. It lies approximately 50 miles east of the Dominican Republic and consists of the main island and over 140 smaller islands and cays. With an estimated population of around 3.2 million people, the capital and largest city is San Juan, which serves as the political, economic and cultural centre. Spanish and English are the official languages, though Spanish is predominant. The United States dollar is the official currency. Shaped by Taíno civilisation, four centuries of Spanish colonial rule and subsequent US sovereignty, Puerto Rico blends deep Indigenous and Hispanic traditions with American influences. Its strategic location, tropical environment and vibrant culture are central to its identity, yet its unresolved political status defines its contemporary challenges and its complex relationship with the United States.

Geography

Puerto Rico occupies a diverse tropical landscape dominated by a central mountain range, the Cordillera Central, with Cerro de Punta as its highest peak. The island features contrasting northern karst terrain and a drier southern coastal plain. Its coastline is fringed by numerous beaches, mangroves and coral reefs. The climate is consistently tropical, moderated by trade winds, with a distinct rainy season. The island is susceptible to Atlantic hurricanes and tropical storms, which have caused significant damage historically. Key natural features include the bioluminescent bays of Vieques and Fajardo, the El Yunque National Forest (the only tropical rainforest within the US National Forest System) and the extensive cave system of the Rio Camuy Cave Park.

History

The history of Puerto Rico begins with its settlement by the Taíno people, who called the island Borikén. It was claimed for Spain by Christopher Columbus in 1493, becoming a strategic military and economic colony. Spanish rule lasted for over 400 years until, following the Spanish-American War of 1898, the island was ceded to the United States under the Treaty of Paris. In 1917, Puerto Ricans were granted US citizenship by the Jones-Shafroth Act. The island's political status evolved with the establishment of its own constitution and self-government as a commonwealth (Estado Libre Asociado) in 1952. The second half of the 20th century saw rapid economic transformation and profound debates over statehood, independence and the current commonwealth arrangement, which remain unresolved.

Government and Politics

Puerto Rico operates under a republican form of government with three branches: executive, legislative and judicial, as defined by its own constitution. The head of government is the Governor, elected by popular vote. It has a bicameral Legislative Assembly. While it exercises broad internal autonomy, the ultimate sovereignty of the United States Congress applies. Puerto Ricans are US citizens but, while residing on the island, cannot vote in US presidential elections and have a non-voting Resident

Commissioner in the US House of Representatives. The dominant political parties are largely organised around the fundamental issue of the island's ultimate political status: statehood, enhanced commonwealth, or independence.

Economy

Puerto Rico's economy is the largest among US territories and was historically industrialised under US tax incentive programs. Manufacturing remains a pillar, particularly pharmaceuticals, electronics and medical devices. Tourism is a major sector and federal transfers and remittances are significant. However, the economy has been mired in a prolonged recession and debt crisis, exacerbated by the phasing out of tax incentives, high energy costs and outmigration. In 2017, the government declared a form of bankruptcy to restructure over $70 billion in public debt under a federal oversight board. Economic challenges include high poverty rates, labour force participation and dependence on imports.

Demographics and Society

With a population of approximately 3.2 million, Puerto Rico is densely populated, with a significant diaspora residing on the US mainland. The population is largely of Spanish and African descent, with Taíno ancestry. Spanish is the primary language of home and public life. While living standards improved dramatically in the mid-20th century, the recent economic crisis has led to population decline and strained social services. Puerto Rican society is characterised by strong family ties, a vibrant cultural identity and resilience in the face of economic and natural challenges.

Culture

Puerto Rican culture is a rich and distinct fusion of Taíno, Spanish and African roots. This is vividly expressed in its music and dance, such as salsa, bomba, plena and the globally popular reggaeton. Its literary and artistic traditions are robust. The national cuisine blends Spanish, African and Caribbean influences. Cultural identity is passionately held and is a central feature of the political discourse surrounding the island's status. Despite

American influences, Puerto Rico maintains a strongly Hispanic national character.

Education and Healthcare

Puerto Rico operates a public education system modelled on the US structure, with instruction primarily in Spanish. It has an extensive network of public and private universities. Healthcare is provided through a mixture of public programs and private insurance, with most residents eligible for federal programs like Medicare and Medicaid. However, the healthcare system faces pressures from the economic crisis, outmigration of medical professionals and the aging population.

Infrastructure

Puerto Rico's infrastructure, including its power grid, roads and water systems, has suffered from chronic underinvestment and was severely damaged by hurricanes Irma and María in 2017. The electric grid, in particular, has been prone to failures. Reconstruction efforts have been slow and costly. The island has major international airports and seaports that are vital for tourism and trade.

Tourism

Tourism is a vital economic sector for Puerto Rico, attracting visitors with its historic sites, beaches, rainforests and cultural festivals. Key attractions include the historic forts and streets of Old San Juan (a UNESCO World Heritage Site), the El Yunque rainforest, the bioluminescent bays and the coastal islands of Culebra and Vieques. The industry is a major focus for economic recovery.

Current Issues and Future Outlook

Puerto Rico faces a defining set of challenges: recovering from natural disasters, restructuring its crippling public debt, reversing economic stagnation and population loss and resolving its century-old political status dilemma. The future outlook hinges on decisions made in both San Juan and Washington D.C., regarding economic policy, disaster recovery funding and, ultimately, whether the island will remain a territory, become the 51st US state or pursue independence.

Overview

Puerto Rico is an island of profound contrasts—rich in culture and natural beauty yet burdened by economic fragility and political ambiguity. Its people have demonstrated remarkable resilience through hurricanes and fiscal crises. As it looks ahead, its path will be determined by how it navigates the complex interplay of self-determination, economic recovery and its enduring relationship with the United States.

DID YOU KNOW...?

Puerto Rico is home to El Yunque National Forest, the only tropical rainforest within the United States National Forest System. Located in the rugged Sierra de Luquillo mountains, El Yunque receives over 200 inches of rainfall annually, fostering immense biodiversity with hundreds of unique plant and animal species, including the endangered Puerto Rican parrot and the tiny, iconic coquí frog. Unlike most rainforests, El Yunque's location on an island and its composition of volcanic rock create a fragile ecosystem that is particularly sensitive to environmental changes. The forest has served as a critical natural laboratory for scientific research for over a century and stands as a symbol of national pride and natural resilience for the Puerto Rican people, embodying the island's unique ecological and cultural identity within the American political framework.

KEY FACTS AND FIGURES

Geography & Environment

• Total area: 9,104 km² (island and smaller adjacent islands).

• Coastline: ≈501 km.

• Climate: Tropical maritime climate; wet and dry seasons; hurricane-prone.

• Highest point: Cerro de Punta (1,338 m).

• Major features: Central mountain range (Cordillera Central), karst region in the north, coastal plains, El Yunque rainforest.

• Wildlife: Coquí frogs, manatees, iguanas, parrots, tropical bird species.

• 1 UNESCO World Heritage site.

Population & Society

• Population: ≈3.1 million (2024 estimate).

• Density: ≈341 persons/km².

• Urbanisation: ≈93%.

• Ethnicity:

o White and Mestizo: ≈75%

o Black and African descent: ≈12%

o Other/mixed: ≈13%

• Languages: Spanish and English (both official).

• Religion: Christian (predominantly Roman Catholic; Protestant minority): ≈85%.

• Literacy: ≈94%.

• Life expectancy: ≈79 years.

Economy

• GDP (nominal): ≈£150 billion.

• GDP per capita (PPP): ≈£48,000.

• Key industries:

o Pharmaceuticals and biotechnology

o Manufacturing (electronics, medical devices)

o Tourism

o Services and finance

• Major exports: Pharmaceuticals, medical devices, electronics, rum.
• Currency: United States dollar (USD).

Government
• Unincorporated territory of the United States.
• System: Representative democracy under US sovereignty.
• Head of State: President of the United States.
• Head of Government: Governor of Puerto Rico.
• Legislature: Legislative Assembly (Senate and House of Representatives).

Infrastructure
• Transport: National road network; public transport in major cities; air and sea transport.
• Major airports: Luis Muñoz Marín International Airport (San Juan).
• Energy mix: Fossil fuels, growing renewable energy (solar, wind).
• Digital connectivity: Well developed across the island.

Major Urban Centres
• San Juan: ≈2.2 million (metro) – Capital, economic and cultural centre.
• Bayamón: ≈200,000 – Industrial and residential hub.
• Ponce: ≈140,000 – Southern regional centre and port city.
• Carolina: ≈160,000 – Tourism and commercial hub.

SAN JUAN PUERTO RICO 'S – CAPITAL, ECONOMIC AND CULTURAL CENTRE

The National Flag

The national flag of the Commonwealth of Puerto Rico features five equal alternating horizontal stripes of red and white, with a blue isosceles triangle based on the hoist side bearing a single white five-pointed star. The blue symbolises the coastal sky and waters, the white stripes represent victory and peace, while the red stripes denote the bloodshed in the struggle for sovereignty. The white star signifies the Commonwealth itself and the triangle reflects the three branches of republican government. The flag as a whole embodies Puerto Rico's identity, its complex political history and its enduring aspirations.

KEY PEOPLE AND PLACES

PEOPLE

Luis Muñoz Marín (1898–1980) Widely regarded as the 'Father of Modern Puerto Rico,' he served as the island's first democratically elected governor from 1949 to 1965. He implemented major economic, social and industrial reforms that shaped mid-20th-century Puerto Rico and strengthened democratic governance.

Pedro Albizu Campos (1891–1965) A nationalist leader and lawyer, Albizu Campos fought for Puerto Rican independence from the United States. He became a symbol of resistance, political activism and Puerto Rican identity, inspiring generations of nationalists while enduring imprisonment and political persecution.

Rafael Hernández Marín (1892–1965) One of Puerto Rico's most celebrated composers, Hernández Marín created music that blends traditional Puerto Rican rhythms with popular Latin genres. His work promoted cultural pride, influenced Caribbean music and continues to represent Puerto Rico's artistic heritage internationally.

Roberto Clemente (1934–1972) A legendary baseball player and humanitarian, Clemente became the first Latin American inducted into the National Baseball Hall of Fame. He is remembered for his athletic achievements and tireless dedication to charitable work benefiting Puerto Rican and Latin American communities.

Sila María Calderón (b. 1942) Governor of Puerto Rico from 2001 to 2005, she was the first woman to hold the office. Calderón implemented social and economic initiatives aimed at reducing poverty, strengthening local governance and improving opportunities for Puerto Rico's disadvantaged communities.

PLACES

San Juan (founded 1521) The capital and largest city of Puerto Rico, San Juan is located on the northeastern coast. Known for its historic old town, colonial architecture, forts, vibrant culture and economic significance, it serves as the political, cultural and commercial hub of the island.

Ponce (founded 1692) A historic city on the southern coast, Ponce is celebrated for its colonial architecture, museums, plazas and cultural institutions. Often called 'La Perla del Sur,' it has played a central role in Puerto Rico's cultural, economic and historical development.

Arecibo Observatory (built 1963) Formerly one of the world's largest radio telescopes, located in northern Puerto Rico, the observatory contributed significantly to astronomy, atmospheric science and radar research. It became a symbol of scientific achievement and global collaboration until its collapse in 2020.

El Yunque National Forest The only tropical rainforest in the United States National Forest System, located in northeastern Puerto Rico. It features rich biodiversity, waterfalls, hiking trails and ecological research opportunities, representing an essential part of Puerto Rico's natural heritage and conservation efforts.

Culebra Island A small island off the east coast of Puerto Rico, known for its pristine beaches, coral reefs and eco-tourism. Culebra attracts divers, snorkelers and visitors seeking natural beauty, recreational activities and an unspoiled Caribbean environment.

Vieques Island An eastern Puerto Rican Island renowned for its natural reserves, bioluminescent bays and historical significance. Vieques is a centre for eco-tourism, cultural preservation and sustainable development, offering visitors unique experiences of Puerto Rico's history, nature and coastal landscapes.

TIMELINE OF EVENTS

c. 1000 BCE – 1493 CE: Indigenous Settlements: The Taíno people settled Puerto Rico, developing agriculture, fishing, trade networks, villages and complex social, political and spiritual systems.

1493: Columbus Arrives in Puerto Rico: Christopher Columbus landed on the island during his second voyage, marking European contact and beginning Spanish colonisation.

1508: Spanish Colonisation Begins: Juan Ponce de León established the first settlement at Caparra, introducing European governance, Catholicism, agriculture and enslaving Indigenous populations.

1521: San Juan Founded: The settlement of San Juan was established, becoming a central port, military hub and administrative centre of Spanish colonial rule.

1590s–1700s: Fortifications and Trade Expansion: Spanish forts were built to protect against pirates, while agriculture and trade expanded, strengthening colonial administration and security.

1800s: Social and Economic Transformation: Puerto Rico developed sugar and coffee plantations, relying on enslaved African labour, reshaping society, economy and social hierarchies significantly.

1898: Spanish-American War: The United States defeated Spain, ending Spanish rule and Puerto Rico was ceded to the United States under the Treaty of Paris.

1900: Foraker Act Implemented: The United States established civil government under the Foraker Act, introducing political, economic and administrative control over Puerto Rico.

1917: Jones Act Granted Citizenship: Puerto Ricans were granted US citizenship, allowing limited political participation while maintaining US federal control over governance and economy.

1930s–1940s: Economic and Social Reforms: Infrastructure, education and health programmes were expanded, modernising the island's economy and improving social conditions under US administration.

1952: Commonwealth Status Established: Puerto Rico became a US Commonwealth, adopting its constitution, providing self-governance while remaining under US federal jurisdiction.

1960s–1980s: Industrialisation and Tourism Growth: Operation Bootstrap and tourism expansion modernised the economy, diversifying industry and improving infrastructure, employment and international trade connections.

1990s: Political and Social Developments: Debates over status, economic reforms and cultural identity shaped Puerto Rico's politics, governance and relations with the United States.

2017: Hurricane Maria Devastates Island: A major hurricane caused widespread destruction, loss of life and severe disruption to electricity, infrastructure, healthcare and daily life.

2020: COVID-19 Pandemic Impact: The pandemic disrupted public health, tourism and the economy, further challenging Puerto Rico's resilience, governance and social services.

ANTIGUA AND BARBUDA

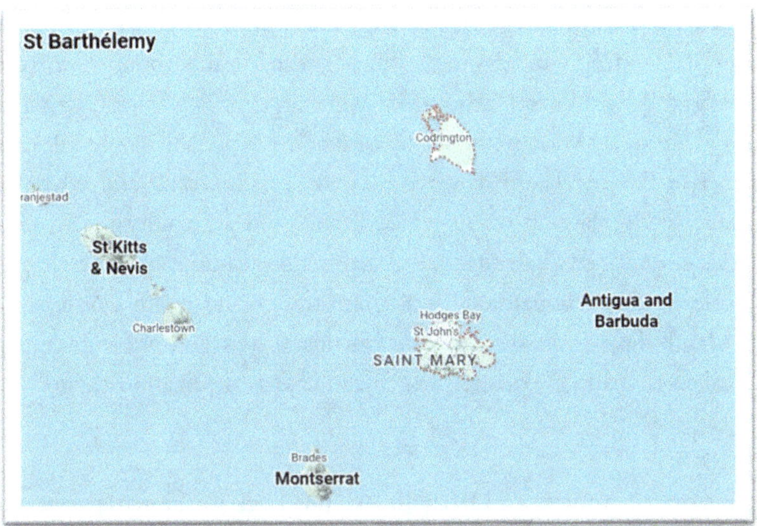

Antigua and Barbuda, known in the local Antiguan and Barbudan Creole as 'Aanteega an' Baabyuuda', is a sovereign archipelagic nation in the Lesser Antilles of the eastern Caribbean Sea, forming part of the Leeward Islands chain. It consists of the two main populated islands—Antigua and Barbuda—and the smaller, uninhabited dependency of Redonda. It is a constitutional monarchy within the Commonwealth, with King Charles III as head of state. With an estimated population of around 105,200, the capital and largest city is St. John's on Antigua, which serves as the political, economic and cultural centre. English is the official language, while Antiguan and Barbudan Creole are widely spoken. The Eastern Caribbean dollar is the official currency. Shaped by Arawak settlement, British colonial history, a legacy of sugar plantations and the modern rise of tourism, Antigua and Barbuda blends a resilient island identity with a cosmopolitan outlook. Its 365 renowned beaches, deep natural harbours and strategic location define its character and its place as a popular destination in the Caribbean.

Geography

Antigua and Barbuda spans a landscape defined by a stark contrast between its two main islands. Antigua is relatively low-lying, a coral island with gentle rolling plains, deeply indented coastlines and natural harbours like English Harbour and Falmouth Harbour. Its highest point is Mount Obama. The island is famously known for its 365 beaches. Barbuda, lying 40 kilometres north, is a flat coral atoll characterised by pristine pink and white sand beaches, a large lagoon on its western side and a significant frigate bird sanctuary. Redonda is a rugged, uninhabited volcanic rock. The climate is tropical maritime, moderated by constant trade winds, with a drier season. The islands lie within the Atlantic hurricane belt and are vulnerable to tropical storms and hurricanes, which can cause significant damage.

History

The history of Antigua and Barbuda extends back to the settlement of the Siboney people over 4,000 years ago, followed by Arawak and later Carib peoples. Christopher Columbus sighted the islands in 1493, naming the main island after the church of Santa María la Antigua in Seville. British colonisation began in 1632, establishing a plantation economy heavily dependent on sugar and the labour of enslaved Africans. Antigua became a strategic naval base for the British Royal Navy in the 18th century, notably at Nelson's Dockyard. Slavery was abolished in 1834. In 1967, Antigua and Barbuda became an associated state of the United Kingdom, gaining full independence on 1 November 1981. The nation has since navigated the challenges of post-colonial development, natural disasters and the evolution of its political landscape.

Government and Politics

Antigua and Barbuda operates as a unitary constitutional monarchy and parliamentary democracy, with the British monarch as the ceremonial head of state, represented locally by a Governor-General. The head of government is the Prime Minister. Legislative power is vested in a bicameral Parliament, consisting of the appointed Senate and the directly elected House of Representatives. The political system is dominated by two main parties, the Antigua and Barbuda Labour Party and the United Progressive

Party. National politics centre on economic management, social welfare, the relationship between Antigua and Barbuda and efforts to diversify the economy.

Economy

Antigua and Barbuda's economy is dominated by services, with tourism contributing the majority of Gross Domestic Product and employment. The country is a premier destination for luxury and yachting tourism, hosting major events like Antigua Sailing Week. The financial services sector is also significant, alongside some limited agriculture. The economy is vulnerable to external shocks, particularly downturns in global travel and the impacts of hurricanes. Key economic challenges include managing high public debt, diversifying away from heavy reliance on tourism, reducing import dependency and fostering inclusive growth.

Demographics and Society

With a population of approximately 105,200, the vast majority reside on Antigua. Barbuda has a much smaller population. The people are predominantly of African descent, reflecting the legacy of the transatlantic slave trade, with minorities of European and mixed heritage. Society is characterised by a strong sense of community, vibrant religious life (predominantly Christian) and a rich oral tradition. While a small middle class exists, economic disparity is a concern. Social challenges include the cost of living, healthcare provision and the need for youth opportunity.

Culture

The culture of Antigua and Barbuda is a spirited fusion of West African heritage and British colonial influences. This is expressed in its music, particularly calypso, soca and the steel pan and in its annual Carnival, a colourful celebration of music, dance and costume. Storytelling, culinary traditions and a deep connection to the sea are central to cultural life. The islands have produced notable figures in literature and music, contributing to a distinct national identity that is both Caribbean and unique within the region.

Education and Healthcare

Education in Antigua and Barbuda is compulsory and free in public schools up to the age of 16. The system follows a British model and the country is home to several offshore medical universities. The University of the West Indies has a campus on Antigua. Healthcare is provided through a mix of public and private facilities, with a main hospital in St. John's. Access can be more limited on Barbuda and the system faces challenges related to funding and the management of non-communicable diseases.

Infrastructure

Antigua and Barbuda's infrastructure is centred on supporting tourism and international connectivity. V.C. Bird International Airport is the main air gateway. The deep natural harbours, especially on Antigua's south coast, are world-class yachting centres. A public bus service operates on Antigua and ferry services connect the main islands. Digital and telecommunications infrastructure is reasonably developed. Critical infrastructure remains vulnerable to hurricane damage, requiring ongoing investment in resilience.

Tourism

Tourism is the lifeblood of the national economy. Antigua's '365 beaches' and historic sites like Nelson's Dockyard, a UNESCO World Heritage Site, are primary attractions. The yachting sector is globally significant, with English Harbour serving as a major base. Barbuda offers an ecotourism experience with its pristine beaches, bird sanctuary and relaxed atmosphere. Sustainable tourism that preserves the islands' natural beauty and benefits local communities is a stated priority.

Current Issues and Future Outlook

Antigua and Barbuda faces the dual challenge of building economic resilience while confronting climate vulnerability. Reducing dependence on tourism, managing public finances and addressing the socio-economic needs of both islands are ongoing priorities. The future outlook hinges on successful economic diversification, investment in climate-resilient infrastructure and the sustainable management of its primary natural asset: its coastline and marine environment.

Overview

Antigua and Barbuda is a nation defined by its breathtaking coastal beauty, a history of endurance and a modern economy built on hospitality. From its origins as a colonial sugar producer to its current status as a tourist haven, it has navigated significant transitions. Looking ahead, balancing development with environmental stewardship and creating a more diversified and resilient economy will be essential for the long-term prosperity of its people.

DID YOU KNOW...?

Antigua and Barbuda is home to Nelson's Dockyard, a restored 18th-century British naval base in English Harbour that is the only continuously working Georgian-era dockyard in the world and a UNESCO World Heritage Site. Named after Admiral Horatio Nelson, who was stationed there in the 1780s, the dockyard was a strategic hub for the Royal Navy during the age of sail, maintaining and repairing warships that patrolled the Caribbean. The site features original buildings—including the Admiral's House, sail lofts and workshops—constructed from brick and timber brought from England as ship's ballast. Its preservation offers a remarkable window into naval history and colonial-era engineering, serving as a striking reminder of imperial maritime power, the strategic importance of the Caribbean and the islands' enduring connection to the sea, which now supports a thriving yachting tourism industry.

KEY FACTS AND FIGURES

Geography & Environment

• Total area: 442 km^2 (two main islands: Antigua and Barbuda, plus smaller islets).
• Coastline: ≈153 km.
• Climate: Tropical marine climate; dry and wet seasons; hurricane-prone.
• Highest point: Mount Obama, Antigua (402 m).
• Major features: Coral reefs, sandy beaches, lagoons, mangroves.
• Wildlife: Frigatebirds, iguanas, sea turtles, tropical fish.
• 0 UNESCO World Heritage sites.

Population & Society

• Population: ≈100,000 (2024 estimate).
• Density: ≈226 persons/km^2.
• Urbanisation: ≈24%.
• Ethnicity:
o Afro-Antiguan and Barbudan: ≈91%
o White: ≈4%
o Mixed and other: ≈5%
• Languages: English (official).
• Religion: Christian (predominantly Anglican and other Protestant denominations): ≈85%.
• Literacy: ≈99%.
• Life expectancy: ≈76 years.

Economy

• GDP (nominal): ≈£2.5 billion.
• GDP per capita (PPP): ≈£25,000.
• Key industries:
o Tourism
o Financial services
o Agriculture (sugar, cotton, vegetables)
o Light manufacturing

• Major exports: Rum, molasses, agricultural products, handicrafts.
• Currency: Eastern Caribbean dollar (XCD; £1 ≈ 4.8 XCD).

Government

• Constitutional monarchy (Commonwealth realm).
• System: Parliamentary democracy.
• Head of State: King Charles III.
• Head of Government: Prime Minister of Antigua and Barbuda.
• Parliament: Bicameral Parliament (House of Representatives and Senate).

Infrastructure

• Transport: Road network on main islands; air and sea transport.
• Major airports: V. C. Bird International Airport (Antigua).
• Energy mix: Fossil fuels with growing solar energy adoption.
• Digital connectivity: Moderate to well developed in main urban and tourist areas; limited on remote islands.

Major Urban Centres

• St. John's: ≈22,000 – Capital, administrative and commercial centre.
• All Saints: ≈3,000 – Regional commercial hub.
• Codrington: ≈1,000 – Main town on Barbuda.
• Potters Village: ≈1,500 – Residential and local trade centre.

ST. JOHN'S – ANTIQUA AND BARBUDA'S CAPITAL, ADMINISTRATIVE AND COMMERCIAL CENTRE

The National Flag

The national flag of Antigua and Barbuda features an inverted black, blue and white triangle at the hoist set against a red field, bearing a golden rising sun with seven points. The red symbolises the dynamism of the people, the black represents the soil and heritage, the blue stands for hope and the sea and the white denotes the nation's beaches. The golden sun signifies the dawn of a new era. The flag as a whole embodies the nation's history, its natural beauty and its triumphant path to independence.

KEY PEOPLE AND PLACES

PEOPLE

Sir Vere Cornwall Bird (1910–1999) Widely regarded as the 'Father of the Nation,' Bird was the first Prime Minister of independent Antigua and Barbuda, serving from 1981 to 1994. He led the country to independence and played a key role in shaping its political and social development.

Sir Lester Bird (1938–2021) Son of Vere Bird, he served as Prime Minister from 1994 to 2004. He continued his father's legacy in governance, promoted economic growth, tourism development and social programmes and was a central figure in Antigua and Barbuda's modern political landscape.

Derek Walcott (1930–2017) A Nobel Prize-winning poet and playwright born on Saint Lucia but influential across the Caribbean, Walcott's works celebrated Caribbean culture, history and identity. His literary achievements contributed to Antigua and Barbuda's cultural heritage and the broader appreciation of Caribbean literature globally.

Sir Vivian Richards (b. 1952) An internationally celebrated cricketer, Richards represented the West Indies with distinction, becoming one of the greatest batsmen in the sport's history. He brought global recognition to Antigua and Barbuda, inspiring generations of athletes across the Caribbean region.

George Walter (1928–2008) A notable politician and advocate for social justice, Walter served in various governmental roles and played an important part in the development of Antigua and Barbuda's democratic institutions, economic policies and education programmes during the early years of independence.

PLACES

St. John's The capital and largest city of Antigua and Barbuda, located on Antigua's northwest coast. St. John's serves as the nation's political, economic and cultural centre, featuring colonial architecture, historic sites, vibrant markets and government institutions, while being the heart of local commerce and tourism.

English Harbour A historic port on Antigua's southern coast, known for its Georgian-era fortifications, a naval past and preserved colonial architecture. English Harbour is a centre for yachting, tourism and cultural heritage, a maritime legacy of Antigua and Barbuda.

Nelson's Dockyard A restored 18th-century naval dockyard located at English Harbour. It is a UNESCO World Heritage site and represents Antigua's colonial maritime history, offering visitors insights into naval operations, shipbuilding and the strategic importance of the Caribbean during the Age of Sail.

Barbuda Island The smaller of the two main islands, Barbuda is known for its pink sand beaches, Frigatebird Sanctuary and relaxed lifestyle. It plays a crucial role in eco-tourism, environmental conservation and preserving the island's natural and cultural heritage.

Devil's Bridge A natural limestone arch located on Antigua's eastern coastline. The site is both a geological wonder and a cultural landmark, attracting visitors for its dramatic Atlantic Ocean waves, scenic beauty and historical significance in folklore and heritage.

Shirley Heights A historic military lookout on Antigua's southern coast, offering panoramic views of English Harbour and the Caribbean Sea. Shirley Heights is celebrated for its scenic landscapes, cultural festivals and historical significance as part of the island's defence system during the colonial period.

TIMELINE OF EVENTS

c. 2400 BCE – 1493 CE: Indigenous Settlements: Archaic peoples, later Arawak and Carib groups, settled Antigua and Barbuda, developing agriculture, fishing, trade networks and organised communities.

1493: Columbus Arrives: Christopher Columbus sighted Antigua and Barbuda during his second voyage, marking European contact and initiating future colonisation by Spain.

1632: British Colonisation Begins: English settlers established permanent colonies on Antigua, introducing European governance, plantations, enslaved African labour and reorganising the islands' social and economic structures.

1666: Expansion of Sugar Economy: Sugar plantations grew rapidly, relying on enslaved Africans, transforming Antigua's economy, society and political power under British colonial administration.

1671: Barbuda Settled for Livestock and Trade: Barbuda was settled to support Antigua's plantations with livestock, timber and trade, remaining under British control and administration.

1700s: Strategic Naval Base Development: Antigua, especially English Harbour, became a key British naval base, enhancing military security, trade and imperial influence in the Caribbean.

1834: Abolition of Slavery: Enslaved Africans were emancipated, radically changing social, economic and political structures, while creating new labour and social dynamics across the islands.

1870s–1900s: Post-Emancipation Development: Antigua and Barbuda gradually rebuilt economies, focusing on agriculture, trade and community organisation after emancipation and colonial reforms.

1951: Universal Adult Suffrage Introduced: Voting rights were extended to all adults, promoting democratic participation, political representation and development of local leadership structures.

1967: Associated State Status Achieved: Antigua and Barbuda gained internal self-government, controlling domestic affairs while Britain retained responsibility for defence and foreign relations.

1981: Independence from Britain: Antigua and Barbuda became an independent nation within the Commonwealth, establishing sovereign governance while retaining the British monarch as ceremonial head.

1980s–1990s: Economic and Tourism Growth: Tourism and services expanded rapidly, diversifying the economy and improving infrastructure, education and social services across both islands.

2000s: Environmental and Cultural Initiatives: The government promoted cultural preservation, heritage tourism and environmental protection, safeguarding natural resources and historical landmarks.

2017: Hurricane Irma Impacts Islands: Hurricane Irma caused widespread destruction, damaging homes, infrastructure and agriculture, requiring extensive recovery, resilience and emergency response efforts.

2020: COVID-19 Pandemic Impact: The pandemic disrupted tourism, trade, public health and daily life, challenging Antigua and Barbuda's economy, healthcare systems and social resilience.

THE FEDERATION OF SAINT KITTS AND NEVIS

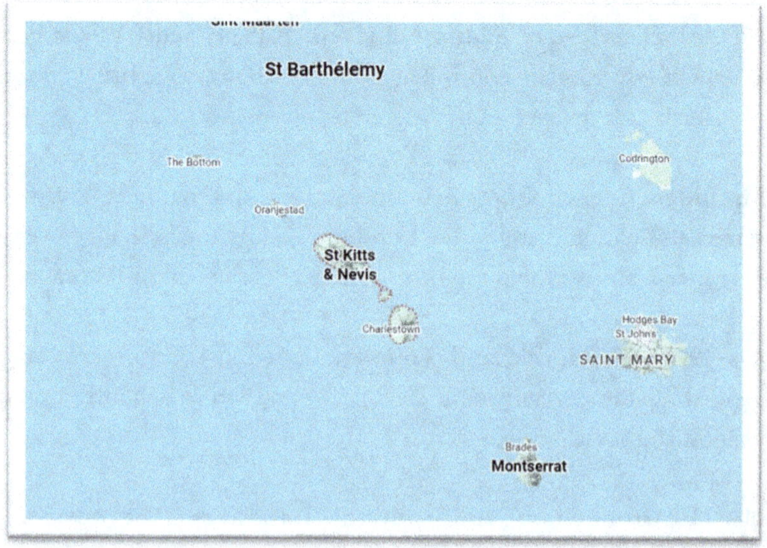

Saint Kitts and Nevis, officially known as the Federation of Saint Kitts and Nevis and often called the Federation, is a sovereign twin-island nation in the Lesser Antilles of the eastern Caribbean Sea. It is the smallest sovereign state in the Americas, both by area and population. It is a constitutional monarchy within the Commonwealth, with King Charles III as head of state. With an estimated population of around 54,800, the capital and largest city is Basseterre on the island of Saint Kitts, which serves as the political, economic and cultural centre. English is the official language. The Eastern Caribbean dollar is the official currency. Shaped by Indigenous Kalinago settlement, British and French colonial rivalry, a pioneering sugar-based economy and the modern evolution of citizenship-by-investment, Saint Kitts and Nevis blends a rich historical legacy with a contemporary focus on sustainable development. Its lush volcanic landscapes, significant historical sites and strategic embrace of economic innovation define its character in the modern Caribbean.

Geography

Saint Kitts and Nevis features a dramatic volcanic geography. The larger island, Saint Kitts, is dominated by the lush, central peak of Mount Liamuiga, a dormant volcano, with a narrow isthmus connecting to a flatter southern peninsula. The landscape includes tropical rainforests, fertile agricultural land and black sand beaches. The smaller island of Nevis is essentially a single, conical volcanic peak (Nevis Peak) surrounded by coral-fringed shores and famous for its golden sand beaches. The climate is tropical, moderated by steady trade winds, with a risk of hurricanes. Both islands are renowned for their natural beauty, from the cloud forests of the central mountains to the coral reefs offshore.

History

The history of Saint Kitts and Nevis begins with the settlement by the Kalinago (Carib) people. Christopher Columbus sighted the islands in 1493, naming Saint Kitts after his patron saint, Christopher. British settlement began in 1623, followed by French arrival, making Saint Kitts the site of the first permanent English and French colonies in the Caribbean. The islands became a pivotal battleground and a model for the plantation system, with sugar cultivation fuelled by enslaved African labour defining the economy for centuries. Slavery was abolished in 1834. The islands were part of the British Leeward Islands colony before entering a federation with neighbouring Anguilla. After Anguilla's secession, Saint Kitts and Nevis achieved full independence on 19 September 1983. The post-independence era has been marked by debates over the political autonomy of Nevis and the development of a novel economic model.

Government and Politics

Saint Kitts and Nevis operates as a federal constitutional monarchy and parliamentary democracy. The British monarch is head of state, represented by a Governor-General. The head of government is the Prime Minister, who is traditionally from Saint Kitts. The federal parliament is unicameral. A unique feature is the constitutional provision for Nevis to secede; it has its own Premier and island assembly, which handles local affairs. National politics have been dominated by the Saint Kitts and Nevis Labour Party and the People's Action Movement, with concerns over inter-island equity, economic management and constitutional reform being perennial themes.

Economy

The economy of Saint Kitts and Nevis has transformed from a historic dependence on sugar, which ended in 2005, to one centred on tourism, financial services and its pioneering Citizenship by Investment (CBI) Programme. Launched in 1984, the CBI programme attracts foreign investment through real estate purchases or contributions to a national fund in exchange for citizenship, becoming a major revenue source. Tourism is vital, focused on cruise ship arrivals, luxury resorts and ecotourism. Agriculture, while diminished, still produces some crops. Key economic challenges include managing the sustainability and reputation of the CBI programme, reducing high public debt, building resilience against external shocks and ensuring balanced development between the two islands.

Demographics and Society

With a population of approximately 54,800, the majority reside on Saint Kitts. The people are predominantly of African descent, with smaller European, mixed-race and Indo-Caribbean communities. Society is close-knit, with strong family and community ties and a vibrant Christian religious life. A significant diaspora exists in the United Kingdom, United States and Canada. Social challenges include addressing cost-of-living pressures, youth unemployment and providing equitable public services across the federation. The relationship between the populations of the two islands, with Nevisians often emphasising a distinct identity, is a subtle but important social dynamic.

Culture

The culture of Saint Kitts and Nevis is a lively fusion of African heritage, British colonial influences and modern Caribbean trends. This is expressed in its annual Carnival celebrations, music (particularly calypso and soca) and colourful folklore. Storytelling, culinary traditions featuring seafood and locally grown produce and a passion for cricket are central to cultural life. The islands maintain a strong sense of history, visible in preserved colonial architecture and sites like the Brimstone Hill Fortress, which serve as touchstones for national pride and identity.

Education and Healthcare

Education in Saint Kitts and Nevis is compulsory and free up to the age of 16. The system follows a British model and the country hosts several offshore medical and veterinary universities. The Clarence Fitzroy Bryant College provides tertiary education. Healthcare is provided through a public system centred on the Joseph N. France General Hospital on Saint Kitts and the Alexandra Hospital on Nevis, supplemented by private clinics. The system works to manage non-communicable diseases and provide consistent care across both islands.

Infrastructure

Infrastructure development supports the tourism and CBI-driven economy. Robert L. Bradshaw International Airport on Saint Kitts and Vance W. Amory International Airport on Nevis provide air links. Port Zante in Basseterre is a major modern cruise ship pier. Road networks are generally good on the main coastlines, though mountain roads can be narrow. Telecommunications are modern and reliable. A passenger ferry provides essential daily transport between the two islands.

Tourism

Tourism is a cornerstone of the economy. Saint Kitts attracts visitors with its UNESCO-listed Brimstone Hill Fortress, rainforest hikes and cruise port. Nevis is known as a more secluded, luxury eco-destination, with historic plantation inns and hot springs. Sustainable tourism that highlights the islands' history, culture and natural environment is a key focus for future growth, alongside the continued development of high-end resort properties.

Current Issues and Future Outlook

Saint Kitts and Nevis faces the ongoing challenge of building a resilient and diversified economy beyond its flagship CBI programme, which faces increasing regional competition and international scrutiny. Managing the fiscal balance, addressing climate vulnerability and ensuring harmonious development between Saint Kitts and Nevis are central priorities. The future outlook depends on successfully transitioning to a more broad-based economic model, investing in human capital and strengthening the federation's unity and international partnerships.

Overview

Saint Kitts and Nevis is a nation defined by its pioneering spirit, from its role as the 'Mother Colony of the West Indies' to its creation of the modern citizenship-by-investment industry. It balances a deep respect for its layered history with a pragmatic approach to economic development. Navigating the path toward sustainable prosperity, while preserving its natural beauty and social cohesion, will shape the future of this small but significant Caribbean federation.

DID YOU KNOW...?

Saint Kitts and Nevis is home to the Brimstone Hill Fortress National Park, a UNESCO World Heritage Site often called the 'Gibraltar of the West Indies.' This monumental 17th- and 18th-century British military fortress was constructed by enslaved Africans using bricks and stone painstakingly carried up the steep hill. Its sophisticated design and sheer scale made it a formidable defensive work intended to secure Britain's valuable sugar colonies. After withstanding a famous siege in 1782, it was eventually captured by the French before being returned under treaty. Today, its extensive ruins—including the iconic Fort George citadel—stand as a powerful testament to European colonial ambition, African engineering skill under duress and the complex military history that shaped the Caribbean, all while offering breathtaking panoramic views of the neighbouring islands.

KEY FACTS AND FIGURES

Geography & Environment

• Total area: 261 km² (two main islands: Saint Kitts and Nevis).
• Coastline: ≈135 km.
• Climate: Tropical marine climate; wet and dry seasons; hurricane-prone.
• Highest point: Mount Liamuiga, Saint Kitts (1,156 m).
• Major features: Volcanic mountains, lush rainforests, coral reefs, sandy beaches.
• Wildlife: Frigatebirds, green vervet monkeys, sea turtles, tropical fish.
• 0 UNESCO World Heritage sites.

Population & Society

• Population: ≈55,000 (2024 estimate).
• Density: ≈211 persons/km².
• Urbanisation: ≈33%.
• Ethnicity:
o Afro-Saint Kitts and Nevis: ≈92%
o White and other: ≈8%
• Languages: English (official).
• Religion: Christian (predominantly Anglican and Methodist): ≈90%.
• Literacy: ≈98%.
• Life expectancy: ≈76 years.

Economy

• GDP (nominal): ≈£1.0 billion.
• GDP per capita (PPP): ≈£18,000.
• Key industries:
o Tourism
o Financial services
o Agriculture (sugarcane, fruits, vegetables)
o Light manufacturing
• Major exports: Sugar, bay oil, electronics, rum.
• Currency: Eastern Caribbean dollar (XCD; £1 ≈ 4.8 XCD).

Government

• Constitutional monarchy (Commonwealth realm).
• System: Parliamentary democracy.
• Head of State: King Charles III.
• Head of Government: Prime Minister of Saint Kitts and Nevis.
• Parliament: Bicameral Parliament (National Assembly and Senate).

Infrastructure

• Transport: Road network on both islands; air and sea transport between islands and internationally.
• Major airports: Robert L. Bradshaw International Airport (Saint Kitts), Vance W. Amory International Airport (Nevis).
• Energy mix: Fossil fuels with growing solar energy adoption.
• Digital connectivity: Moderate to well developed in main towns and tourist areas; limited in remote areas.

Major Urban Centres

• Basseterre: ≈15,500 – Capital, administrative and commercial centre.
• Charlestown: ≈1,500 – Capital of Nevis and regional hub.
• Dieppe Bay Town: ≈1,000 – Local fishing and trade centre.
• Sandy Point Town: ≈1,200 – Port and community hub on Saint Kitts.

BASSETERRE – ST. KITTS AND NEVIS'S CAPITAL, ADMINISTRATIVE AND COMMERCIAL CENTRE

The National Flag

The national flag of the Federation of Saint Kitts and Nevis features a green field with a red chevron edged in black, bearing two white stars. The green symbolises the fertile land, the red denotes the struggle from slavery and colonialism to freedom and the black represents the people's African heritage. The white stars stand for the islands of Saint Kitts and Nevis, embodying hope and liberty. The flag as a whole embodies the nation's history, its dual-island unity and its optimistic future.

KEY PEOPLE AND PLACES

PEOPLE

Sir Robert Llewellyn Bradshaw (1916–1978) Widely regarded as the 'Father of the Nation,' Bradshaw served as the first Premier of Saint Kitts and Nevis. He led the federation toward self-governance, championed workers' rights and played a crucial role in establishing the country's political and social institutions.

Sir Kennedy Simmonds (b. 1936) The first Prime Minister of independent Saint Kitts and Nevis from 1983 to 1995, Simmonds guided the country through independence, promoted economic growth, tourism and international relations and helped strengthen the democratic and institutional framework of the young nation.

Dr. Denzil Douglas (b. 1953) A prominent political leader and physician, Douglas served as Prime Minister from 1995 to 2015. He implemented healthcare reforms, education initiatives and economic development programmes, contributing to the country's political stability and modernisation over two decades of leadership.

Joan 'Josie' Douglas A cultural and community leader, she is recognised for her contributions to preserving the heritage, music and traditions of Saint Kitts and Nevis. Her work in education, civic engagement and cultural promotion has strengthened the islands' sense of identity and national pride.

Sir Cuthbert Sebastian (1921–2017) Governor-General of Saint Kitts and Nevis from 1996 to 2013, he played a key ceremonial and stabilising role in the country's governance, promoting education, community service and national unity while representing the federation internationally.

PLACES

Basseterre (founded 1627) The capital and largest city of Saint Kitts, Basseterre is located on the island's southern coast. It serves as the political, cultural and economic centre of the federation, featuring historic architecture, government institutions, commercial districts and cultural festivals that highlight the nation's heritage.

Charlestown The capital of Nevis, Charlestown is known for its colonial-era buildings, historic sites and scenic harbour. It is the administrative, cultural and commercial hub of Nevis, offering insight into the island's history, architecture and role within the federation.

Brimstone Hill Fortress A UNESCO World Heritage site on Saint Kitts, Brimstone Hill Fortress is a well-preserved colonial fortification that demonstrates the strategic military history of the Caribbean. It is a major cultural and tourist site, offering panoramic views and historical education.

Nevis Peak A dormant volcanic mountain in the centre of Nevis, it dominates the island's landscape. Nevis Peak is important for its biodiversity, hiking trails and eco-tourism, offering visitors spectacular views of the surrounding island, coastlines and Caribbean Sea.

Frigate Bay A popular coastal area on Saint Kitts, Frigate Bay is known for its beaches, resorts and recreational activities. It attracts tourists and locals alike for swimming, water sports and leisure, contributing significantly to the federation's tourism economy.

Indian Castle Church A historic Anglican church on Nevis built during the colonial period, representing the island's religious and cultural heritage. The site highlights the early European influence on Nevis, colonial architecture and the preservation of historical landmarks for tourism and education.

TIMELINE OF EVENTS

c. 2000 BCE – 1493 CE: Indigenous Settlements: Kalinago and Arawak peoples settled Saint Kitts and Nevis, developing agriculture, fishing, trade networks, villages and complex social structures.

1493: Columbus Arrives: Christopher Columbus sighted Saint Kitts and Nevis during his second voyage, marking European contact and initiating future colonisation of the islands.

1623–1624: British and French Colonisation: British and French settlers established colonies on Saint Kitts, introducing European governance, plantations and enslaved African labour, creating rival colonial settlements.

1666: Conflict Between Colonial Powers: Britain and France contested control over Saint Kitts, with warfare and agreements shaping the islands' political boundaries and administration.

1700s: Expansion of Plantation Economy: Sugar plantations grew, relying heavily on enslaved African labour, transforming Saint Kitts' and Nevis' economies, society and hierarchical structures.

1834: Abolition of Slavery: Enslaved Africans were emancipated, fundamentally altering social and economic systems, creating new labour dynamics and reshaping communities across the islands.

1870s–1900s: Post-Emancipation Recovery: Saint Kitts and Nevis gradually rebuilt economies and communities, focusing on sugar production, trade and local governance after emancipation.

1946: Universal Adult Suffrage Introduced: Voting rights were extended to all adults, promoting democratic participation, political representation and local leadership development across the federation.

1958–1962: West Indies Federation Membership: Saint Kitts and Nevis joined the short-lived West Indies Federation, participating in regional political unity and governance experiments.

1967: Associated Statehood Achieved: The federation gained internal self-government, controlling domestic affairs while Britain retained responsibility for defence and foreign relations.

1983: Independence from Britain: Saint Kitts and Nevis became a fully independent nation within the Commonwealth, establishing sovereign governance while retaining the British monarch as head of state.

1980s–1990s: Economic and Tourism Development: Sugar remained important, but tourism and services expanded, improving infrastructure, education, employment and economic diversification across both islands.

2000s: Cultural and Environmental Initiatives: The government promoted cultural heritage, historical preservation and environmental protection, safeguarding natural resources and tourism potential.

2017: Hurricane Irma and Other Storms: Hurricanes and tropical storms caused severe damage to homes, infrastructure and agriculture, requiring extensive recovery and disaster resilience measures.

2020: COVID-19 Pandemic Impact: The pandemic disrupted tourism, public health, economy and daily life, testing Saint Kitts and Nevis' social resilience, healthcare and government services.

THE COMMONWEALTH OF DOMINICA

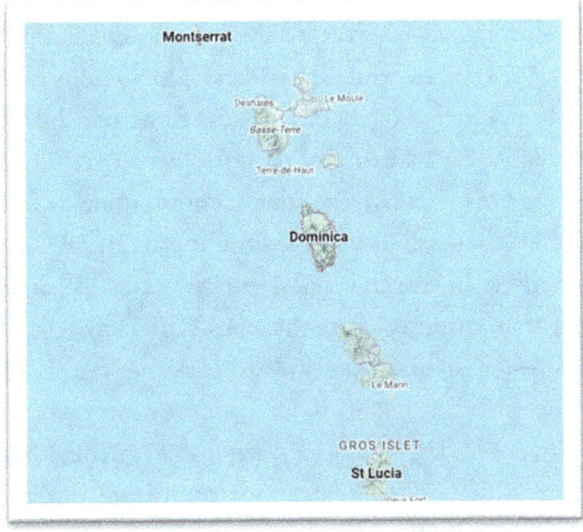

Dominica is a mountainous tropical island located in the eastern Caribbean Sea, situated between the French overseas territories of Guadeloupe to the north and Martinique to the south. With an estimated population of approximately 72,000 people, the capital city is Roseau, while Portsmouth functions as the island's second-largest town and an important administrative and economic centre. English is the official national language, while a French-based creole known as Dominican Creole or Kwéyòl is widely spoken across the island in everyday life. The Eastern Caribbean Dollar serves as the national currency. Shaped by centuries of Indigenous Kalinago civilisation, prolonged resistance to European settlement and later French and British colonial rule, Dominica has developed a historical identity distinct from many of its Caribbean neighbours. Renowned for its environmental richness, cultural continuity and resilience in the face of adversity, the island blends deep historical roots with a strong connection to nature. This combination of endurance, cultural pride and environmental stewardship defines the national identity of Dominica.

Geography

Spanning a compact yet exceptionally rugged landscape, Dominica exhibits some of the most dramatic geographical features in the Caribbean. The island is dominated by a central spine of steep volcanic mountains, dense rainforest and deeply incised river valleys. Morne Diablotins, the highest peak, rises to 1,447 metres, while the Morne Trois Pitons massif contains geothermal features including boiling lakes, fumaroles and hot springs. Dominica is notable for its extraordinary freshwater resources, with over 365 rivers and streams flowing year-round, contributing to fertile soils and lush vegetation. The coastline stretches for approximately 148 kilometres and is characterised by rugged cliffs, rocky headlands and black sand beaches, rather than extensive coral beaches. The climate is tropical, with high rainfall throughout the year and a hurricane season from June to November. The island is highly biodiverse, hosting numerous endemic plant and animal species, but faces significant natural hazards from hurricanes, landslides and flooding. Environmental challenges include forest conservation, watershed protection and coastal erosion.

History

The history of Dominica begins with the Kalinago people, who settled the island centuries before European contact and maintained control over much of its territory longer than on most Caribbean islands. Christopher Columbus sighted the island in 1493, naming it Dominica after the day of his arrival. For more than two centuries, Dominica remained largely outside sustained European settlement, serving as a stronghold of Indigenous resistance. French and British powers later contested the island, with shifting control until Britain secured formal possession in 1763. A plantation economy developed on a limited scale, based on coffee, sugar and cotton and sustained by enslaved African labour. Slavery was abolished in 1834 and Dominica became notable for early Black political participation during the colonial period. The 20th century saw growing demands for self-government, culminating in full independence from the United Kingdom in 1978. Since independence, Dominica has navigated democratic governance alongside economic vulnerability and repeated environmental shocks.

Government and Politics

Dominica is a unitary parliamentary democracy and a republic, with a President serving as ceremonial head of state and a Prime Minister as head of government. Political authority is centralised, with local administration organised through 10 parishes. The political system consists of three branches: executive, legislative and judicial. Executive power is exercised by the Prime Minister and Cabinet, drawn from the elected members of the House of Assembly. Legislative authority rests with the unicameral Parliament, comprising elected representatives and appointed senators. The judiciary operates independently under English common law, with final appellate jurisdiction vested in the Caribbean Court of Justice. Political life is dominated by two principal parties, the Dominica Labour Party (DLP) and the United Workers Party (UWP). Domestically, political debate focuses on economic management, disaster recovery and development policy, while internationally Dominica maintains active membership in CARICOM, the OECS, the Commonwealth and the United Nations.

Economy

Dominica possesses a small, open and service-oriented economy, traditionally supported by agriculture, tourism and public sector activity. Agriculture has historically been dominated by banana production, supplemented by crops such as plantains, citrus fruits, cocoa and root vegetables. Tourism has grown steadily but is deliberately oriented towards eco-tourism and low-density development, rather than mass resort tourism. The services sector accounts for the majority of economic output, complemented by remittances and a citizenship-by-investment programme that provides significant government revenue. Despite these income sources, the economy has long faced challenges including limited diversification, small domestic markets and vulnerability to external shocks, particularly hurricanes. The Eastern Caribbean Dollar is managed by the Eastern Caribbean Central Bank. Ongoing economic policy emphasises fiscal stability, climate resilience, renewable energy development and sustainable long-term growth.

Demographics and Society

With a population of approximately 72,000, Dominica is among the least populous sovereign states in the Caribbean. The population is predominantly of African descent, reflecting the legacy of the transatlantic slave trade, with a small but culturally significant Indigenous Kalinago population residing primarily within the Kalinago Territory on the east coast. The national motto, 'Après Bondié, C'est La Ter' ('After God, the Earth'), reflects the island's strong spiritual and environmental values. Society is largely rural, with settlements dispersed across mountainous terrain and coastal villages. English is the official language, while Dominican Creole functions as the principal language of daily interaction. Christianity predominates, particularly Roman Catholicism. Social challenges include outward migration, limited employment opportunities and disaster vulnerability, though communities are characterised by strong family ties, social cohesion and cultural pride.

Culture

Dominican culture has achieved growing international recognition, shaped by African, Kalinago, French and British influences and a deep relationship with the natural environment. Music plays a central role, with genres such as cadence-lypso and bouyon forming key expressions of national identity. Cultural traditions are prominently displayed during Carnival, locally known as *Mas Domnik* and through events such as the World Creole Music Festival, which attracts regional and international audiences. Cuisine reflects the island's agricultural base, featuring dishes such as callaloo soup, roasted breadfruit, freshwater fish and mountain chicken. Dominican Creole remains a vital medium for storytelling, music and oral tradition. Cultural expression is closely linked to environmental awareness and the preservation of heritage.

Education and Healthcare

Dominica maintains an education system based on the British model, comprising primary, secondary and tertiary levels. Literacy rates are relatively high and tertiary education is provided primarily through Dominica State College. Healthcare services are delivered mainly through a publicly funded system offering universal access, supported by private clinics and practitioners. While basic healthcare coverage is widespread, specialised services are limited and serious medical cases often require treatment overseas. Key public health challenges include managing non-communicable diseases such as diabetes and hypertension. Policy discussions focus on improving healthcare infrastructure, workforce capacity and resilience to natural disasters.

Infrastructure

Infrastructure development in Dominica reflects the challenges posed by its mountainous terrain and exposure to extreme weather. A national road network connects most communities, though maintenance is complicated by landslides and storm damage. The island has no railway system. Seaports in Roseau and Portsmouth support trade and inter-island transport, while Douglas–Charles Airport provides international air access. Energy production has traditionally relied on imported fossil fuels, prompting efforts to expand geothermal and other renewable energy sources. Telecommunications infrastructure has improved, though internet access remains uneven in remote areas. Infrastructure priorities include strengthening water supply systems and enhancing climate resilience.

Tourism

Tourism is important to Dominica's economy and international image. Attractions include the rainforests and waterfalls of Morne Trois Pitons National Park, geothermal features such as the Boiling Lake and rich marine environments suitable for diving and whale watching. Cultural sites, village experiences and heritage attractions add depth to the visitor offering. Unique to Dominica, it has limited large-scale resort development, instead promoting eco-lodges, guesthouses and community-based tourism. Sustainable tourism initiatives aim to balance environmental protection with economic benefits for local communities.

Current Issues and Future Outlook

Dominica faces a defined set of challenges alongside its considerable natural and cultural strengths. Central concerns include climate vulnerability, economic diversification, population decline due to emigration and the ongoing recovery from hurricane damage. Internationally, climate advocacy and development partnerships play a critical role. The country benefits from political stability, social cohesion and a strong global reputation for environmental leadership. The future outlook replies on successful climate adaptation, renewable energy development and investment in human capital.

Overview

Dominica is a nation defined by its environmental abundance, cultural depth and historical resilience. Rooted in Indigenous heritage and shaped by a complex colonial past, it has emerged as a distinctive Caribbean state committed to sustainability and cultural preservation. Its island geography presents both developmental challenges and unique opportunities. Looking ahead, the nation seeks to harness its natural assets, strengthen economic resilience and preserve social cohesion while maintaining democratic institutions and environmental stewardship.

DID YOU KNOW...?

Dominica is home to the Sisserou parrot, one of the rarest parrots in the world and the national bird of Dominica. Endemic to the island's mountainous rainforests, this vividly coloured species is so culturally significant that it appears prominently on the national flag. Traditionally regarded as a symbol of resilience and environmental guardianship, the Sisserou represents Dominica's extraordinary biodiversity, Indigenous legacy and enduring connection between its people and the natural world.

KEY FACTS AND FIGURES

Geography & Environment

• Total area: 751 km².

• Coastline: ≈148 km.

• Climate: Tropical marine climate; wet and dry seasons; hurricane-prone.

• Highest point: Morne Diablotins (1,447 m).

• Major features: Volcanic mountains, rainforests, hot springs, rivers, Boiling Lake.

• Wildlife: Sisserou parrot (national bird), Agouti, iguanas, tropical amphibians.

• 1 UNESCO World Heritage site.

Population & Society

• Population: ≈72,000 (2024 estimate).

• Density: ≈96 persons/km².

• Urbanisation: ≈70%.

• Ethnicity:

o Afro-Dominican: ≈86%

o Mixed: ≈9%

o Carib Indigenous: ≈4%

o Other: ≈1%

• Languages: English (official); Kwéyòl (Creole) widely spoken.

• Religion: Christian (predominantly Roman Catholic and Protestant): ≈90%.

• Literacy: ≈94%.

• Life expectancy: ≈77 years.

Economy

• GDP (nominal): ≈£0.9 billion.

• GDP per capita (PPP): ≈£12,500.

• Key industries:

o Agriculture (bananas, cocoa, coconuts)

o Tourism (eco-tourism focus)

o Light manufacturing

o Services
• Major exports: Bananas, citrus, coconuts, bay oil.
• Currency: Eastern Caribbean dollar (XCD; £1 ≈ 4.8 XCD).

Government
• Constitutional monarchy (Commonwealth realm).
• System: Parliamentary democracy.
• Head of State: King Charles III.
• Head of Government: Prime Minister of Dominica.
• Parliament: House of Assembly (unicameral).

Infrastructure
• Transport: Road network across main island; air and sea transport.
• Major airports: Douglas-Charles Airport (formerly Melville Hall), Canefield Airport.
• Energy mix: Primarily fossil fuels; developing geothermal energy.
• Digital connectivity: Moderate; better in urban and tourist areas, limited in remote regions.

Major Urban Centres
• Roseau: ≈16,500 – Capital, administrative and commercial centre.
• Portsmouth: ≈6,500 – Northern regional hub and port.
• Marigot: ≈2,500 – Coastal community and local trade centre.
• Salisbury: ≈2,000 – Residential and regional service town.

ROSEAU – DOMINICA'S CAPITAL, ADMINISTRATIVE AND COMMERCIAL CENTRE

The National Flag

The national flag of the Commonwealth of Dominica features a green field with a central red disc bearing a Sisserou parrot, encircled by ten green stars on a yellow, black and white cross. The green symbolises the island's lush forest, the red disc represents social justice and the parrot stands for national flight toward lofty aspirations. The ten green stars denote the island's ten parishes and the cross reflects the Trinity and Christian faith. The flag as a whole embodies Dominica's natural heritage, its commitment to justice and its sovereign identity.

KEY PEOPLE AND PLACES

PEOPLE

Sir Edward Oliver LeBlanc (1923–2001) Widely regarded as the 'Father of the Nation,' LeBlanc served as Premier from 1967 to 1978. He championed social reform, rural development and self-governance, laying the foundation for Dominica's independence and strengthening the country's democratic institutions.

Patrick John (1938–2021) The first Prime Minister of independent Dominica, serving from 1978 to 1979, John guided the country through the initial stages of sovereignty, focusing on nation-building, public administration and establishing the structures necessary for governance, social development and economic progress.

Eugenia Charles (1919–2005) The first female Prime Minister in Dominica and the Caribbean, serving from 1980 to 1995, she was a strong advocate for democratic governance, rule of law and regional cooperation and she gained international recognition for her leadership during crises.

Phyllis Shand Allfrey (1908–1986) A pioneering writer, politician and journalist, Allfrey contributed to Dominica's political and cultural life, promoting social reform, education and literary expression. She remains celebrated for her novels and advocacy of equality, justice and Caribbean identity.

Rosie Douglas (1941–2000) A social activist, politician and international diplomat, Douglas was committed to social justice, human rights and Caribbean solidarity. His advocacy for economic reform and regional integration left a lasting influence on Dominica's political and international development.

PLACES

Roseau (founded 1635) The capital and largest city of Dominica, located on the southwestern coast. Roseau is the political, cultural and economic hub of the country, featuring historic colonial architecture, government institutions, markets and cultural centres that showcase the nation's vibrant heritage.

Portsmouth (founded 1722) The second-largest town on the northern coast, Portsmouth serves as a historical and commercial centre. It is notable for its colonial-era structures, maritime history, proximity to Indian River and Cabrits National Park and role in regional trade and tourism.

Morne Trois Pitons National Park A UNESCO World Heritage site located in central Dominica, this protected area features volcanic peaks, hot springs, rainforests, rivers and endemic wildlife. It is renowned for its ecological significance, biodiversity, eco-tourism and cultural importance to Indigenous and local communities.

Boiling Lake A unique volcanic crater lake sits in Morne Trois Pitons National Park. Boiling Lake, the world's second-largest of its kind, attracts hikers and nature enthusiasts while highlighting Dominica's volcanic activity, natural beauty and eco-tourism potential.

Trafalgar Falls A famous twin waterfall located near the village of Trafalgar. These natural landmarks are celebrated for their stunning scenery, hiking trails and eco-tourism opportunities, offering insight into Dominica's volcanic geology and lush rainforest ecosystems.

Cabrits National Park A historic and ecological park located near Portsmouth, featuring 18th-century Fort Shirley, tropical forests and diverse marine habitats. Cabrits National Park is an important site for heritage preservation, environmental protection and tourism in Dominica.

TIMELINE OF EVENTS

c. 500–1492 CE: Indigenous Settlements: Kalinago (Carib) peoples settled Dominica, developing agriculture, fishing, trade networks, villages and complex social, cultural and spiritual systems across the islands.

1493: Columbus Arrives: Christopher Columbus sighted Dominica during his second voyage, marking European contact and initiating future colonisation attempts in the Caribbean.

1600s: Early European Colonisation Attempts: French and British settlers attempted to establish colonies, facing resistance from the Kalinago and harsh tropical environments.

1690s: French Influence Strengthens: France established more permanent settlements, introducing plantations, European governance and Catholicism while competing with British colonial interests.

1763: Treaty of Paris: France ceded Dominica to Britain, officially establishing British colonial administration and controlling governance, trade and security on the island.

1800s: Expansion of Plantation Economy: Sugar, coffee and other crops were cultivated on plantations using enslaved African labour, transforming society, economy and social hierarchies.

1834: Abolition of Slavery: Enslaved Africans were emancipated, changing labour systems, social structures and economic patterns across Dominica's plantations and communities.

1870s–1900s: Post-Emancipation Development: Dominica gradually rebuilt its economy, focusing on agriculture, trade and community organisation while adapting to colonial governance.

1946: Universal Adult Suffrage Introduced: Voting rights were extended to all adults, promoting democratic participation, political representation and the emergence of local leadership structures.

1967: Associated Statehood Achieved: Dominica gained internal self-government, controlling domestic affairs while Britain retained responsibility for defence and foreign relations.

1978: Independence from Britain: Dominica became an independent nation within the Commonwealth, establishing full sovereignty while retaining the British monarch as ceremonial head of state.

1980s–1990s: Economic and Social Development: Agriculture remained important, but tourism and services expanded, improving infrastructure, education, employment and economic diversification across Dominica.

2000s: Environmental and Cultural Initiatives: The government promoted environmental protection, heritage preservation and sustainable tourism, safeguarding natural resources and cultural landmarks.

2017: Hurricane Maria Devastates Island: Hurricane Maria caused widespread destruction, damaging homes, infrastructure, agriculture and public services, prompting extensive recovery and disaster resilience measures.

2020: COVID-19 Pandemic Impact: The pandemic disrupted tourism, public health, economy and daily life, testing Dominica's resilience, healthcare systems and social and governmental services.

SAINT LUCIA

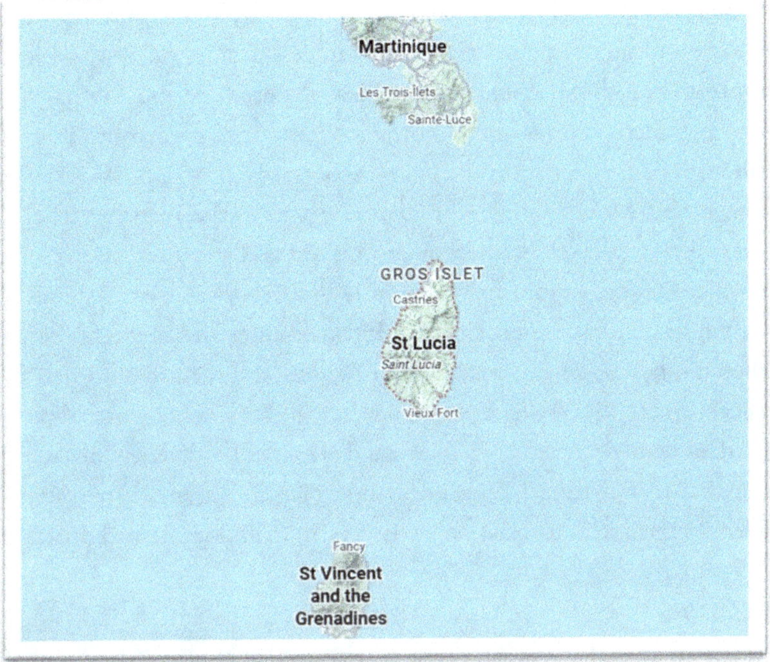

Saint Lucia is a mountainous tropical island nation located in the eastern Caribbean Sea, positioned between Martinique to the north and Saint Vincent and the Grenadines to the south. With an estimated population of approximately 184,000 people, the capital city is Castries, which also serves as the island's principal port and commercial centre. Other notable towns include Gros Islet, Soufrière and Vieux Fort, each playing important roles in tourism, industry and regional administration. English is the official national language, while a French-based creole known as Saint Lucian Creole or Kwéyòl is widely spoken in everyday life. The Eastern Caribbean Dollar serves as the national currency. Shaped by Indigenous Arawak and Kalinago heritage, prolonged French and British colonial rivalry and African diaspora influences, Saint Lucia blends deep historical roots with a rich cultural tradition. Its dramatic landscapes, cultural vibrancy and resilience have helped define Saint Lucia's distinctive national identity.

Geography

Despite its modest size, Saint Lucia possesses a strikingly varied and dramatic physical landscape. The island is dominated by a central mountain range of volcanic origin, with steep ridges, fertile valleys and dense rainforest. The most iconic geographical features are the Pitons—Gros Piton and Petit Piton—twin volcanic spires rising sharply from the Caribbean Sea near Soufrière and recognised as a UNESCO World Heritage Site. Mount Gimie, the highest point on the island, reaches 950 metres above sea level. Numerous short rivers and streams descend rapidly from the interior, supporting agriculture and freshwater ecosystems. The coastline stretches for approximately 158 kilometres and alternates between sheltered sandy beaches, rocky headlands and coral reefs. Saint Lucia has a tropical climate with a wet season from June to November, coinciding with the Atlantic hurricane season. The island is rich in biodiversity but remains vulnerable to hurricanes, landslides and volcanic activity. Environmental challenges include deforestation, coastal erosion and watershed protection.

History

The history of Saint Lucia begins with the Indigenous Arawak and later Kalinago peoples, who inhabited the island long before European contact. Christopher Columbus is believed to have sighted the island in 1502, though early European settlement was limited due to Kalinago resistance. During the 17th and 18th centuries, Saint Lucia became a focal point of rivalry between France and Britain, changing hands fourteen times before Britain gained permanent control in 1814. A plantation economy developed based on sugar production and enslaved African labour. Slavery was abolished in 1834, profoundly reshaping social and economic relations. The post-emancipation period was marked by economic hardship and limited political representation. The 20th century saw gradual constitutional reform and the growth of nationalist movements. Saint Lucia achieved full independence from the United Kingdom in 1979. Since independence, the country has maintained democratic governance while navigating economic vulnerability and environmental risk.

Government and Politics

Saint Lucia is a unitary parliamentary democracy and a constitutional monarchy, with the British monarch serving as ceremonial head of state, represented locally by a Governor-General. Political authority is centralised, with local administration organised through 11 districts. The political system consists of executive, legislative and judicial branches. Executive power is exercised by the Prime Minister and Cabinet, drawn from the elected House of Assembly. Legislative authority rests with a bicameral Parliament, comprising the elected House of Assembly and an appointed Senate. The judiciary operates independently under English common law, with the Eastern Caribbean Supreme Court serving as the superior court system and final appeals heard by the Caribbean Court of Justice. Political life is dominated by two major parties, the Saint Lucia Labour Party (SLP) and the United Workers Party (UWP). Domestically, political debate focuses on economic management, crime, social services and development, while internationally Saint Lucia is an active member of CARICOM, the OECS, the Commonwealth and the United Nations.

Economy

Saint Lucia has a small, open and service-oriented economy, with tourism as its primary economic driver. Agriculture, once dominated by banana production, has declined in relative importance but continues to contribute through crops such as bananas, cocoa, coconut and root vegetables. Tourism accounts for a significant share of employment and foreign exchange earnings, supported by cruise tourism, luxury resorts and eco-tourism ventures. The services sector dominates economic output, supplemented by remittances and offshore financial services. Despite these strengths, the economy faces persistent challenges, including limited diversification, high public debt and vulnerability to external shocks such as hurricanes and global economic downturns. The Eastern Caribbean Dollar is managed by the Eastern Caribbean Central Bank. Economic policy priorities include fiscal reform, private sector development and enhancing climate resilience.

Demographics and Society

With a population of approximately 184,000, Saint Lucia is one of the smaller sovereign states in the Caribbean. The population is predominantly of African descent, reflecting the legacy of the transatlantic slave trade, with smaller communities of mixed European, East Indian and Indigenous ancestry. The national motto, 'The Land, The People, The Light,' reflects the country's emphasis on unity, identity and progress. Society is moderately urbanised, with a significant proportion of the population living in or around Castries. English is the official language, while Saint Lucian Creole remains widely spoken and culturally significant. Christianity predominates, particularly Roman Catholicism, though religious diversity exists. Social challenges include youth unemployment, crime and economic inequality, but communities are often characterised by strong family ties, religious faith and social cohesion.

Culture

Saint Lucian culture reflects a rich blend of African, French and British influences, shaped by history and reinforced through language, music and festival traditions. Music plays a central role, with genres such as calypso, soca and traditional folk music forming important expressions of cultural identity. The annual Saint Lucia Jazz & Arts Festival is internationally recognised and showcases both local and global talent. Carnival celebrations, particularly those held in July, are major cultural events marked by music, dance and masquerade. Cuisine highlights local produce and flavours, with dishes such as green fig and saltfish (the national dish), callaloo soup and bouyon. Saint Lucian Creole is a vital medium for storytelling and oral tradition. Cultural life is closely tied to national pride and historical memory.

Education and Healthcare

Saint Lucia maintains an education system based on the British model, comprising primary, secondary and tertiary levels. Education is compulsory at the primary level and literacy rates are relatively high. Sir Arthur Lewis Community College serves as the island's principal tertiary institution. Healthcare is delivered through a public system offering universal access, supported by private clinics and practitioners. While basic healthcare services are widely available, specialised medical care is limited, often requiring overseas referral. Key public health challenges include managing non-communicable diseases such as diabetes and hypertension. Policy discussions focus on improving healthcare infrastructure, access and workforce capacity.

Infrastructure

Infrastructure development in Saint Lucia reflects the challenges of its mountainous terrain and exposure to natural hazards. A national road network connects most communities, though steep gradients and landslides complicate maintenance. The island has no railway system. Major ports in Castries and Vieux Fort support trade and cruise tourism, while Hewanorra International Airport and George F. L. Charles Airport provide international and regional air access. Energy production has traditionally relied on imported fossil fuels, prompting efforts to expand renewable energy sources such as solar and geothermal power. Telecommunications infrastructure is relatively well developed, though internet access can be uneven in rural areas. Infrastructure priorities include improving water supply reliability and strengthening disaster resilience.

Tourism

Tourism is the cornerstone of Saint Lucia's economy and a key component of its global image. Natural attractions include the iconic Pitons, lush rainforests, waterfalls and volcanic features such as the Sulphur Springs near Soufrière. The island is also known for its luxury resorts, honeymoon tourism and yachting facilities, particularly around Rodney Bay and Marigot Bay. Cultural tourism, heritage sites and community-based initiatives add depth to the visitor experience. Sustainable tourism strategies aim to balance environmental protection with economic benefits, recognising the island's ecological sensitivity and reliance on natural beauty.

Current Issues and Future Outlook

Saint Lucia faces challenges alongside its notable strengths. Key national concerns include economic diversification, youth unemployment, crime, public debt and vulnerability to climate change. Hurricanes, coastal erosion and rising sea levels pose risks to infrastructure and livelihoods. Internationally, maintaining development partnerships and regional cooperation is essential. At the same time, Saint Lucia benefits from political stability, strong institutions and a well-established tourism brand. The future outlook depends on successful economic reform, investment in human capital and infrastructure and effective climate adaptation strategies. These challenges will shape the country's long-term resilience and prosperity.

Overview

Saint Lucia is a nation of dramatic landscapes, cultural richness and complex colonial legacy. From its Indigenous roots and centuries of European rivalry to a modern day independent Caribbean state, the island has forged a strong sense of identity. Its geography presents both development constraints and opportunities, particularly in tourism. Saint Lucia seeks to harness its cultural and natural assets to promote inclusive growth, strengthen resilience and sustain democratic governance.

DID YOU KNOW...?

Saint Lucia is the only sovereign country in the world named after a woman—Saint Lucy of Syracuse, a Christian martyr. The island's name reflects its French colonial heritage and is a unique distinction among nations. This symbolic naming underscores Saint Lucia's blend of history, culture and identity, contributing to its distinctive place within the Caribbean and the wider world.

KEY FACTS AND FIGURES

Geography & Environment

• Total area: 616 km².

• Coastline: ≈158 km.

• Climate: Tropical marine climate; wet and dry seasons; hurricane-prone.

• Highest point: Mount Gimie (950 m).

• Major features: Pitons (UNESCO-listed), volcanic mountains, rainforests, beaches, rivers.

• Wildlife: Saint Lucia parrot (Amazona versicolor), agouti, bats, tropical amphibians and reptiles.

• 1 UNESCO World Heritage site.

Population & Society

• Population: ≈180,000 (2024 estimate).

• Density: ≈292 persons/km².

• Urbanisation: ≈20%.

• Ethnicity:

o Afro-Saint Lucian: ≈85%

o Mixed: ≈10%

o Indo-Caribbean and other: ≈5%

• Languages: English (official); Saint Lucian Creole French widely spoken.

• Religion: Christian (predominantly Roman Catholic; Protestant minorities): ≈90%.

• Literacy: ≈90%.

• Life expectancy: ≈77 years.

Economy

• GDP (nominal): ≈£2.5 billion.

• GDP per capita (PPP): ≈£14,000.

• Key industries:

o Tourism

o Agriculture (banana, cocoa, coconut, vegetables)

o Light manufacturing

o Services

- Major exports: Bananas, cocoa, coconuts, vegetables.
- Currency: Eastern Caribbean dollar (XCD; £1 ≈ 4.8 XCD).

Government

- Constitutional monarchy (Commonwealth realm).
- System: Parliamentary democracy.
- Head of State: King Charles III.
- Head of Government: Prime Minister of Saint Lucia.
- Parliament: House of Assembly (unicameral).

Infrastructure

- Transport: Road network across main island; air and sea transport.
- Major airports: Hewanorra International, George F. L. Charles Airport.
- Energy mix: Predominantly fossil fuels; growing solar energy.
- Digital connectivity: Moderate; better in urban and tourist areas.

Major Urban Centres

- Castries: ≈20,000 – Capital, administrative and commercial centre.
- Vieux Fort: ≈14,000 – Southern industrial and tourism hub.
- Soufrière: ≈8,000 – Tourism and cultural centre.
- Gros Islet: ≈10,000 – Coastal town and tourism hotspot.

CASTRIES – SAIT LUCIA'S CAPITAL, ADMINISTRATIVE AND COMMERCIAL CENTRE

The National Flag

The national flag of Saint Lucia features a cerulean blue field with a central triangular design of gold, black and white. The blue symbolises the Caribbean Sea and the Atlantic Ocean, while the gold represents the sunshine and prosperity. The black and white denote the island's cultural harmony between peoples and the specific triangular shapes evoke the famous Pitons mountains. The flag as a whole embodies the nation's natural beauty, its racial unity and its bright, hopeful future.

KEY PEOPLE AND PLACES

PEOPLE

Sir John Compton (1925–2007) Widely regarded as the 'Father of the Nation,' Compton served multiple terms as Prime Minister, leading Saint Lucia to independence in 1979. He played a key role in political development, nation-building and strengthening democratic institutions and governance.

Derek Walcott (1930–2017) A Nobel Prize-winning poet and playwright born in Saint Lucia, Walcott celebrated Caribbean culture, history and identity through his literature. His work brought international recognition to the island, highlighting its cultural richness and influencing generations of Caribbean writers and artists.

Kenny Anthony (b. 1951) Served as Prime Minister for multiple terms, implementing economic reforms, education initiatives and social development programmes. He strengthened Saint Lucia's political and economic institutions, promoted regional integration and represented the island in international diplomacy and development efforts.

Daren Sammy (b. 1983) An internationally acclaimed cricketer and captain of the West Indies team, Sammy brought global attention to Saint Lucia through his sporting achievements, inspiring young athletes and becoming a national symbol of pride, leadership and dedication to the community.

Dionne Brand (b. 1953) Though primarily associated with Canada, Brand was born in Saint Lucia and her literary and activist work reflects Caribbean identity, social justice and cultural heritage. She has brought international recognition to the island through her poetry, novels and advocacy.

PLACES

Castries (founded 1650) The capital and largest city of Saint Lucia, on the northwest coast. It is the political, economic and cultural hub of the island with government institutions, historic sites, markets, ports and centres for commerce, tourism and cultural events.

Soufrière A historic town on the southwestern coast, Soufrière is known for its colonial architecture, Caribbean heritage and proximity to natural landmarks such as the Pitons, Sulphur Springs and botanical gardens, attracting eco-tourists, historians and visitors seeking cultural and natural experiences.

The Pitons Two striking volcanos, Gros Piton and Petit Piton, located near Soufrière. A UNESCO World Heritage site, These are central to Saint Lucia's natural heritage, tourism, hiking and conservation, symbolising the island's unique geological and ecological features.

Pigeon Island National Landmark A historic site and park located on the northern coast, featuring colonial fortifications, scenic trails and beaches. Pigeon Island preserves Saint Lucia's military, cultural and natural history while providing recreational opportunities and panoramic views of the Caribbean Sea.

Marigot Bay A picturesque bay on the west coast, renowned for its natural beauty, marina facilities and calm waters. Marigot Bay attracts tourists, sailors and eco-tourists, offering opportunities for leisure, recreation and appreciation of Saint Lucia's coastal landscapes and tropical environment.

Sulphur Springs A geothermal area near Soufrière featuring hot springs, mud baths and volcanic activity. Sulphur Springs is a major eco-tourism site, attracting visitors for health, recreation and scientific interest, while highlighting Saint Lucia's unique volcanic and geological environment.

TIMELINE OF EVENTS

c. 2000 BCE – 1492 CE: Indigenous Settlements: Arawak and later Kalinago peoples settled Saint Lucia, developing agriculture, fishing, trade networks, villages and complex social, cultural and spiritual systems.

1492: Columbus Sightings: Christopher Columbus sighted Saint Lucia during his voyages, marking European contact and initiating future attempts at colonisation of the island.

1600s: Early European Colonisation Attempts: French and British settlers attempted to establish colonies, facing resistance from Kalinago populations and challenges from harsh tropical environments.

1660s–1700s: French and British Rivalries: Control of Saint Lucia alternated between France and Britain, with treaties and conflicts shaping colonial administration and territorial boundaries.

1763: Treaty of Paris: France ceded Saint Lucia to Britain temporarily, although the island continued to change hands frequently during subsequent Anglo-French conflicts.

1790s: Expansion of Plantation Economy: Sugar plantations grew under British and French influence, relying on enslaved African labour, transforming Saint Lucia's economy, society and hierarchical structures.

1834: Abolition of Slavery: Enslaved Africans were emancipated, changing labour systems, social structures and plantation economies while shaping post-emancipation society on the island.

1870s–1900s: Post-Emancipation Development: Saint Lucia gradually rebuilt its economy and society, focusing on agriculture, trade, education and local governance after emancipation.

1946: Universal Adult Suffrage Introduced: Voting rights were extended to all adults, promoting democratic participation, political representation and development of local leadership structures.

1967: Associated Statehood Achieved: Saint Lucia gained internal self-government, controlling domestic affairs while Britain retained responsibility for defence and foreign relations.

1979: Independence from Britain: Saint Lucia became an independent nation within the Commonwealth, establishing full sovereignty while retaining the British monarch as ceremonial head of state.

1980s–1990s: Economic and Social Development: Agriculture remained important, but tourism and services expanded, improving infrastructure, education, employment and economic diversification.

2000s: Environmental and Cultural Initiatives: The government promoted heritage preservation, environmental protection and sustainable tourism, safeguarding natural resources and cultural landmarks across the island.

2017: Hurricane Maria Devastates Island: Hurricane Maria caused extensive damage to homes, infrastructure, agriculture and public services, requiring major recovery and disaster resilience efforts.

2020: COVID-19 Pandemic Impact: The pandemic disrupted tourism, public health, economy and daily life, testing Saint Lucia's resilience, healthcare systems and governmental capacity.

SAINT VINCENT AND THE GRENADINES

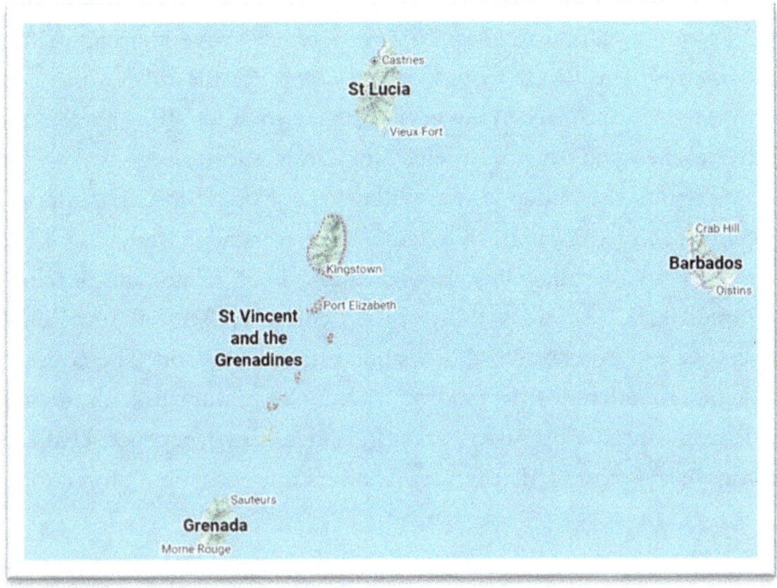

Saint Vincent and the Grenadines is a volcanic island nation located in the eastern Caribbean Sea, forming part of the Lesser Antilles. The country consists of the main island of Saint Vincent and a chain of smaller islands known as the Grenadines, stretching southward towards Grenada. With an estimated population of approximately 110,000 people, the capital city is Kingstown, which also serves as the principal port and administrative centre. Other significant towns include Georgetown, Barrouallie and Chateaubelair on the main island, as well as Port Elizabeth on Bequia. English is the official national language, while Vincentian Creole is widely spoken in everyday life. The Eastern Caribbean Dollar serves as the national currency. Shaped by Indigenous Kalinago heritage, prolonged resistance to European settlement and later French and British colonial rule, the nation blends deep historical roots with a strong maritime and island identity. Its cultural traditions, natural environment and resilience in the face of natural hazards define the identity of Saint Vincent and the Grenadines.

Geography

Spanning a compact but topographically dramatic landscape, Saint Vincent and the Grenadines displays significant geographical diversity. The main island of Saint Vincent is dominated by a rugged central mountain range of volcanic origin, culminating in La Soufrière, an active volcano rising to 1,234 metres. The island features steep slopes, fertile valleys and dense rainforest, while the Grenadines are characterised by low-lying coral islands, sandy beaches and shallow reefs. Numerous short rivers and streams descend from the mountainous interior of Saint Vincent, supporting agriculture and freshwater ecosystems. The coastline is varied, with black sand beaches along the windward side and calmer, white-sand beaches in the Grenadines. The climate is tropical, with a wet season from June to November and exposure to the Atlantic hurricane season. The country is rich in marine and terrestrial biodiversity but faces natural hazards including hurricanes, volcanic eruptions and landslides. Environmental challenges include coastal erosion, deforestation and marine ecosystem protection.

History

The history of Saint Vincent and the Grenadines begins with the Kalinago people, who inhabited the islands long before European contact and successfully resisted colonisation for centuries. Saint Vincent became known as 'Hairoun,' meaning 'Land of the Blessed,' and served as a stronghold of Indigenous resistance. European contact began in the late 15th century, but sustained settlement was delayed due to Kalinago opposition. French settlers arrived in the 18th century, followed by British expansion, leading to prolonged conflict. Britain gained control in 1763, though resistance continued through the Carib Wars, culminating in the forced deportation of the Black Caribs, later known as the Garifuna, in 1797. A plantation economy based on sugar developed, reliant on enslaved African labour. Slavery was abolished in 1834. The 20th century saw the gradual emergence of representative government, leading to full independence from the United Kingdom in 1979. Since independence, the nation has pursued democratic governance while confronting economic and environmental challenges.

Government and Politics

Saint Vincent and the Grenadines is a unitary parliamentary democracy and a constitutional monarchy, with the British monarch serving as head of state, represented by a Governor-General. Political authority is centralised, with administrative divisions organised into parishes. The political system comprises executive, legislative and judicial branches. Executive power is vested in the Prime Minister and Cabinet, drawn from the elected House of Assembly. Legislative authority rests with a unicameral Parliament, consisting of elected representatives and appointed senators. The judiciary is independent and based on English common law, operating under the Eastern Caribbean Supreme Court, with final appeals heard by the Caribbean Court of Justice. Political life is dominated by two major parties, the Unity Labour Party (ULP) and the New Democratic Party (NDP). Domestically, political debate focuses on economic development, social services and disaster preparedness, while internationally the country maintains active membership in CARICOM, the OECS, the Commonwealth and the United Nations.

Economy

Saint Vincent and the Grenadines has a small, open and service-oriented economy, traditionally supported by agriculture, tourism and public sector employment. Agriculture has historically centred on banana production, alongside root crops, arrowroot and spices, though its relative importance has declined. Tourism plays an increasingly significant role, particularly in the Grenadines, which are known for yachting, luxury resorts and marine tourism. The services sector accounts for the majority of economic output, supplemented by remittances and construction activity. Despite these strengths, the economy faces ongoing challenges, including limited diversification, high vulnerability to external shocks and natural disasters. The Eastern Caribbean Dollar is managed by the Eastern Caribbean Central Bank. Economic policy priorities include fiscal stability, sustainable tourism development and enhancing climate resilience.

Demographics and Society

With a population of approximately 110,000, Saint Vincent and the Grenadines is one of the smaller sovereign states in the Caribbean. The population is predominantly of African descent, reflecting the legacy of the transatlantic slave trade, with smaller communities of mixed, East Indian and Indigenous ancestry. The national motto, 'Pax et Justitia' ('Peace and Justice'), reflects the country's social values. Society is moderately urbanised, with a significant proportion of the population residing in and around Kingstown. English is the official language, while Vincentian Creole is widely used in daily communication. Christianity predominates, particularly Protestant denominations, though religious diversity exists. Social challenges include outward migration, unemployment and economic inequality, but communities are characterised by strong family ties and social cohesion.

Culture

The culture of Saint Vincent and the Grenadines reflects a rich blend of African, Indigenous and European influences. Music plays a central role in national life, with calypso and soca particularly prominent, alongside traditional folk forms such as string band and big drum music. Carnival, known locally as *Vincy Mas*, is the most significant cultural event of the year, featuring music, dance, costume and street parades. Cuisine draws heavily on local agricultural produce and seafood, with dishes such as roasted breadfruit, fried jackfish, callaloo soup and pepper pot. Vincentian Creole serves as an important medium for oral tradition, storytelling and song. Cultural expression is closely linked to national identity and historical memory.

Education and Healthcare

Saint Vincent and the Grenadines maintains an education system based on the British model, encompassing primary, secondary and tertiary levels. Education is compulsory at the primary level and literacy rates are relatively high. The St. Vincent and the Grenadines Community College serves as the main tertiary institution. Healthcare services are delivered primarily through a publicly funded system offering universal access, supported by private providers. While basic healthcare is widely available, specialised medical services are limited, often requiring overseas referral. Public health challenges include managing non-communicable diseases such as diabetes and hypertension. Policy efforts focus on strengthening healthcare infrastructure and improving access across all islands.

Infrastructure

Infrastructure development in Saint Vincent and the Grenadines reflects the challenges of a multi-island state and exposure to natural hazards. A road network connects communities on Saint Vincent, while inter-island transport relies on ferries and small aircraft. The country has no railway system. Major ports in Kingstown and the Grenadines facilitate trade and tourism, while Argyle International Airport provides international air access. Energy production has traditionally relied on imported fossil fuels, prompting efforts to expand renewable energy sources such as solar and geothermal power. Telecommunications infrastructure has improved, though internet access remains uneven across smaller islands. Infrastructure priorities include strengthening transport links, water supply systems and disaster resilience.

Tourism

Tourism is a vital component of the economy of Saint Vincent and the Grenadines, particularly within the Grenadines. Attractions include pristine beaches, coral reefs, sailing and yachting opportunities, as well as hiking and eco-tourism on Saint Vincent. Popular destinations include Bequia, Mustique, Canouan and Union Island. Cultural festivals, heritage sites and community-based tourism initiatives add depth to the visitor experience. Sustainable tourism strategies aim to balance economic development with environmental protection and local community benefits.

Current Issues and Future Outlook

Saint Vincent and the Grenadines faces a range of challenges alongside its natural and cultural strengths. Key concerns include economic diversification, climate vulnerability, disaster recovery and population decline through emigration. Volcanic activity, particularly the 2021 eruption of La Soufrière, underscores the country's exposure to natural hazards. At the same time, the nation benefits from political stability, strong social cohesion and growing international recognition for sustainable tourism. The future outlook depends on effective disaster preparedness, climate adaptation, investment in human capital and regional cooperation. How these issues are addressed will shape the country's resilience and long-term development.

Overview

Saint Vincent and the Grenadines is a nation defined by its volcanic landscapes, maritime character and resilient people. Rooted in Indigenous heritage and shaped by colonial rivalry and struggle, it has developed a distinct national identity across its islands. While its geography presents significant development challenges, it also offers unique economic opportunities. Moving forward, the country seeks to strengthen economic resilience, preserve cultural heritage and protect its natural environment while sustaining democratic governance.

DID YOU KNOW...?

Saint Vincent and the Grenadines is home to La Soufrière, one of the most active volcanoes in the Caribbean. Its eruptions, most recently in 2021, have profoundly shaped the island's landscape and history. Revered and feared in equal measure, La Soufrière stands as a powerful symbol of the nation's resilience, natural forces and enduring capacity to rebuild in the face of adversity.

KEY FACTS AND FIGURES

Geography & Environment

• Total area: 389 km² (main island St. Vincent plus smaller Grenadine islands).

• Coastline: ≈84 km.

• Climate: Tropical marine climate; wet and dry seasons; hurricane-prone.

• Highest point: La Soufrière (1,234 m).

• Major features: Volcanic mountains, rainforests, beaches, coral reefs.

• Wildlife: Saint Vincent parrot, bats, birds, marine turtles, iguanas.

• 0 UNESCO World Heritage sites.

Population & Society

• Population: ≈110,000 (2024 estimate).

• Density: ≈283 persons/km².

• Urbanisation: ≈54%.

• Ethnicity:

o Afro-Saint Vincentian and Grenadian: ≈66%

o Mixed: ≈19%

o Indigenous Carib: ≈6%

o Other: ≈9%

• Languages: English (official); Vincentian Creole widely spoken.

• Religion: Christian (predominantly Anglican, Roman Catholic, Methodist): ≈90%.

• Literacy: ≈95%.

• Life expectancy: ≈74 years.

Economy

• GDP (nominal): ≈£1.0 billion.

• GDP per capita (PPP): ≈£9,500.

• Key industries:

o Agriculture (bananas, arrowroot, vegetables, cocoa)

o Tourism

o Light manufacturing and services

o Fishing

• Major exports: Bananas, arrowroot, cocoa, vegetables.

• Currency: Eastern Caribbean dollar (XCD; £1 ≈ 4.8 XCD).

Government

• Constitutional monarchy (Commonwealth realm).

• System: Parliamentary democracy.
• Head of State: King Charles III.
• Head of Government: Prime Minister of Saint Vincent and the Grenadines.
• Parliament: House of Assembly (unicameral).

Infrastructure
• Transport: Road network on main islands; air and sea transport between islands.
• Major airports: Argyle International Airport (Saint Vincent).
• Energy mix: Predominantly fossil fuels; growing solar energy.
• Digital connectivity: Moderate; concentrated in urban and tourist areas, limited on remote Grenadine islands.

Major Urban Centres
• Kingstown: ≈16,500 – Capital, administrative and commerce.
• Georgetown: ≈1,500 – Grenada-based regional hub.
• Barrouallie: ≈1,200 – Coastal town and fishing centre.
• Chateaubelair: ≈1,000 – Northern town and local service hub.

KINGSTOWN – SAINT VINCENT AND THE GRENADINES' CAPITAL, ADMINISTRATIVE AND COMMERCIAL CENTRE

The National Flag

The national flag of Saint Vincent and the Grenadines feature three vertical diamonds of green, gold and green on a blue field, with the central gold diamond bearing a green breadfruit leaf. The blue symbolises the sky and sea, the green represents the islands' lush vegetation and the enduring vitality of the people and the gold stands for the golden sands and the bright spirit of the islanders. The breadfruit leaf commemorates the historical breadfruit plants brought to the islands and signifies the nation's rich agricultural heritage. The flag as a whole embodies the nation's natural resources, its history and its vibrant, hopeful character.

KEY PEOPLE AND PLACES

PEOPLE

Sir Milton Cato (1915–1997) Widely regarded as the 'Father of the Nation,' Cato served as the first Prime Minister of Saint Vincent and the Grenadines after independence in 1979. He played a pivotal role in achieving sovereignty, developing political institutions and shaping the nation's early governance.

Arnhim Eustace (b. 1944) A prominent political leader and economist, Eustace served as Prime Minister and held several key governmental roles. He contributed to national economic planning, education initiatives and public administration, promoting political stability and sustainable development in Saint Vincent and the Grenadines.

Ralph Gonsalves (b. 1946) Serving as Prime Minister from 2001, Gonsalves has been a central figure in the country's politics, advocating for social reform, economic development, regional integration and international diplomacy, while maintaining a focus on education, infrastructure and healthcare improvements.

Sir James Fitz-Allen Mitchell (1924–2016) A distinguished political leader, Mitchell served as Prime Minister for multiple terms, guiding national development, implementing agricultural and infrastructural programmes and fostering regional cooperation. His leadership helped strengthen Saint Vincent and the Grenadines' political and economic institutions.

Shevern 'Shevy' Christian A cultural activist and community leader, Christian has contributed to preserving the music, dance and traditions of Saint Vincent and the Grenadines. Her work highlights the nation's cultural identity and promotes education and awareness of Caribbean heritage for future generations.

PLACES

Kingstown (founded 1722) The capital and largest city of Saint Vincent and the Grenadines, located on the island of Saint Vincent. Kingstown serves as the nation's political, economic and cultural centre, featuring historic buildings, government institutions, commercial hubs, markets and vibrant urban life.

Bequia The largest of the Grenadine islands, Bequia is known for its scenic beauty, yachting, beaches and cultural festivals. It attracts tourists, sailors and eco-travellers while maintaining strong local traditions and contributing to the nation's tourism economy.

La Soufrière Volcano An active volcano on Saint Vincent, La Soufrière is both a natural landmark and a source of geothermal activity. It has historical, ecological and cultural significance, attracting scientists, hikers and tourists interested in the island's volcanic landscapes and biodiversity.

Mustique A private island in the Grenadines, Mustique is celebrated for its luxury resorts, exclusive villas and pristine beaches. The island plays a significant role in high-end tourism, attracting international visitors while showcasing the natural beauty and exclusivity of the Grenadines.

Union Island A southern Grenadine Island known for its vibrant culture, picturesque beaches and sailing opportunities. Union Island supports local fishing communities, eco-tourism and recreational activities, offering visitors a glimpse into the natural, cultural and maritime heritage of Saint Vincent and the Grenadines.

Wallilabou Bay A scenic bay on Saint Vincent's western coast, known for its natural beauty, historic significance and use as a filming location for international productions. Wallilabou Bay attracts tourists and sailors while preserving aspects of the island's heritage and coastal environment.

TIMELINE OF EVENTS

c. 2000 BCE – 1498 CE: Indigenous Settlements: Arawak and later Kalinago peoples settled Saint Vincent and the Grenadines, developing agriculture, fishing, trade networks and complex social, cultural systems.

1498: Columbus Sightings: Christopher Columbus sighted Saint Vincent during his third voyage, marking European contact and initiating future colonisation attempts in the Caribbean.

1600s: Early European Colonisation Attempts: French and British settlers attempted to establish colonies on Saint Vincent, facing strong resistance from the Kalinago population and harsh tropical conditions.

1719–1763: French and British Rivalries: Control of Saint Vincent alternated between France and Britain, with treaties and military conflicts shaping colonial administration and territorial boundaries.

1763: Treaty of Paris: France ceded Saint Vincent to Britain, establishing formal British colonial administration, trade regulation and governance structures on the island.

1770s–1800s: Expansion of Plantation Economy: Sugar plantations expanded under British control, relying heavily on enslaved African labour, transforming Saint Vincent's economy, society and social hierarchies.

1834: Abolition of Slavery: Emancipation of enslaved Africans changed labour systems, social structures and plantation economies, reshaping post-emancipation society across Saint Vincent and the Grenadines.

1870s–1900s: Post-Emancipation Development: Saint Vincent gradually rebuilt its economy, focusing on agriculture, trade, education and local governance after emancipation and colonial reforms.

1946: Universal Adult Suffrage Introduced: Voting rights were extended to all adults, promoting democratic participation, political representation and the emergence of local leadership structures.

1969: Associated Statehood Achieved: Saint Vincent and the Grenadines gained internal self-government, controlling domestic affairs while Britain retained responsibility for defence and foreign relations.

1979: Independence from Britain: The country became a fully independent nation within the Commonwealth, establishing sovereign governance while retaining the British monarch as ceremonial head of state.

1980s–1990s: Economic and Social Development: Agriculture remained central, but tourism and services expanded, improving infrastructure, education, employment and economic diversification across the islands.

2000s: Environmental and Cultural Initiatives: The government promoted heritage preservation, environmental protection and sustainable tourism, safeguarding natural resources and cultural landmarks throughout the country.

2017: Hurricane Maria Devastates Islands: Hurricane Maria caused extensive destruction, damaging homes, infrastructure, agriculture and public services, requiring major recovery and disaster resilience efforts.

2020: COVID-19 Pandemic Impact: The pandemic disrupted tourism, public health, economy and daily life, testing Saint Vincent and the Grenadines' resilience, healthcare and governmental systems.

BARBADOS

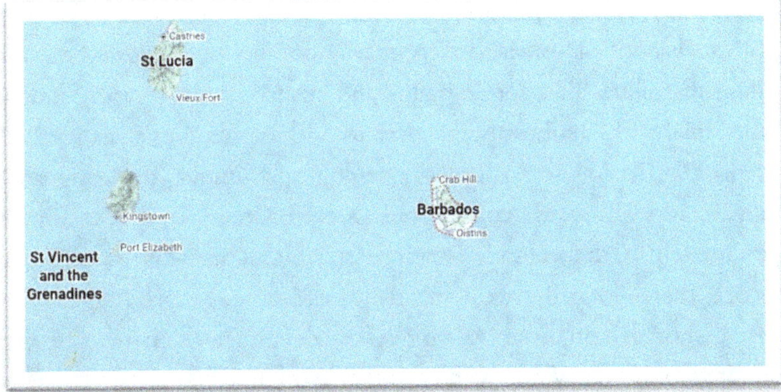

Barbados is a coral island nation located in the western Atlantic Ocean, forming the easternmost boundary of the Caribbean region. Situated east of the Windward Islands, it occupies a strategic position along historic Atlantic trade routes. With an estimated population of approximately 281,000 people, the capital city is Bridgetown, which also serves as the country's principal port, commercial hub and cultural centre. Other notable urban areas include Speightstown, Oistins and Holetown, each playing important roles in commerce, tourism and local administration. English is the official national language, spoken throughout the island. The Barbadian Dollar serves as the national currency. Shaped by Indigenous Amerindian presence, early British colonisation, a plantation economy and the African diaspora, Barbados blends deep historical foundations with a stable institutional legacy. Renowned for its democratic traditions, cultural expression and tourism appeal, the nation projects a strong sense of continuity, resilience and national pride.

Geography

Despite its relatively small size, Barbados possesses a distinctive and comparatively gentle physical landscape when contrasted with many Caribbean islands. The island is primarily composed of coral limestone, resulting in rolling hills, fertile plains and relatively few steep mountains. Mount Hillaby, the highest point, rises to 340 metres above sea level. The Scotland District in the northeast is geologically unique, featuring rugged terrain, clay soils and coastal cliffs. Barbados has a coastline of approximately 97 kilometres, characterised by calm, white-sand beaches and coral reefs along the west and south coasts and more rugged, wave-exposed shores along the Atlantic east coast. The climate is tropical, moderated by trade winds, with a wet season from June to November. While Barbados lies east of the main hurricane belt, it remains vulnerable to storms, coastal erosion and water scarcity. Environmental challenges include freshwater management, coral reef protection and climate change adaptation.

History

The history of Barbados begins with Indigenous Amerindian peoples, including the Saladoid and Arawak, who inhabited the island prior to European contact. The island was uninhabited when the British established a permanent settlement in 1627. Barbados rapidly developed into a major sugar-producing colony, reliant on enslaved African labour and characterised by an entrenched plantation system. It became one of Britain's most profitable colonies in the Americas. Slavery was abolished in 1834, followed by a period of social and economic transition marked by limited political power for the formerly enslaved population. The 20th century saw the rise of labour movements and demands for political reform. Barbados achieved full independence from the United Kingdom in 1966. In 2021, the country transitioned from a constitutional monarchy to a parliamentary republic. Since independence, Barbados has maintained political stability and strong democratic institutions.

Government and Politics

Barbados is a unitary parliamentary democracy and a republic, with a President serving as head of state and a Prime Minister as head of government. Political authority is centralised, with local administration organised through constituencies rather than formal parish councils, though the island retains historic parish divisions. The political system comprises executive, legislative and judicial branches. Executive power is exercised by the Prime Minister and Cabinet, drawn from the elected House of Assembly. Legislative authority rests with a bicameral Parliament, consisting of the elected House of Assembly and an appointed Senate. The judiciary is independent and based on English common law, with the Caribbean Court of Justice serving as the final appellate court. Political life is dominated by two major parties, the Barbados Labour Party (BLP) and the Democratic Labour Party (DLP). Domestically, political debate centres on economic management, social policy and climate resilience, while internationally Barbados is an active member of CARICOM, the Commonwealth and the United Nations.

Economy

Barbados possesses a diversified, service-oriented economy, with tourism, international business and financial services as key pillars. Historically reliant on sugar production, agriculture now plays a smaller role, though sugarcane remains culturally significant. Tourism accounts for a substantial share of employment and foreign exchange earnings, supported by luxury resorts, cruise tourism and sports tourism. The services sector dominates economic output, complemented by remittances and creative industries. Despite its strengths, the economy faces challenges including high public debt, vulnerability to global economic fluctuations and climate-related risks. The Barbadian Dollar is managed by the Central Bank of Barbados. Economic policy priorities include fiscal consolidation, economic diversification and investment in renewable energy and human capital to support long-term resilience.

Demographics and Society

With a population of approximately 281,000, Barbados is one of the more densely populated Caribbean nations. The population is predominantly of African descent, reflecting the legacy of the transatlantic slave trade, with smaller communities of mixed, European and Asian ancestry. The national motto, 'Pride and Industry,' reflects the country's emphasis on self-reliance and achievement. Barbados is highly urbanised, with a large proportion of the population living in or around Bridgetown and along the south and west coasts. English is universally spoken, complemented by Barbadian Creole, commonly known as Bajan, in informal settings. Christianity predominates, particularly Anglicanism, though religious diversity exists. Social challenges include ageing demographics and economic inequality, but the society is widely regarded for its social cohesion, educational attainment and civic engagement.

Culture

Barbadian culture reflects a rich blend of African heritage and British institutional influence, expressed through music, language, festivals and social traditions. Music plays a central role, with calypso and soca featuring prominently alongside spouge, a uniquely Barbadian genre. The annual Crop Over Festival is the island's most significant cultural event, celebrating the end of the sugar harvest through music, dance and costume. Barbadian cuisine features dishes such as flying fish and cou-cou (the national dish), macaroni pie and pudding and souse. Bajan Creole serves as an important medium for humour, storytelling and oral expression. Sport is central to national identity, with cricket holding particular cultural importance and producing internationally renowned players.

Education and Healthcare

Barbados maintains a well-developed education system based on the British model, encompassing primary, secondary and tertiary levels. Education is compulsory and literacy rates are among the highest in the Caribbean. The University of the West Indies, Cave Hill campus, is a major regional institution. Healthcare is delivered through a publicly funded system offering universal access, supplemented by private providers. The system provides a broad range of services, though pressures exist related to ageing populations and non-communicable diseases. Public health priorities include managing chronic conditions such as diabetes and hypertension and maintaining healthcare quality and sustainability.

Infrastructure

Infrastructure in Barbados reflects its relatively flat terrain and high level of development. A comprehensive road network connects all parts of the island, though traffic congestion is a growing concern. There is no railway system. The Port of Bridgetown supports cruise and cargo traffic, while Grantley Adams International Airport serves as a major aviation hub for the eastern Caribbean. Energy production has traditionally relied on imported fossil fuels, prompting efforts to expand solar and other renewable energy sources. Telecommunications infrastructure is advanced, with widespread broadband and mobile access. Infrastructure priorities include improving water security, upgrading public transport and strengthening climate resilience.

Tourism

Tourism is the primary engine of Barbados's economy and a defining feature of its global image. The island is renowned for its beaches, coral reefs and favourable climate, attracting visitors from Europe and North America. Cultural attractions include historic Bridgetown and its Garrison, a UNESCO World Heritage Site, as well as plantation houses and museums. Sports tourism, culinary tourism and festivals further diversify the sector. Sustainable tourism initiatives increasingly focus on environmental protection, community engagement and cultural preservation to ensure long-term benefits.

Current Issues and Future Outlook

Barbados faces a set of challenges alongside its economic and institutional strengths. Key concerns include managing public debt, addressing climate change impacts, ensuring water security and adapting to global economic volatility. At the same time, the country benefits from political stability, strong governance and a highly educated population. Internationally,

Barbados has taken a prominent role in climate advocacy and financial reform discussions. The future outlook depends on continued economic reform, investment in renewable energy and infrastructure and strengthening social resilience. How effectively these priorities are managed will shape Barbados's long-term prosperity and sustainability.

Overview

Barbados is a nation defined by its stability, cultural richness and historical continuity. From its early colonial development to its modern status as a parliamentary republic, it has forged strong institutions and a distinctive national identity. Its geography supports tourism and settlement, while its people have cultivated a reputation for education, diplomacy and resilience. Looking forward, Barbados seeks to balance economic innovation with social equity and environmental stewardship while maintaining its democratic traditions.

DID YOU KNOW...?

Barbados is often referred to as the 'Birthplace of Rum', with a rum-making tradition dating back to the 17th century. Mount Gay Distillery, established in 1703, is recognised as the oldest commercial rum distillery in the world. This enduring legacy reflects Barbados's historical role in global trade and its lasting cultural influence well beyond the Caribbean.

KEY FACTS AND FIGURES

Geography & Environment

• Total area: 430 km².

• Coastline: ≈97 km.

• Climate: Tropical marine climate; wet and dry seasons; hurricane-prone.

• Highest point: Mount Hillaby (336 m).

• Major features: Coral limestone plateau, rolling plains, coastal beaches, small ponds and wetlands.

• Wildlife: Green monkeys, tropical birds, sea turtles, coral reef fish.

• 0 UNESCO World Heritage sites.

Population & Society

• Population: ≈290,000 (2024 estimate).

• Density: ≈674 persons/km² (one of the highest in the Caribbean).

• Urbanisation: ≈32%.

• Ethnicity:

o Afro-Barbadian: ≈92%

o White: ≈4%

o Mixed and other: ≈4%

• Languages: English (official); Bajan Creole widely spoken.

• Religion: Christian (predominantly Anglican, Catholic, Methodist): ≈95%.

• Literacy: ≈99%.

• Life expectancy: ≈77 years.

Economy

• GDP (nominal): ≈£5.0 billion.

• GDP per capita (PPP): ≈£17,500.

• Key industries:

o Tourism

o Agriculture (sugarcane, vegetables, rum production)

o Financial and offshore services

o Light manufacturing

- Major exports: Sugar, rum, chemicals, molasses, manufactured goods.
- Currency: Barbadian dollar (BBD; £1 ≈ 2.0 BBD).

Government

- Constitutional monarchy (Commonwealth realm).
- System: Parliamentary democracy.
- Head of State: King Charles III.
- Head of Government: Prime Minister of Barbados.
- Parliament: Bicameral Parliament (Senate and House of Assembly).

Infrastructure

- Transport: Road network throughout the island; air and sea transport.
- Major airports: Grantley Adams International Airport (Bridgetown).
- Energy mix: Predominantly fossil fuels; growing solar energy adoption.
- Digital connectivity: Well developed, particularly in tourist areas.

Major Urban Centres

- Bridgetown: ≈110,000 – Capital, administrative and commercial centre.
- Speightstown: ≈4,500 – Northern coastal town and fishing hub.
- Oistins: ≈5,000 – Coastal town and tourism centre.
- Holetown: ≈3,000 – Tourism and commercial hub.

BRIDGETOWN – BARBADOS'S CAPITAL, ADMINISTRATIVE AND COMMERCIAL CENTRE

The National Flag

The national flag of Barbados features three vertical panels of ultramarine, gold and ultramarine, with a broken trident centred on the gold panel. The ultramarine symbolises the sky and sea, while the gold represents the nation's sandy beaches. The broken trident denotes Barbados's break from its colonial past and its full independence. The flag as a whole embodies the nation's natural environment, its history and its sovereign status.

KEY PEOPLE AND PLACES

PEOPLE

Errol Barrow (1920–1987) Widely regarded as the 'Father of Independence,' Barrow served as the first Prime Minister of Barbados. He led the country to independence in 1966, promoted social and economic reforms, education and democratic institutions and strengthened national identity.

Owen Arthur (1949–2020) Prime Minister of Barbados from 1994 to 2008, Arthur oversaw economic development, trade liberalisation, infrastructure projects and regional diplomacy. His leadership contributed to national growth, international relations and the consolidation of democratic governance in Barbados during the late 20th and early 21st centuries.

Sir Garfield Sobers (b. 1936) An internationally celebrated cricketer, Sobers is widely regarded as one of the greatest all-rounders in cricket history. He brought global recognition to Barbados, inspiring generations of athletes and becoming a national icon of sporting excellence and pride.

Dame Nita Barrow (1916–1995) A pioneering educator, social worker and diplomat, Barrow served as Governor-General of Barbados. She promoted education, women's empowerment, social welfare and community development, leaving a lasting legacy in advancing social justice and public service on the island.

Rihanna (Robyn Rihanna Fenty) (b. 1988) A globally renowned singer, entrepreneur and philanthropist, Rihanna was born in Barbados. She has brought international recognition to the island through her music, business ventures and charitable work, becoming a symbol of Barbadian culture and global influence.

PLACES

Bridgetown (founded 1628) The capital and largest city of Barbados, Bridgetown is a political, economic and cultural centre. Located on the southwestern coast, it features colonial architecture, government institutions, historic sites, a busy port and vibrant commercial and cultural activity.

Holetown (founded 1627) The first British settlement on Barbados, Holetown is historically significant as the site of early colonial development. It now serves as a cultural and tourism hub, offering heritage sites, shopping and beach resorts that reflect the island's colonial past.

Bathsheba A coastal village on the east coast known for its dramatic rock formations, surfing beaches and scenic beauty. Bathsheba attracts tourists, photographers and nature enthusiasts while preserving aspects of traditional Barbadian fishing culture and rural coastal life.

Harrison's Cave A spectacular limestone cave system located in central Barbados, featuring stalactites, stalagmites, streams and underground waterfalls. Harrison's Cave is a major tourist attraction, providing insight into the island's geology, natural history and eco-tourism opportunities.

St. Nicholas Abbey A historic plantation house on the northern part of the island, dating back to the 17th century. It is a cultural and architectural landmark, offering visitors a glimpse into colonial history, rum production and Barbadian heritage.

Animal Flower Cave Located at the northernmost point of Barbados; this sea cave features natural rock formations and ocean views. It serves as a tourist destination, showcasing the island's coastal geology, marine biodiversity and scenic landscapes for visitors and researchers alike.

TIMELINE OF EVENTS

c. 1600 BCE – 1625 CE: Indigenous Settlements: Arawak and Carib peoples settled Barbados, developing agriculture, fishing, trade networks, villages and complex social, cultural and spiritual systems.

1625: British Colonisation Begins: English settlers established permanent colonies in Barbados, introducing European governance, plantations, enslaved African labour and reshaping the island's social and economic structures.

1640s–1700s: Expansion of Sugar Economy: Sugar plantations expanded rapidly, relying on enslaved African labour, transforming Barbados' economy, society, political influence and hierarchical colonial structures.

1650s: Consolidation of British Control: Britain strengthened governance, military presence and trade regulations, establishing Barbados as a key colonial hub in the Caribbean.

1834: Abolition of Slavery: Enslaved Africans were emancipated under British law, radically transforming social, economic and labour systems across Barbados' plantations and communities.

1870s–1900s: Post-Emancipation Development: Barbados gradually rebuilt its economy and communities, focusing on agriculture, trade, education and local governance after emancipation and reforms.

1944: Universal Adult Suffrage Introduced: Voting rights were extended to all adults, promoting democratic participation, political representation and development of local leadership across the island.

1950s–1960s: Political and Social Reforms: Labour and social movements advanced workers' rights, education and political representation, shaping Barbados' path toward self-governance and democracy.

1966: Independence from Britain: Barbados became an independent nation within the Commonwealth, establishing full sovereignty while retaining the British monarch as ceremonial head of state.

1970s–1990s: Economic and Tourism Development: Agriculture remained important, but tourism and services expanded, improving infrastructure, education, employment and economic diversification across Barbados.

2000s: Cultural and Environmental Initiatives: The government promoted cultural preservation, heritage tourism and environmental protection, safeguarding natural resources and historical landmarks across the island.

2017: Hurricane and Storm Preparedness: Hurricanes and tropical storms tested infrastructure and disaster management, prompting resilience strategies, emergency response and community preparedness across Barbados.

2020: COVID-19 Pandemic Impact: The pandemic disrupted tourism, trade, public health and daily life, testing Barbados' healthcare systems, economy and social resilience nationwide.

GRENADA

Grenada is a mountainous tropical island nation located in the southeastern Caribbean Sea, forming part of the Lesser Antilles. Situated at the southern end of the Windward Islands, it lies north of Trinidad and Tobago and south of Saint Vincent and the Grenadines. With an estimated population of approximately 125,000 people, the capital city is St. George's, widely regarded as one of the most picturesque harbours in the Caribbean. Other important towns include Grenville and Gouyave, which serve as regional commercial and agricultural centres. English is the official national language, while Grenadian Creole English and French-based Creole are widely spoken in daily life. The Eastern Caribbean Dollar serves as the national currency. Shaped by Indigenous Kalinago heritage, French and British colonial rule, plantation agriculture and the African diaspora, Grenada blends deep historical foundations with a strong cultural identity. Known internationally as the 'Spice Isle,' its agricultural legacy, natural beauty and resilience define the character of Grenada.

Geography

Grenada spans a compact but geologically diverse landscape characterised by volcanic terrain, mountainous interiors and fertile lowlands. The island's central highlands are dominated by extinct volcanic peaks, with Mount Saint Catherine rising to 840 metres as the highest point. Numerous rivers, streams and waterfalls flow from the interior, supporting agriculture and lush rainforest ecosystems. Grenada's coastline stretches for approximately 121 kilometres, featuring sheltered bays, coral reefs and sandy beaches, particularly along the southwest coast, contrasted with more rugged shores in the north and east. The climate is tropical, with a wet season from June to November and moderating trade winds. While located near the southern edge of the hurricane belt, Grenada remains vulnerable to severe storms, as demonstrated by Hurricane Ivan in 2004. The island is rich in biodiversity but faces environmental challenges including deforestation, coastal erosion and coral reef degradation.

History

The history of Grenada begins with the Kalinago people, who inhabited the island long before European contact and resisted colonisation. Christopher Columbus sighted the island in 1498, naming it Concepción, though Spanish settlement did not follow. French settlers established a permanent colony in the mid-17th century, displacing Indigenous populations and developing a plantation economy based on sugar and enslaved African labour. Britain gained control of Grenada in 1763 following the Treaty of Paris, though French rule briefly returned before British dominance was secured. Slavery was abolished in 1834, leading to significant social transformation. The 20th century saw the emergence of labour movements and political reform. Grenada achieved independence from the United Kingdom in 1974. The post-independence period was marked by political instability, including the 1979 revolution and subsequent 1983 United States-led intervention. Since then, Grenada has re-established democratic governance and political stability.

Government and Politics

Grenada is a unitary parliamentary democracy and a constitutional monarchy, with the British monarch serving as head of state, represented by a Governor-General. Political authority is centralised, with local administration organised through parishes and constituencies. The political system comprises executive, legislative and judicial branches. Executive power is vested in the Prime Minister and Cabinet, drawn from the elected House of Representatives. Legislative authority rests with a bicameral Parliament, consisting of the elected House of Representatives and an appointed Senate. The judiciary operates independently under English common law, with the Eastern Caribbean Supreme Court serving as the superior court and final appeals heard by the Caribbean Court of Justice. Political life is dominated by two major parties, the New National Party (NNP) and the National Democratic Congress (NDC). Domestically, political debate focuses on economic management, debt reduction and social development, while internationally Grenada is an active member of CARICOM, the OECS, the Commonwealth and the United Nations.

Economy

Grenada possesses a small, open and service-oriented economy, with tourism, agriculture and public services as its primary pillars. Agriculture remains culturally and economically significant, with the island producing spices such as nutmeg and mace, as well as cocoa, bananas and root crops. Tourism is the main driver of economic growth, supported by beach resorts, yachting and cruise tourism, as well as eco-tourism and heritage attractions. The services sector accounts for the majority of economic output, supplemented by remittances and construction. Despite these strengths, the economy faces challenges including limited diversification, high public debt and vulnerability to external shocks and natural disasters. The Eastern Caribbean Dollar is managed by the Eastern Caribbean Central Bank. Economic policy priorities include fiscal sustainability, tourism diversification and strengthening climate resilience.

Demographics and Society

With a population of approximately 125,000, Grenada is a small but socially cohesive Caribbean nation. The population is predominantly of African descent, reflecting the legacy of the transatlantic slave trade, with smaller communities of mixed European, East Indian and Indigenous ancestry. The national motto, 'Ever Conscious of God We Aspire, Build and Advance as One People,' reflects the country's emphasis on unity and spiritual values. Society is moderately urbanised, with a significant proportion of the population living in or around St. George's. English is the official language, while Grenadian Creole is widely spoken in informal settings. Christianity predominates, particularly Roman Catholicism and Protestant denominations. Social challenges include unemployment, outward migration and economic inequality, but Grenadian society is widely regarded for its strong family structures, community solidarity and cultural pride.

Culture

Grenadian culture reflects a rich blend of African, Indigenous and European influences, expressed through music, dance, festivals and culinary traditions. Music plays a central role, with calypso and soca featuring prominently, alongside traditional forms such as *big drum* music rooted in African heritage. Carnival, known locally as *Spicemas*, is the island's most important cultural event, celebrating emancipation and cultural identity through music, masquerade and street performance. Grenadian cuisine highlights local produce and spices, featuring dishes such as oil down (the national dish), nutmeg-flavoured sweets and fresh seafood. Grenadian Creole is an important medium for oral traditions and storytelling. Cultural expression remains a key component of national identity and international recognition.

Education and Healthcare

Grenada maintains an education system based on the British model, encompassing primary, secondary and tertiary levels. Education is compulsory at the primary level and literacy rates are relatively high. St. George's University, an internationally recognised medical institution, plays a significant role in higher education and the national economy. Healthcare is delivered primarily through a publicly funded system offering universal access, supported by private providers. While basic healthcare services are widely available, specialised care is limited, often requiring overseas treatment. Public health challenges include managing non-communicable diseases such as diabetes and hypertension. Policy discussions focus on improving healthcare infrastructure and workforce capacity.

Infrastructure

Infrastructure development in Grenada reflects the challenges of a mountainous island state exposed to extreme weather events. A national road network connects most communities, though road quality and maintenance remain ongoing concerns. The island has no railway system. The Port of St. George's supports cargo and cruise traffic, while Maurice Bishop International Airport provides international air connectivity. Energy production has traditionally relied on imported fossil fuels, prompting efforts to expand renewable energy sources such as solar and wind power. Telecommunications infrastructure is relatively well developed, though internet access can be uneven in rural areas. Infrastructure priorities include improving water supply reliability and strengthening disaster resilience.

Tourism

Tourism is the primary engine of Grenada's economy and a defining element of its global identity. Natural attractions include white-sand beaches, coral reefs, waterfalls and rainforest-covered mountains. Cultural and historical sites such as Fort George and plantation estates add depth to the visitor experience. Yachting, diving and eco-tourism are particularly prominent. Sustainable tourism initiatives aim to balance economic growth with environmental protection and community involvement, recognising the island's ecological sensitivity and reliance on natural beauty.

Current Issues and Future Outlook

Grenada faces a set of challenges alongside its natural and cultural strengths. Key concerns include economic diversification, public debt management, climate vulnerability and disaster recovery. Hurricanes and external economic shocks pose ongoing risks. At the same time, the country benefits from political stability, a strong tourism brand and international recognition for its agricultural products. The future outlook depends on effective economic reform, climate adaptation and continued investment in human capital and infrastructure. How these priorities are managed will shape Grenada's long-term resilience and development.

Overview

Grenada is a nation defined by its natural beauty, cultural richness and complex modern history. From its Indigenous roots and plantation past to its revolutionary period and democratic recovery, the island has forged a resilient national identity. Its geography supports both agriculture and tourism, while its people maintain strong social cohesion and cultural pride. Looking ahead, Grenada seeks to strengthen economic resilience, preserve its environment and sustain democratic governance.

DID YOU KNOW...?

Grenada is one of the world's leading producers of nutmeg and mace, earning it the nickname the 'Spice Isle.' Nutmeg is so central to national identity that it appears on the country's flag, making Grenada the only nation in the world to feature this spice on its national emblem. Introduced during the colonial era, nutmeg cultivation has since become deeply rooted in the island's landscape and way of life, shaping rural communities and traditional farming practices. This aromatic spice symbolises Grenada's rich agricultural heritage, its ability to recover from natural disasters and economic challenges, and the pride of generations of farmers who sustain the industry. Nutmeg has long connected Grenada to global trade networks, with its spices exported worldwide for use in cooking, medicine and cosmetics. Beyond its economic value, nutmeg represents endurance, cultural identity and Grenada's lasting presence in the global spice trade.

KEY FACTS AND FIGURES

Geography & Environment

• Total area: 344 km² (main island Grenada plus smaller Grenadine islands).

• Coastline: ≈121 km.

• Climate: Tropical marine climate; wet and dry seasons; hurricane-prone.

• Highest point: Mount Saint Catherine (840 m).

• Major features: Volcanic mountains, rainforests, rivers, beaches, coral reefs.

• Wildlife: Grenada dove (endemic), agouti, tropical birds, sea turtles, iguanas.

• 0 UNESCO World Heritage sites.

Population & Society

• Population: ≈115,000 (2024 estimate).

• Density: ≈334 persons/km².

• Urbanisation: ≈33%.

• Ethnicity:

o Afro-Grenadian: ≈82%

o Mixed: ≈13%

o Indo-Grenadian and other: ≈5%

• Languages: English (official); Grenadian Creole widely spoken.

• Religion: Christian (predominantly Roman Catholic and Anglican): ≈90%.

• Literacy: ≈96%.

• Life expectancy: ≈75 years.

Economy

• GDP (nominal): ≈£1.2 billion.

• GDP per capita (PPP): ≈£10,500.

• Key industries:

o Tourism

o Agriculture (nutmeg, cocoa, bananas, vegetables)

o Light manufacturing

o Services
• Major exports: Nutmeg, cocoa, bananas, vegetables.
• Currency: Eastern Caribbean dollar (XCD; £1 ≈ 4.8 XCD).

Government
• Constitutional monarchy (Commonwealth realm).
• System: Parliamentary democracy.
• Head of State: King Charles III.
• Head of Government: Prime Minister of Grenada.
• Parliament: House of Assembly (unicameral).

Infrastructure
• Transport: Road network on main island; air and sea transport.
• Major airports: Maurice Bishop International Airport (Point Salines).
• Energy mix: Predominantly fossil fuels; some solar energy development.
• Digital connectivity: Moderate; concentrated in main urban and tourist areas.

Major Urban Centres
• St. George's: ≈33,000 – Capital, administrative and commercial centre.
• Grenville: ≈10,000 – Eastern regional hub and commercial centre.
• Gouyave: ≈4,000 – Agriculture and fishing centre.
• Victoria: ≈2,000 – Northern local town and service centre.

ST. GEORGE'S – GRENADA'S CAPITAL, ADMINISTRATIVE AND COMMERCIAL CENTRE

The National Flag

The national flag of Grenada features a red border with six yellow stars, a field divided into yellow and green triangles, a central yellow star on a red disc and a nutmeg symbol at the hoist. The red symbolises courage and harmony, the yellow represents the sun and wisdom and the green stands for the island's vegetation. The six stars denote the nation's parishes and the central star its capital. The nutmeg signifies Grenada's historical spice industry. The flag as a whole embodies Grenada's natural beauty, its unity and its path to independence.

KEY PEOPLE AND PLACES

PEOPLE

Sir Eric Gairy (1922–1997) Widely regarded as a founding figure in Grenada's independence movement, Gairy served as the country's first Prime Minister after independence in 1974. He championed workers' rights, social reform and political development, shaping Grenada's early post-colonial governance and national identity.

Maurice Bishop (1944–1983) A revolutionary leader and Prime Minister from 1979 to 1983, Bishop led the New Jewel Movement and sought to implement social, economic and educational reforms. His assassination marked a turning point in Grenada's political history and remains a symbol of struggle and resistance.

Sir Paul Scoon (1935–2013) Governor-General of Grenada from 1978 to 1992, Scoon played a key stabilising role during political crises, including the 1983 U.S.-led intervention. He worked to maintain constitutional order, national unity and the transition from conflict to civilian governance.

Keith Mitchell (b. 1946) A prominent political leader who served multiple terms as Prime Minister, Mitchell oversaw economic development, infrastructure improvements and public service reforms. He strengthened Grenada's international relations, tourism and regional cooperation while promoting stability and sustainable growth.

George Brizan (1942–2012) An economist and politician, Brizan briefly served as Prime Minister and contributed significantly to policy development, education and economic planning in Grenada. He was recognised for his scholarly work and commitment to national development and governance.

PLACES

St. George's (founded 1650) The capital and largest city of Grenada, located on the southwestern coast. St. George's is the political, cultural and economic centre of the country, featuring colourful colonial architecture, historic forts, government institutions, marketplaces and vibrant maritime activity.

Grand Anse Beach A famous white sand beach near St. George's, known for its scenic beauty, recreational opportunities and popularity with tourists. Grand Anse Beach is a key driver of Grenada's tourism economy and represents the island's coastal charm and natural attractions.

Carriacou The largest of Grenada's smaller islands, Carriacou is celebrated for its beaches, sailing culture, traditional festivals and fishing communities. The island contributes to Grenada's cultural heritage, eco-tourism and maritime activities, preserving aspects of Caribbean Island life.

Petite Martinique A small island northeast of Grenada, Petite Martinique is known for its fishing villages, quiet beaches and rural lifestyle. It offers visitors a glimpse of traditional Caribbean culture and natural beauty while contributing to the Grenadian maritime economy.

Mount Saint Catherine The highest peak in Grenada, located in the northern part of the island. This volcanic mountain is significant for its biodiversity, hiking trails and eco-tourism, offering panoramic views of the island, the Caribbean Sea and Grenada's lush rainforest environment.

Fort George A historic military fort overlooking St. George's harbour, built during the colonial period. Fort George is a key heritage site, representing Grenada's colonial history, strategic importance and tourism appeal, while providing scenic views and cultural insight for visitors.

TIMELINE OF EVENTS

c. 1000 BCE – 1498 CE: Indigenous Settlements: Arawak and later Kalinago peoples settled Grenada, developing agriculture, fishing, trade networks, villages and complex social, cultural and spiritual systems.

1498: Columbus Sightings: Christopher Columbus sighted Grenada during his third voyage, marking European contact and initiating future colonisation attempts in the Caribbean region.

1600s: Early European Colonisation Attempts: French and British settlers attempted to establish colonies, facing resistance from Kalinago populations and harsh tropical environments on Grenada.

1649–1763: French Colonial Rule: France established permanent settlements, introducing plantations, enslaved African labour, European governance and Catholicism while competing with British colonial ambitions.

1763: Treaty of Paris: France ceded Grenada to Britain, officially establishing British colonial administration, trade regulation and governance across the island.

1700s–1800s: Expansion of Plantation Economy: Sugar, cocoa and nutmeg plantations grew under British control, relying on enslaved African labour, reshaping Grenada's economy, society and hierarchies.

1834: Abolition of Slavery: Enslaved Africans were emancipated, altering labour systems, social structures and economic patterns, while shaping post-emancipation society on the island.

1870s–1900s: Post-Emancipation Development: Grenada gradually rebuilt its economy and communities, focusing on agriculture, trade, education and local governance after emancipation and reforms.

1946: Universal Adult Suffrage Introduced: Voting rights were extended to all adults, promoting democratic participation, political representation and the emergence of local leadership structures.

1967: Associated Statehood Achieved: Grenada gained internal self-government, controlling domestic affairs while Britain retained responsibility for defence and foreign relations.

1974: Independence from Britain: Grenada became an independent nation within the Commonwealth, establishing full sovereignty while retaining the British monarch as ceremonial head of state.

1980s–1990s: Economic and Social Development: Agriculture remained central, but tourism and services expanded, improving infrastructure, education, employment and economic diversification across the island.

2000s: Environmental and Cultural Initiatives: The government promoted heritage preservation, environmental protection and sustainable tourism, safeguarding natural resources and cultural landmarks throughout Grenada.

2004–2017: Hurricane Impacts: Hurricanes and tropical storms caused widespread destruction to homes, infrastructure and agriculture, prompting major recovery, resilience and disaster preparedness efforts.

2020: COVID-19 Pandemic Impact: The pandemic disrupted tourism, public health, economy and daily life, testing Grenada's resilience, healthcare systems and governmental capacity.

THE REPUBLIC OF TRINIDAD AND TOBAGO

Trinidad and Tobago is a twin-island republic located at the southernmost edge of the Caribbean, just off the northeastern coast of Venezuela. Trinidad, the larger and more industrialised island, lies only a few kilometres from the South American mainland, while Tobago sits to the northeast, known for its smaller scale and tourism appeal. With an estimated population of approximately 1.4 million people, the capital city is Port of Spain, which functions as the political and economic centre. Other significant urban centres include San Fernando, Arima and Scarborough on Tobago. English is the official national language, alongside a rich linguistic landscape that includes Trinidadian Creole, Tobagonian Creole and influences from Indian languages. The Trinidad and Tobago Dollar is the national currency. Shaped by Indigenous heritage, Spanish and British colonial rule, plantation agriculture, indentured labour and the African and Indian diasporas, the nation reflects a complex multicultural identity. Its global energy industry, vibrant festivals and cultural creativity define Trinidad and Tobago's international profile.

Geography

Trinidad and Tobago displays notable geographical diversity despite its relatively small land area. Trinidad features a varied landscape of plains, low mountain ranges and wetlands, including the Northern Range, Central Range and Southern Range, while Tobago is dominated by a central mountain spine, the Main Ridge, one of the oldest protected rainforests in the Western Hemisphere. Trinidad's Caroni Swamp, a vast mangrove wetland, supports rich biodiversity and is home to the national bird, the scarlet ibis. The country's coastline stretches for approximately 437 kilometres, featuring sandy beaches, mangroves and rocky headlands. The climate is tropical, with a distinct wet season from June to December and relatively mild exposure to hurricanes compared to other Caribbean states. Biodiversity is high, particularly due to Trinidad's proximity to South America, though environmental pressures include industrial pollution, deforestation and coastal degradation.

History

The history of Trinidad and Tobago begins with Indigenous Amerindian peoples, including the Arawak and Carib, who inhabited the islands long before European arrival. Christopher Columbus sighted Trinidad in 1498, claiming it for Spain, though sustained settlement remained limited for centuries. Spanish rule persisted until 1797, when Britain captured the island. Tobago changed hands multiple times between European powers before becoming British in 1814. The plantation economy relied on enslaved African labour, followed by the introduction of indentured workers from India, China and Madeira after emancipation in 1834. This migration profoundly shaped the country's demographic and cultural composition. Trinidad and Tobago achieved independence from Britain in 1962 and became a republic in 1976. Since then, it has maintained democratic governance while navigating economic growth driven by energy resources and evolving social dynamics.

Government and Politics

Trinidad and Tobago is a unitary parliamentary democracy and a republic, with a President serving as ceremonial head of state and a Prime Minister exercising executive authority. The political system is based on the Westminster model and consists of executive, legislative and judicial branches. Executive power is vested in the Prime Minister and Cabinet, drawn from the elected House of Representatives. Legislative authority rests with a bicameral Parliament comprising the House of Representatives and an appointed Senate. The judiciary operates independently under common law, with final appellate jurisdiction resting with the Caribbean Court of Justice. Political life is largely dominated by two major parties, the People's National Movement (PNM) and the United National Congress (UNC), often reflecting ethnic and socio-economic alignments. Tobago enjoys a degree of internal self-governance through the Tobago House of Assembly. Internationally, Trinidad and Tobago is an active member of CARICOM, the Commonwealth and the United Nations.

Economy

Trinidad and Tobago possesses one of the most industrialised economies in the Caribbean, driven primarily by its energy sector. Oil and natural gas production form the backbone of the economy, supporting petrochemicals, liquefied natural gas (LNG) exports and downstream manufacturing. The services sector, including finance, trade and public administration, also contributes significantly to GDP. While agriculture once played a central role, it now represents a smaller share of economic output, though crops such as cocoa retain cultural importance. The country's wealth has enabled comparatively high living standards, but economic volatility linked to global energy prices remains a challenge. The Trinidad and Tobago Dollar is managed by the Central Bank of Trinidad and Tobago. Economic diversification, private sector development and sustainability are central policy priorities.

Demographics and Society

With a population of approximately 1.4 million, Trinidad and Tobago is one of the most culturally diverse societies in the Caribbean. The population is primarily composed of people of African and Indian descent, with significant mixed, European, Chinese and Middle Eastern communities. This diversity is reflected in the national motto, 'Together We

Aspire, Together We Achieve.' Society is highly urbanised, particularly in the Port of Spain–San Fernando corridor. English is the official language, while Creole speech patterns dominate everyday communication. Religious life is notably pluralistic, encompassing Christianity, Hinduism, Islam and other faiths, all of which are recognised through public holidays. Social challenges include crime, inequality and youth unemployment, but the country is also characterised by strong community networks and cultural cohesion.

Culture

Trinidad and Tobago is internationally renowned for its vibrant and influential cultural traditions. The nation is the birthplace of calypso, soca and steelpan music, the latter being the only acoustic musical instrument invented in the 20th century. Carnival is the most significant cultural event, blending African, European and Indigenous traditions through music, masquerade and performance. Cuisine reflects multicultural influences, featuring dishes such as pelau, doubles, roti and callaloo. Language, humour and storytelling are central to cultural expression. The arts play a significant role in national identity, reinforcing Trinidad and Tobago's reputation as the cultural heartbeat of the Caribbean.

Education and Healthcare

Trinidad and Tobago maintains a comprehensive education system based on the British model, offering free education from primary through tertiary levels. Literacy rates are high and institutions such as the University of the West Indies and the University of Trinidad and Tobago serve as regional centres of higher learning. Healthcare is provided through a publicly funded system offering universal access, complemented by private facilities. The country has relatively well-developed healthcare infrastructure, though challenges remain in service efficiency and specialist availability. Public health concerns include non-communicable diseases such as diabetes and cardiovascular illness. Ongoing reforms aim to improve service delivery and workforce development.

Infrastructure

Infrastructure in Trinidad and Tobago reflects its status as an industrialised Caribbean nation. An extensive road network connects urban and industrial centres, though congestion remains a concern. The country has no active passenger railway system. Major ports such as Port of Spain and Point Lisas support industrial exports and trade, while Piarco International Airport and A.N.R. Robinson International Airport provide air connectivity. Energy infrastructure is advanced, supporting domestic consumption and exports. Telecommunications and broadband access are widespread, particularly in urban areas. Infrastructure priorities include transport modernisation, digital expansion and climate resilience.

Tourism

Tourism plays a smaller but increasingly important role in the economy of Trinidad and Tobago. Tobago serves as the primary tourism destination, known for its beaches, coral reefs and eco-tourism offerings. Trinidad attracts visitors for cultural tourism, particularly Carnival, festivals and culinary experiences. Nature tourism, including birdwatching and rainforest exploration, is also growing. Sustainable tourism initiatives aim to balance economic development with environmental protection and community involvement.

Current Issues and Future Outlook

Trinidad and Tobago faces a range of challenges alongside its economic advantages. Dependence on energy exports exposes the country to global price volatility, while crime and social inequality remain pressing concerns. Climate change and environmental management are increasingly important policy issues. At the same time, the country benefits from strong institutions, human capital and cultural influence. The future outlook depends on successful economic diversification, crime reduction strategies and sustainable development planning.

Overview

Trinidad and Tobago is a nation defined by its economic strength, cultural innovation and complex social fabric. Rooted in Indigenous heritage and shaped by colonialism, slavery and indentureship, it has developed into one of the Caribbean's most influential states. Its energy resources underpin prosperity, while its cultural contributions resonate globally. Looking ahead, the country seeks to balance economic transformation with social cohesion and environmental sustainability.

DID YOU KNOW...?

Trinidad and Tobago is the birthplace of the steelpan, the only acoustic musical instrument invented in the 20th century. Originating from the ingenuity of working-class communities, the steelpan has become a global symbol of creativity, resilience and cultural pride, reflecting the nation's enduring contribution to world music, and showcasing the innovative spirit that transformed everyday materials into powerful expressions of rhythm, unity, and national identity worldwide today.

KEY FACTS AND FIGURES

Geography & Environment

• Total area: 5,131 km² (two main islands: Trinidad and Tobago).
• Coastline: ≈362 km.
• Climate: Tropical; wet and dry seasons; hurricane-prone.
• Highest point: El Cerro del Aripo (940 m).
• Major features: Northern Range, Caroni Swamp, Pitch Lake, coral reefs.
• Wildlife: Howler monkeys, ocelots, scarlet ibis, leatherback turtles, birds.
• 0 UNESCO World Heritage sites.

Population & Society

• Population: ≈1.4 million (2024 estimate).
• Density: ≈273 persons/km².
• Urbanisation: ≈55%.
• Ethnicity:
o Indo-Trinidadian and Tobagonian: ≈35%
o Afro-Trinidadian and Tobagonian: ≈34%
o Mixed: ≈23%
o Other (including European, Chinese, Syrian/Lebanese): ≈8%
• Languages: English (official); Trinidadian and Tobagonian Creole English widely spoken.
• Religion: Christian (≈63%), Hindu (≈18%), Muslim (≈5%), other and non-religious (≈14%).
• Literacy: ≈98%.
• Life expectancy: ≈73 years.

Economy

• GDP (nominal): ≈£30 billion.
• GDP per capita (PPP): ≈£21,000.
• Key industries:
o Oil and natural gas production
o Petrochemicals and manufacturing
o Tourism
o Agriculture (sugar, cocoa, citrus)

• Major exports: Petroleum, petrochemicals, LNG, cocoa, sugar.
• Currency: Trinidad and Tobago dollar (TTD; £1 ≈ 9 TTD).

Government

• Republic within the Commonwealth.
• System: Parliamentary democracy.
• Head of State: President of Trinidad and Tobago.
• Head of Government: Prime Minister of Trinidad and Tobago.
• Parliament: Bicameral Parliament (Senate and House of Representatives).

Infrastructure

• Transport: Road network across main islands; sea and air transport.
• Major airports: Piarco International Airport (Trinidad), A.N.R. Robinson International Airport (Tobago).
• Energy mix: Predominantly natural gas and oil.
• Digital connectivity: Well-developed in urban areas.

Major Urban Centres

• Port of Spain: ≈37,000 – Capital, administrative centre.
• San Fernando: ≈50,000 – Industrial and commercial centre.
• Chaguanas: ≈80,000 – Largest town, commercial and residential hub.
• Scarborough: ≈20,000 – Capital of Tobago and service centre.

PORT OF SPAIN – TRINIDAD AND TOBAGO'S CAPITAL

The National Flag

The national flag of the Republic of Trinidad and Tobago features a red field with a black diagonal band edged in white, running from the top left to the bottom right. The red symbolises the sun, courage and the vitality of the people, the black represents the earth, dedication and unity of purpose, while the white denotes the sea, purity and the equality of all. The flag as a whole embodies the nation's character, its natural elements and the harmony of its diverse population.

KEY PEOPLE AND PLACES

PEOPLE

Dr. Eric Williams (1911–1981) Widely regarded as the 'Father of the Nation,' Williams served as the first Prime Minister of independent Trinidad and Tobago from 1962 until his death in 1981. He played a pivotal role in leading the country to independence, shaping national policy and promoting education, industry and social development.

Basdeo Panday (b. 1933) A prominent political leader and former Prime Minister, Panday was the first Indo-Trinidadian to hold the office. He promoted social inclusion, economic reform and democratic governance, contributing to national unity and representing the diverse population of Trinidad and Tobago.

Patrick Manning (1946–2016) Served as Prime Minister for multiple terms, Manning was influential in economic planning, infrastructure development and international diplomacy. His policies helped modernise industry, strengthen the energy sector and foster regional and global partnerships for Trinidad and Tobago.

Kamla Persad-Bissessar (b. 1952) The first female Prime Minister of Trinidad and Tobago, serving from 2010 to 2015. She championed social reform, gender equality, education and economic development, becoming a leading figure in national politics and a role model for women in the Caribbean.

Hasely Crawford (b. 1950) Trinidad and Tobago's first Olympic gold medallist, winning the 100 metres at the 1976 Montreal Olympics. Crawford became a national icon for sporting excellence, inspiring generations of athletes and enhancing the country's international reputation in track and field.

PLACES

Port of Spain (founded 1560s) The capital city of Trinidad and Tobago, located on the northwest coast of Trinidad. Port of Spain serves as the political, cultural and economic hub, featuring government institutions, commercial districts, historic architecture and hosting the internationally renowned Carnival festival.

San Fernando The second-largest city in Trinidad, located in the southwest. San Fernando is an industrial, commercial and cultural centre, playing a key role in the oil and gas sector while providing vibrant community life, entertainment and urban development.

Scarborough The capital of Tobago, Scarborough is the administrative and economic centre of the smaller island. It features colonial architecture, a scenic harbour, cultural institutions and serves as a hub for tourism, government services and local commerce.

The Pitch Lake Located in La Brea, Trinidad, the Pitch Lake is the largest natural asphalt deposit in the world. It has historical, economic and geological significance, attracting researchers, tourists and industries while representing a unique natural wonder of Trinidad and Tobago.

Maracas Bay A famous beach on the northern coast of Trinidad, Maracas Bay is renowned for its scenic beauty, recreational opportunities and local food culture, including the popular 'bake and shark' dish. It attracts tourists and locals seeking sun, sea and leisure.

The Nylon Pool A shallow white sand area in the middle of Buccoo Reef, Tobago, accessible only by boat. The Nylon Pool is celebrated for its crystal-clear waters, marine biodiversity and recreational appeal, making it one of the country's premier eco-tourism attractions.

TIMELINE OF EVENTS

c. 500 BCE – 1498 CE: Indigenous Settlements: Arawak and Carib peoples settled Trinidad and Tobago, developing agriculture, fishing, trade networks, villages and complex social, cultural and spiritual systems.

1498: Columbus Arrives in Trinidad: Christopher Columbus reached Trinidad during his third voyage, marking European contact and initiating future colonisation by Spain in the region.

1530s–1590s: Spanish Colonisation: Spain established settlements in Trinidad, introducing European governance, Catholicism, agriculture and enslaving Indigenous populations, reshaping society, culture and economy significantly.

1797: British Take Control of Trinidad: Britain seized Trinidad from Spain, establishing colonial administration, plantations and introducing African slave labour into the island's economy.

1802: Treaty of Amiens: Spain formally ceded Trinidad to Britain, confirming colonial status and enabling the development of agriculture, trade and governance under British rule.

1834: Emancipation of Slaves: Enslaved Africans were emancipated, transforming labour systems, social structures and plantation economies, profoundly reshaping Trinidad and Tobago's society.

1889: Crown Colony Administration: Colonial governance was centralised under Britain, with local councils having limited power while Britain controlled administration, law and economic policies.

1919: Labour and Political Movements Begin: Workers and social movements emerged to demand better conditions, political representation and reforms in governance, education and society.

1962: Independence from Britain: Trinidad and Tobago became an independent nation within the Commonwealth, establishing full sovereignty while retaining the British monarch as ceremonial head of state.

1970: Black Power Movement: Social and political activism highlighted inequalities, sparking reforms in governance, education, culture and empowerment of historically marginalised communities.

1980s–1990s: Economic Diversification: The country expanded oil, gas and industrial sectors, balancing energy production with tourism, international trade and sustainable economic development.

2010: Climate and Environmental Focus: Efforts increased to manage coastal erosion, protect biodiversity and promote sustainable energy and environmental awareness nationwide.

2019: Regional Leadership Initiatives: Trinidad and Tobago strengthened its role in CARICOM and regional diplomacy, asserting economic, political and cultural influence in the Caribbean region.

2020: COVID-19 Pandemic Impact: The pandemic disrupted public health, economy, tourism and daily life, testing Trinidad and Tobago's resilience, healthcare systems and governance capacity.

APPENDIX 1 - TIMELINE OF MAJOR NORTH AMERICAN EVENTS

c. 13,000 BCE onward: Early Human Migrations – The initial peopling of the continent via the Bering Land Bridge, leading to the development of diverse and complex indigenous civilisations across North America.

c. 1000 CE: Norse Exploration – The establishment of a short-lived Norse settlement at L'Anse aux Meadows in Newfoundland, representing the first documented European contact with North America.

1492: Columbian Voyage – Christopher Columbus's first transatlantic expedition, sponsored by Spain, which initiated lasting European exploration and colonisation of the Americas.

1607: Jamestown Founded – The establishment of the first permanent English settlement in the Americas at Jamestown, Virginia, marking the beginning of England's colonial venture in North America.

1775–1783: American Revolutionary War – A conflict whereby thirteen British colonies secured independence, establishing the United States of America and profoundly influencing Atlantic-world politics.

1803: Louisiana Purchase – The acquisition by the United States of a vast territory from France, dramatically expanding its western frontier and shaping the continent's geopolitical future.

1812–1815: War of 1812 – A military conflict fought between the United States and the United Kingdom, cementing US sovereignty and solidifying the northern border with British North America (Canada).

1830: Indian Removal Act – A US policy leading to the forced relocation of numerous Native American nations from the southeastern United States, an event known as the Trail of Tears.

1846–1848: Mexican-American War – A conflict between the United States and Mexico resulting in significant US territorial gains in the southwest, reshaping the borders of both nations.

1861–1865: American Civil War – A pivotal internal conflict in the United States over slavery and states' rights, culminating in the abolition of slavery and a strengthened federal government.

1867: Canadian Confederation – The union of three British colonies into the Dominion of Canada, creating a self-governing entity within the British Empire and a major step toward modern nationhood.

1898: Spanish-American War – A brief conflict between the United States and Spain that ended Spanish colonial rule in the Americas and established the US as a significant Pacific and Caribbean power.

1914: Panama Canal Opens – The completion of the strategic canal, fundamentally altering global maritime trade routes and cementing US influence in Central America.

1929–1939: The Great Depression – A severe worldwide economic depression originating in the United States, leading to widespread unemployment, social upheaval and transformative government policies.

1942–1945: Alaska Highway Construction – The rapid building of a strategic military route through Canada, connecting the contiguous US to Alaska and demonstrating Allied wartime cooperation.

1955–1975: Civil Rights Movement – A decades-long struggle in the United States to end institutionalised racial segregation and discrimination, achieving major legislative and social reforms.

1962: Cuban Missile Crisis – A 13-day confrontation between the United States and the Soviet Union over Soviet ballistic missiles in Cuba, marking the Cold War's closest approach to nuclear conflict.

1965: Immigration and Nationality Act – A landmark US law that abolished the national-origins quota system, dramatically altering the demographic composition of the United States.

1982: Patriation of the Canadian Constitution – The process by which Canada gained full control over its constitution, culminating in the Canada Act and the establishment of the Canadian Charter of Rights and Freedoms.

1994: North American Free Trade Agreement (NAFTA) – The implementation of a trilateral trade bloc between Canada, the United States and Mexico, deeply integrating the continent's economies.

September 2001: 9/11 Attacks – A series of coordinated terrorist attacks on the United States, leading to the US-led 'War on Terror' and significant shifts in domestic and foreign policy.

APPENDIX 2 - GLOSSARY OF TERMS

American Civil War: A pivotal internal conflict (1861–1865) in the United States over issues of slavery, states' rights and federal authority, leading to the abolition of slavery and a profound transformation of the nation.

American Revolutionary War: The war (1775–1783) whereby thirteen British colonies in North America secured independence, establishing the United States and inspiring subsequent anti-colonial movements.

Black Tuesday: The date of the Wall Street stock market crash (29 October 1929), which signalled the onset of the decade-long Great Depression in the United States and around the world.

Canadian Confederation: The political process (culminating in 1867) that united three British North American colonies into the Dominion of Canada, creating a self-governing federation within the British Empire.

Civil Rights Movement: A decades-long struggle (peaking 1955–1968) in the United States to end institutionalised racial segregation and discrimination against African Americans, achieving landmark legislative reforms.

Cuban Missile Crisis: A major 13-day confrontation (October 1962) between the United States and the Soviet Union over the latter's deployment of ballistic missiles in Cuba, marking the Cold War's closest brush with nuclear war.

Federalist Papers: A series of 85 essays (1787–1788) written by Alexander Hamilton, James Madison and John Jay promoting the ratification of the United States Constitution and articulating key principles of American governance.

First Nations: A collective term for the diverse indigenous peoples of Canada who are neither Inuit nor Métis, encompassing numerous distinct nations with unique histories, cultures and legal statuses.

Great Depression: A severe worldwide economic depression (1929–1939) that originated in the United States, causing massive unemployment, social dislocation and leading to President Franklin D. Roosevelt's New Deal.

Hart-Celler Act / Immigration and Nationality Act of 1965: A landmark US law that abolished the national-origins quota system, fundamentally changing immigration patterns and the demographic makeup of the United States.

Indian Removal Act: A US law passed in 1830 authorising the federal government to negotiate the forced removal of Native American tribes from the southeastern United States to lands west of the Mississippi River.

Louisiana Purchase: The 1803 acquisition by the United States of approximately 828,000 square miles of French territory west of the Mississippi River, doubling the size of the nation.

Manifest Destiny: A 19th-century cultural belief prevalent in the United States that American settlers were destined to expand across the North American continent, justifying territorial acquisition.

Mexican-American War: An armed conflict (1846–1848) between the United States and Mexico following US annexation of Texas, resulting in significant US territorial gains in the southwest.

Monroe Doctrine: A US foreign policy principle (introduced 1823) declaring opposition to European colonialism in the Americas while asserting US political influence over the Western Hemisphere.

NAFTA (North American Free Trade Agreement): A trilateral trade bloc (implemented 1994) between Canada, the United States and Mexico, creating one of the world's largest free-trade zones and deeply integrating the continent's economies.

New Deal: A series of programmes, public works projects, financial reforms and regulations enacted by President Franklin D. Roosevelt (1933–1939) in response to the Great Depression.

9/11 Attacks: A series of coordinated terrorist attacks by al-Qaeda against the United States on 11 September 2001, leading to the US-led 'War on Terror' and significant shifts in global security policy.

Panama Canal: An artificial 82-kilometre waterway completed in 1914, connecting the Atlantic and Pacific Oceans, which revolutionised global maritime trade and solidified US strategic influence.

Patriation of the Canadian Constitution: The process (achieved in 1982) by which Canada gained full legal autonomy, culminating in the Canada Act and the establishment of the Canadian Charter of Rights and Freedoms.

Pueblo Revolt: A successful uprising (1680) of most of the indigenous Pueblo people against Spanish colonisers in the province of Santa Fe de Nuevo México, temporarily expelling the Spanish for over a decade.

Spanish-American War: A brief conflict (1898) between the United States and Spain that ended Spanish colonial rule in the Americas, resulting in US acquisition of territories in the Caribbean and the Pacific.

The Trail of Tears: The forced displacement during the 1830s of approximately 60,000 Native Americans of the 'Five Civilised Tribes' from their ancestral homelands in the southeastern United States to Indian Territory (present-day Oklahoma).

Transcontinental Railroad: The first continuous railroad line (completed 1869) connecting the existing eastern US rail network to the Pacific coast, dramatically accelerating the settlement and economic development of the American West.

Treaty of Paris (1783): The agreement that formally ended the American Revolutionary War, in which Great Britain recognised the sovereignty of the United States over territory bounded by the Mississippi River.

US Constitution: The supreme law of the United States, drafted in 1787 and ratified in 1788, establishing the framework of the national government and its relationship to the states and the people.

Vietnam War: A prolonged, divisive conflict (1955–1975) in which the United States supported South Vietnam against the communist North, becoming the focal point of major Cold War-era domestic and international protest.

War of 1812: A military conflict (1812–1815) fought between the United States and the United Kingdom over issues including trade restrictions and British support for Native American tribes, which cemented US sovereignty.

APPENDIX 3 – BIBLIOGRAPHY AND FURTHER READING

Books

North America: A Continental History by Alan Taylor (2020): A comprehensive synthesis exploring the intertwined histories of Indigenous nations, European empires, and the modern United States, Canada, and Mexico from pre-contact to the present.

1491: New Revelations of the Americas Before Columbus by Charles C. Mann (2005): A groundbreaking work that radically reinterprets the scope, sophistication, and population of the pre-Columbian Americas.

Bury My Heart at Wounded Knee: An Indian History of the American West by Dee Brown (1970): A seminal and powerful narrative history of the displacement and destruction of Native American peoples in the late nineteenth century.

What Hath God Wrought: The Transformation of America, 1815–1848 by Daniel Walker Howe (2007): A Pulitzer Prize–winning history of a formative era marked by rapid technological innovation, territorial expansion, and political democratisation.

The Canadian Frontier, 1534–1760 by W. J. Eccles (1983): A classic study of New France, focusing on the French colonial experience, Indigenous alliances, and the fur trade economy.

The Republic for Which It Stands: The United States During Reconstruction and the Gilded Age, 1865–1896 by Richard White (2017): A detailed examination of the tumultuous post–Civil War era, tracing the rise of industrial capitalism and the struggles over race, citizenship, and political power.

The Labyrinth of Solitude by Octavio Paz (1950): A profound and influential collection of essays by the Mexican Nobel laureate analysing Mexican history, identity, and psychology.

Articles

'The Unfinished Legacy of the New Deal' (*The Atlantic*, 2020): Analyses the enduring impact of 1930s-era policies on the modern American state and contemporary social welfare debates.

'Borders and Belonging: A History of the US–Canada Frontier' (*Journal of American History*, 2019): Examines the creation and meaning of the world's longest undefended border and its role in shaping national identities.

'NAFTA to USMCA: The Re-negotiation of North American Trade' (*Foreign Affairs*, 2021): Assesses the political and economic implications of updating the continental trade agreement.

'Reconciling Histories: The Truth and Reconciliation Commission of Canada' (*The Guardian*, 2018): Explores the process and challenges of addressing the legacy of the residential school system for Indigenous peoples.

Documentaries

The Civil War (PBS, 1990): Ken Burns' landmark documentary series chronicling the defining conflict in American history through archival photographs, letters, and firsthand accounts.

Canada: A People's History (CBC, 2000): A sweeping documentary series tracing the story of Canada from earliest times to the twentieth century, emphasising diverse perspectives.

The West (PBS, 1996): A documentary series by Stephen Ives and Ken Burns exploring the conquest and mythology of the American West and its impact on the national character.

The Mexican Revolution (BBC, 2010): A series examining the complex social, political, and military struggles that defined Mexico in the early twentieth century.

13th (Netflix, 2016): Ava DuVernay's critically acclaimed documentary tracing a historical line from the abolition of slavery to the modern era of mass incarceration in the United States.

Online Resources

Library and Archives Canada (https://www.bac-lac.gc.ca/): The premier source for Canadian historical documents, genealogy, and digital collections.

Digital Public Library of America (https://dp.la/): A massive, free digital library aggregating millions of photographs, manuscripts, books, and artefacts from American libraries, archives, and museums.

National Museum of the American Indian (Smithsonian) (https://americanindian.si.edu/): Online collections and educational resources dedicated to the history, culture, and art of Native peoples of the Western Hemisphere.

The Avalon Project (Yale Law School) (https://avalon.law.yale.edu/): A collection of digital documents relevant to law, history, economics, politics, diplomacy, and government, with extensive North American primary sources.

APPENDIX 4 -
ACKNOWLEDGEMENTS AND CREDITS

The author gratefully acknowledges the individuals, institutions and organisations whose scholarship, resources and generosity contributed to the research and presentation of this work.

Institutional and archival support was provided by the Library of Congress (United States), Library and Archives Canada, the National Institute of Anthropology and History (INAH, Mexico), the Smithsonian Institution and the David Rumsey Map Collection. Additional access to digitised historical materials was facilitated by the Digital Public Library of America, the Avalon Project at Yale Law School, the National Archives (United States) and the McCord Stewart Museum (Montreal).

This study has been informed by the published scholarship of Alan Taylor, Tiya Miles, Margaret MacMillan and Daniel J. Hopkins, as well as by the reporting and historical analysis of journalists and editors at *The Atlantic*, *The Globe and Mail*, *Nexos* and *The New York Times*.

The author also acknowledges the contributions of cultural and community institutions, including the National Museum of the American Indian, the Gilder Lehrman Institute of American History, Historica Canada and representatives of the Métis Nation, for their ongoing work in preserving and presenting diverse historical narratives.

Gratitude is extended to individuals who shared personal recollections and lived experiences, including descendants of the Great Migration, veterans of the Normandy campaigns, former participants in the Civil Rights Movement and members of agricultural communities in the Canadian Prairies and the American Midwest.

Visual materials reproduced in this volume have been drawn from publicly accessible archival collections, including Wikimedia Commons, and from stock image repositories such as Unsplash.com, in accordance with applicable licensing terms. Base maps and contemporary cartographic imagery depicting the locations of North American countries are derived from Google Maps and were captured in 2026 via screen capture.

Some illustrative images and visual aids were produced using artificial intelligence tools (including ChatGPT, developed by OpenAI) under the author's direction. These tools were used to assist in the creation of supporting visual material only. The author retains full responsibility for the accuracy, selection, interpretation and presentation of all visual and textual content in this work.

www.ingramcontent.com/pod-product-compliance
Lightning Source LLC
LaVergne TN
LVHW020553110826
845149LV00002B/253